10 Days to Golden Triangle

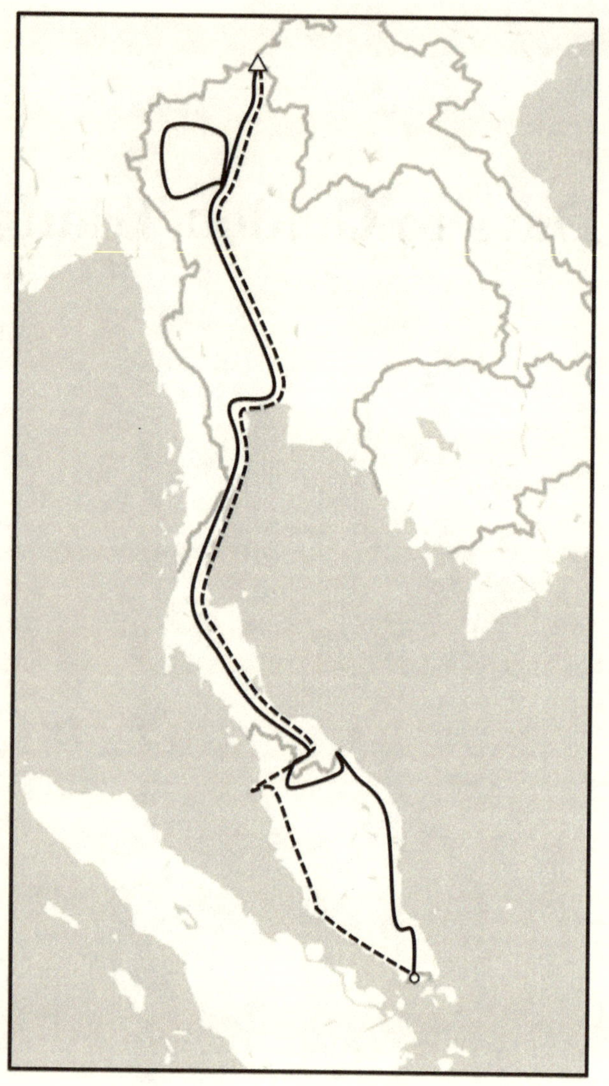

10 Days to Golden Triangle

An Endeavour to Create a Better Life Story

by

Mohamad Khair

Contents

Preface   vii

Part 1: An Endeavour

1   My Boring Life   1
2   The Start of a New Journey   9
3   Life Hints   19
4   Game Plan   25
5   Preparation   35

Part 2: An Endeavour to Create

6   Black Figure   41
7   What Do You Mean By Enjoy?   65
8   Cowboy Town   99
9   When Plans Don't Go as Planned   117
10   Crazy Traffic   135
11   A Bottle of Good Memory   149
12   Teeth Chattering Ride   163
13   Certificate of Conquest   185
14   Not What I had Expected   203
15   Tiger What?   217

Part 3: An Endeavour to Create a Better Life Story

16   Not Like Movies   229
17   False Meditation   249
18   Double the Trouble   269

19   The Final Ride   287

Part 4: The Aftermath

20   All You Have to Do Is Try   303

About the Author   308
Appendix   309

Preface

I spent countless hours pondering whether there was a need to write a detailed history, such as the historical site I had come across. With the advent of Google and other search engines, not to mention AI chatbots, what's the point of explaining the history where full information can be easily searched for, right? That was my rationale when writing this book, aiming to omit unnecessary details. However, fear not, names of the sites and locations I visited are clearly stated, which could be helpful for future travellers.

The story unfolds chronologically, capturing various events along the way. You won't find yourself jumping back and forth between numerous different scenes, with the exception of a few moments where the humour may prompt you to regress and reread certain sections.

Lastly, in some instances, I refer motorcycle as "bike" for readability. I won't spoil any further as this is a quickie preface. So, sit back, relax, and I hope you have a pleasant journey to my endeavour.

Part 1: An Endeavour

1

My Boring Life

My two years of National Service (NS) in Singapore – a mandatory military service for all male Singaporeans, unless exempted, had finally ended. I found myself on a ferry heading back to mainland Singapore from an island where much of my service took place. Contrary to the expected euphoria one might feel after finishing such a commitment, my mind was not buzzing with thoughts of celebration or extravagance. Instead, I was grappling with a sense of uncertainty about what the future held for me.

I once served as a sergeant, relishing the chance to assert authority and raise my voice at recruits – for valid reasons. Upon the ferry's arrival in mainland Singapore, that chapter closed abruptly. I transitioned from being a sergeant to simply a twenty-four-year-old man – though to some observers, I might have seemed more like an immature adult. It's ironic, considering the transformative nature of NS, which supposedly moulds boys to men. Yet, here I stood feeling like an exception to that rule. Guess it was just me.

Stepping out of the ferry terminal, jobless, financially strained, and plagued by the overarching question: What would my life lead to? It was something I couldn't unravel or grasp in my current position. With a diploma certificate in aeronautical and aerospace technology, which is kept somewhere in my closet, I was still clueless about what I wanted to do in life. But there was one pressing question that echoed in my mind loudly: To work or to study?

***

It was definitely work for me as I was poor in cash. I emailed various engineering companies a few months before ending my NS. Not one email came from the aerospace company. But there were few replies came with obscure roles: Vacuum cleaner technician? Printer technician? And somehow, strangely, flyer distributor? Really?

Even if I were to get hired by one of the obscure jobs, none of the benefits and the working hours were appreciable for the peanut salary I would probably receive. Then it came to my mind; there was another option where I could give it a try. During the days when I could book out from camp and be back on the mainland of Singapore, I attentively observed the many delivery riders on the roads delivering food orders, which nudged me to look for a job in a delivery fleet.

Several companies run a food delivery fleet in Singapore, and they were in their hiring mode and in need of more delivery personnel as their fleet was expanding fast. The per-order-rate fee was attractive, and also the companies were giving out weekly incentives for those riders who completed the stipulated number of orders for the day or the week or even for the month.

Even though it isn't a typical ladder-climbing job, it somehow nudges me to get into it for some quick cash first, as I was poor in cash and still clueless about what I wanted to do in life. But there was an issue with it. Not the food delivery fleet, but me. The modes of delivery options were a motorcycle, electric scooter (e-scooter) or bicycle. Of all the modes of transport, I own none of which.

That was when I purchased a 250-watt e-scooter with my savings as the mode of delivery. It was a standing-type of e-scooter with a foot-placing platform dimension of roughly one and a half feet in length, and both the wheels' diameters were just six inches wide. Moreover, it could carry my weight through six hours of ride on an even gradual terrain.

The food delivery company pays different delivery rates for various towns in Singapore and it's commonly called zones. The zones with higher per-delivery rates are those in the central business district or the zones that are closer to the major malls in Singapore. Consequently, I opted to work in those higher-rate zones. I mean, who wouldn't want right?

After a few weeks of working as a delivery rider, I was astonished by how much I was making. I was getting a decent salary and was so glad I didn't sign up for obscure jobs that would have given me a peanut salary. And again, flyer distributor?

But in hindsight, it induced me to work more than 10 hours. With that said, earning a good income didn't come with small surprises. It was sheer hard work delivering under Singapore's hot and humid weather.

As I mentioned earlier, the e-scooter only had enough power to bring me around for only 6 hours. So, how did I manage to work over 10 hours? Whenever I see a downslope path, I would not power the scooter but let it roll down from my weight that acts as a gravitational force. And for upslopes, I would grasp the handlebar tightly and run up hastily, pushing the e-scooter beside me. Doing just that would save a great deal of battery power for the e-scooter for at least an hour, and I would continually do it whenever I see upslopes. But the battery power still didn't add up to over 10 hours of work time, right? Well, that's when I would become a ninja.

During my break, I would secretly head to a shopping mall with the e-scooter and find a secluded area with a landline port to charge the e-scooter's battery. Apparently, e-scooters weren't allowed to be charged in malls as there was much news regarding fire breaking out from e-scooter batteries due to being faulty or other problems that could potentially cause the e-scooter to catch fire. With the many possibilities of an e-scooter catching fire, the shopping malls' securities were fully alerted and stopped people from charging in the malls. But for the sake of getting additional hours of work time and also to cool myself from the mall's air conditioning after baking myself under the dreaded heat, why not?

Shouldn't I add an additional battery pack to the e-scooter to give more extended battery usage than being a ninja in a mall? Unfortunately, it wasn't possible. The e-scooter alone weighs about 20 kilograms, and adding an additional battery pack would weigh more than 2 kilograms (the lightest battery pack on sale at that time) which exceeds the 20 kilograms regulation for the e-scooter maximum weight set by a relevant authority in Singapore.

Breaking the rules was something that I wanted to avoid, especially when my only source of income came from food delivery job. And it wasn't only for that reason. Getting apprehended by the relevant authority who catches errant e-scooter users who disregard the rules can be a pain in the butt. One could be rewarded with a hefty fine or, worse, have their e-scooter towed away. It is all these that I wanted to avoid, and I could not afford to lose my e-scooter.

***

Delivery orders came in all the time, and I tirelessly worked, taking only a single off day in a week. Sometimes, I would just work on the off days as the money that I was receiving was too good not to work a single day. This went on for months, and my adrenaline remained fixed in me like gold that wouldn't want to run away from me.

But something wasn't right. Something bothered me a lot. It lingered in my mind all the time while I picked up the orders from the vendors, scooted to the delivery addresses, and even at times when delivering the orders to the customer's door front. It wasn't a life-threatening thing, but it had something to do with the lifestyle I have, and I always ponder about it.

Apparently, it's the boring life I have.

***

Ever since I was a twelve-year-old kid, I had already started to work. Working at the age of 12 is considered illegal in Singapore. However, it was more of a work-for-fun and a way to earn some quick cash. It was an odd job I did that gave me some cash in my pocket: a car wash job.

The job was introduced by a friend of mine, and it wasn't a full-time job. Whenever there was a slot for us to work, we would work. We would work night till dawn cleaning the cars – especially taxis – till we exhausted the heck out of ourselves. But at times, police patrol vehicles would sometimes come into the venue to do their routine checks. But we were smart kids. There was this drainage that had more than enough space for us to get into, and it was just adjacent to the washing bay just next a fence. We don't have to climb over the fence. We already have a pre-made body size hole at the bottom of the fence where we would crawl past the fence, climb down the drainage, and hide till the police vehicle goes off. It was this nonsense that we would do whenever the police patrol vehicle was to come.

It was fun back then doing this stuff. But little did I know, it was the start of the boring lifestyle I would have.

Since then, I have been working odd jobs whenever there was a school term break or working after school to get some cash. I did jobs like folding Microsoft licence key boxes, distributing flyers (well, not going to lie, I did once before), tried selling stuff door-to-door, been a food runner in a restaurant – carrying dishes and sending to the customer's table, a cashier in a noodle restaurant, and many other obscure jobs before enlisting to the army at the age of 22.

My life would conclude just like this: Work, study, work, study, work, study, and the same repetitive thing over and over again. Since most of the jobs are odd jobs that don't give a huge salary, it was just enough to get by to buy the necessary stuff for myself, for school, and at times, treating myself to good food – usually fast food.

Going out with friends was infrequent for me. I couldn't get along with many as I was considered a poor kid from whatever group I was in. So, most of the time, I'm all alone in my world, struggling to get by. I would wander around by myself, eating meals alone, watching movies alone, and doing much of everything all by myself. However, as I grew older, I somehow preferred being on my own, finding solace and fulfillment in my own company.

With that said, if I were to have a best friend, that best friend is definitely me.

Singapore is a tiny country. Not getting out of the country can be questionable as Singapore has one of the best passports in the world – not promoting Singapore, but it's a fact. But sadly, travelling wasn't a thing in my family. As my parents weren't educated much and worked as odd-job workers, *everything was just enough* to raise four children – me being the youngest. And when everything was just enough, my parents never brought anyone out of the country. With that said, I never really had the urge or the dog-wagging tail that yearns to get out of the country. But I have to say; it can be tough getting along with people.

Whenever people I know start talking about their travels, I often find myself drifting away from the conversation. In those moments, I become the one who seems distant, turning my head toward them without fully engaging. I was always on the losing side for this and would always be seen as a pitiful boy.

But I've always been a curious person. Curious to see what's there outside Singapore. However, I never found the courage to venture out of the country. That changed when I decided to take a bold step before enlisting in the army. I mustered the determination to obtain my passport and embarked on my first-ever solo trip. It was to Bangkok, Thailand. All alone.

I can still recall the moment in the arrival hall in Thailand where the Thai immigration officer looked at me oddly because I smiled peculiarly. I was that new. New to a world of travelling.

Upon returning to Singapore after the first trip, my eyes were wide open to the vast possibilities and myriad of experiences awaiting exploration. However, as I was so accustomed to my boring lifestyle, I reverted back to my normal lifestyle and didn't think much afterwards. But there will be times when I would have nudges in my brain urging me to sprout out an idea to do something remarkable. Something remarkable enough to remember them and to tell myself, "Dude, you have an awesome life, not a boring one."

But I just didn't know what would that be.

***

Back to delivering orders with my e-scooter, there came a new problem that bothered me much, in which I had to do something about it.

Mall security guards became more aware that people were charging their e-scooter in malls. I would get kicked out by the guards, but then, I would continue to hop from mall to mall, doing the same thing. But unfortunately, I would get kicked out by the guards repeatedly. Aside from that, my energy-saving method for the e-scooter from running up slopes also started to exhaust me a lot – partly due to the dreaded heat in Singapore, which made me despise doing delivery on an e-scooter.

Then there came a day while sprinting up the slope gasping for breath, with a pumping brain and a fast-pumping heart, I murmured to myself a holy grail for a change, "When will I ever stop using this shit!"

Then a wisdom of fine words sprinkled in my head: Get a fucking motorcycle you idiot!

2

The Start of a New Journey

Enrolling myself in Singapore Safe Driving Centre (SSDC) to learn motorcycle Class 2B (a class category where it allows me to ride motorcycles up to 200cc) is a new game changer. Holding the pocket-size practical lesson booklet, I leafed through its pages with a bewildered expression, trying to absorb the reality that I was about to embark on learning a whole new machine. It somehow compelled me to recollect an old memory of mine.

I remembered being a pillion passenger on my friend's motorcycle, gripping tightly onto the top box rack beneath the seat as we zoomed down the highway. My friend's speed made me regret not closing the helmet's visor, subjecting me to obnoxious headwinds and my spectacles pressed tightly on my nose bridge. The oversized helmet produced rough whistling sounds, and the rush of wind created a cacophony in my ears, making me feel as if my skin might tear apart at any moment. Amidst this chaos, I couldn't help but holler, "BRO! TOO FAST, TOO FAST!" In response, he turned over his right shoulder, erupted laughter at me, and then without mercy, throttled even faster. That brought me jerking back to the top box behind me and grabbing the rack even more tightly.

After that moment, I affirmed that I wasn't the type of guy who was fond of motorcycles. Whenever someone asks me if I ride a motorcycle, I say, "I'm a car type of person."

Well, at least a remote-controlled car.

Back to the waiting area for my first motorcycle practical lesson with full protective gears on, I mentally giggled to myself at what I had perceived before.

"Come forward and pass your booklets!" One of the instructors shouted across the floor to the awaiting learners. And that was when the start of the pursuit to motorcycle venture began.

***

It took me almost four months to obtain my class 2B licence. It wasn't a fruitful experience going through the practical lesson frivolously. It was just a pain in my pocket as I failed more lessons than I had passed, which annoyed me much. Besides that, I was taking the lessons between my work timing, and I was always rushing for time.

Completing the last delivery orders before 2 pm and then locking up my e-scooter at the bicycle stand at my work zone, then taking the train to the driving school, then going through the lessons, rushing back to the train again after the lesson, and then back to work by 6 pm or sometimes later. Then carry on with delivery and end my day after 10 pm or slightly later. It was the routine I was adhering to until I got my licence. It was exceptionally tiring and mentally exhausting.

But when the day arrived to receive my licence from the instructor, I carefully held up the piece of card, pinching both edges with my thumbs and index fingers. A peculiar smile sprouted on my face for achieving something I had never thought of. Flipping the card to its back, my eyes met the print of the passing date: 30 November 2018. Another peculiar smile adorned my face, accompanied by a shift in perception: "I'm no longer a boy, I'm a man now."

But what motorcycle should I get?

I considered opting for a Yamaha R15, a 200cc sport bike that aligns with the maximum capacity allowed by the class 2B licence limit. It's a bike I wanted to get, as it seemed like I could be the cool guy on the road. However, much introspection, it didn't fit my style of delivery. All I wanted was a bike that I could get the parts cheaply, place both my feet flat on the ground, and a reasonably priced motorcycle. That was all I needed.

I'd been observing several other food delivery riders on the road with different bikes in the same zone as I. Watching them closely for several months prior before getting the licence to see which bike suited me well. It came to my mind that the "kapcai" bike (a name commonly used in Singapore and Malaysia that depicts lower capacity bikes like 125cc Honda cub bikes or other lower capacity bikes) appeared more reliable and easier to handle than the other bikes on the road.

After numerous conversations with other delivery riders on the road and extensive searches on Carousell – an online application, I finally found the machine that I wanted. It's a second-hand motorcycle, or perhaps after passing through several previous owners, I found a bike that fits my needs: a Yamaha Spark T135. A clutch-less motorcycle that has been on the road for over ten years and has an engine displacement of 135cc. It's a simple straightforward bike where all I got to do was to change the gears with my left foot, use my right hand to throttle down to accelerate, and the bike would move. I don't need the hassle of meddling with the clutch, nor do I need to think about stalling the engine at a U-turn junction for wrongly controlling the clutch.

I went over to have a look at the bike. Upon meeting the seller, who then brought me over to the bike's location, I saw the machine that I had in mind. However, I was apprehensive and didn't know what to inquire from the seller about the bike.

With eyes wide open, I walked around the bike, running my hands over it and trying to appear knowledgeable about what I was checking on. Unfortunately, I was in a sheltered car park that wasn't well-lit. Nevertheless, the seller turned on the flashlight on his phone and walked around with me while explaining the bike's performance and why he was selling the bike away.

"I use this bike go JB (Johor Bahru) then come back to office almost every day. My wife now pregnant. We want to sell this bike and buy a car." I nod to his saying, and he continues, "Actually, I don't want to sell. But my wife wants me to sell this bike. She says too dangerous."

I looked at him with a poker face and my mind was like: Dude, I just got my licence, and you're telling me too dangerous?

"This bike got into any accident before?" I asked curiously.

"So far, NO (the NO he said was kind of loud). I buy this bike from shop 6 months ago. So far… NO," he said. But the NO was oddly loud again.

We squat down next to the engine, and he flashed the phone light on some parts near the engine.

He knocked on the engine casing and looked at me confidently, saying, "See. All OK," then showed me a thumbs up, "Engine, good".

I was somehow impressed with the answer but was still sceptical about how he tried to convince me that the bike hadn't had any problem nor gotten into any accidents.

"You want to test?" He asked.

"Yes, yes," I said apprehensively.

"You got licence, right?" He asked as though doubting me that I would ride away with his bike. I chuckled and took out my licence to assure him I had one, and we both chuckled. But it felt cringy.

As I sat on the bike to test the bike, I somehow felt that I would eventually own this bike. Turning the ignition key on, then finding where the heck the electric starter switch at, "Bro, this one. Press for one second then release. The engine will start," he said. I pressed the switch button for a second, and the engine started like a charm. I was so amused by it, like a kid getting his first toy.

Gripping tightly on the handlebar grip, back peddling the bike with my feet on the ground to face the car park's road direction. Then my left foot kicked down to set the gear to one. As I throttled down the accelerator slightly, the bike moved. When I further increased the throttle down, my balancing went off and the bike veered automatically to the left. My left foot dropped to the ground, and I went pondering, "Why did the bike veer to the left? Maybe it's my first time riding this bike?"

I tried again. Slight throttle down, place my feet back on the footrest and increase the throttle again. The bike wobbled and veered to the left again despite trying to target riding straight.

Whether the problem lies in my riding skills or the problem lies on the bike, it was 50-50 to me. I had recently passed my licence, and the only bike I had practised with was the bike from the driving centre. The driving centre doesn't have a kapcai as the bike to learn on. So, I didn't know if riding a kapcai would be different from what I have learned from the driving centre.

I rode back to the seller wobbling with the bike, and asked about the issue. He gave me a bewildered look at me and then replied, "It's like that. Starting will slightly wobble. When you ride above 50-60 km/h the bike won't wobble. Very smooth."

I couldn't convince myself what he'd just said, but I just nodded to it.

"I think the steering cone bearing a bit loose. I can ask my mechanic at JB to tighten. You want?" He asked.

"Oh...Ok, ok. Then just ask them to tighten it," I said in a way like it's a small matter.

"Don't worry. I one time change engine oil for you and take pictures show you."

With nothing else to ask, I said "OK" with a handshake and left.

After two weeks of waiting and the numerous reasons to hold back on selling the bike to me – probably making full use of the bike to traverse back and forth to JB, we finally met up again to transfer the bike's ownership. I paid $3,400 for the bike (which was a reasonable price at that time) and with a COE period of 4 years 6 months left. (A Certificate of Entitlement (COE) gives the rights to own a vehicle and the rights to use a vehicle on the road of Singapore. As the bike standard COE has passed the 10-year mark since the first registration in 2008, the extension of COE can only be done once with a choice between 5 or 10 years. Since the seller extended to only 5 years and used it for 6 months only, I have left with 4 years and 6 months to make use of the bike before sending it to a scrapyard. What a pity.)

I got the key, and a final handshake was done with a farewell wave from the seller before he left. At that very moment, I had mixed feelings but felt fulfilled to upgrade from an e-scooter to a motorcycle. Before riding off, an important thing to stick on the bike was the probatory plate sticker (a squared sticker to show to the other road users that I am a novice rider on the road). I took the probatory plate sticker from my drawstring bag and pasted one at the front wheel fairing and another at the rear wheel mudguard. That made the bike fully legal for me to be used on the road.

The ignition key turned to ON, pressed the starter switch, "PEEP," which wasn't the right button. That was the horn button.

Pressing the correct starter button, the engine started. A huge smile sprouted on my face, but at the same time, freaking out that I had to ride the bike back to my home.

As I throttled, the bike moved. My smile was still intact. But after a few seconds, my huge smile turned off, and I dropped my feet on the ground.

"Damn it! Nothing changed."

I was upset. The wobbly ride kept occurring. But I thought about the times when the seller traversed back and forth from Singapore to Johor Bahru. Not once, but many times. So why should I be upset about the wobbly feel from the bike when the seller wasn't perturbed by it? Or perhaps, was he just trying to pretend like it's normal to cover up an issue? I could possibly create many reasons and be at the car park without a resolution. So, what made sense to me at that moment was to just "leave it as it was."

However, I hesitated to take the bike out of the car park immediately. Instead, I practiced riding round and round the car park till I gained confidence on straights and did many U-turns practices so as to not embarrass myself by dropping the bike out on the main road.

With many practices and face wipes on my shirt to clear my sweat, I eventually reached a moment where everything clicked in my mind, which got me to handle the bike confidently. And with that, I made my way out of the car park to the main road.

That was it. Another accomplishment for the year 2018 for owning a motorcycle.

***

My delivery job was still ongoing but with a new machine. I felt like a superstar on the roads, and the delivery riders who knew me congratulated me for the transition to riding a motorcycle. I was flattered by much praise from them, but I did not become complacent about it. It was just something that I didn't get a lot in life. So, I cherished that moment.

Not only did I receive praise for the transition, but I also got invitations from several riders who wanted to take me to JB to show me the servicing shops there.

Then, came a time when I asked a fellow delivery rider if his bike had any steering issues. He was baffled by my question, for which he went over to my bike to rock the handlebar back and forth and swivelled the handle left and right.

"Bro, how you ride the bike? The steering cone bearing broken lah. You got skill ah, still do delivery," he said with much amusement on his face, but I wondered to myself if he was rather being sarcastic. Well, he wasn't sarcastic after he said this: "Come, I bring you to JB. I also need to service my bike."

I was right all the while. The seller had partially deceived me. However, I didn't feel resented about it as I was enthralled to hear that I would ride over to JB. It was something that I was looking forward to, and saying no to him wasn't an option in my mind.

Days later, on 10 January 2019, the fellow rider and I crossed the border to Johor Bahru via Woodlands checkpoint in Singapore. On that very day, my novice ride on the road to Malaysia elevated my curiosity about what is out there in Malaysia.

The fellow delivery rider brought me to '*Lorong Bapok*' (the English translation will be 'Gay Street'. I don't know why the fellow rider called the street name as that – probably many years back then, it was something else on the street. Who knows). The actual name of the street is Jalan Tun Abdul Razak (Susur 4), where a stretch of motorcycle servicing outlets can be seen, and it is where many Singaporean bikers would come by here to service their bike.

My bike's steering cone bearing was fixed at a random shop there recommended by the fellow rider. My new ride was smooth like silk, and my ride was like how I had learned from the driving centre. Well, I have to say; I was indeed deceived by the seller who sold the bike to me after all.

Putting the incident behind me, my focus went on observing what was around as I knew that I couldn't possibly ask the fellow rider to bring me over to JB whenever I wanted. It would be on my own the next time I come to service in JB. So, I familiarized myself with various road signboards, grasped the border crossing procedures, and most importantly, understand the style of how Malaysians drive their vehicles on the road to avoid using Singaporean habits on Malaysian roads.

***

Not long after, I had my first solo ride to JB to service the bike. Once every bi-weekly, I would head to JB alone to service the bike as I was clocking between 700 to 1,000 kilometres just by delivering orders in a week. All thanks to fellow riders on the road who popped by to chat with me and advise me on how to care for the bike. From the advises, I established a personal agreement to change the engine oil every 2000 kilometres or once every two weeks.

After some months passed, it became a habit for me to ride over to JB, not only for bike servicing but also to hop from different food store to another, have affordable Thai massage – prices that could never be matched with Singapore prices – and purchase a stash of snacks to indulge back in Singapore. It became addictive to do this, but I liked my time riding to JB as it frees me from work.

But at times, I would get lost on the roads of JB. I would wander around without using Google Maps as I find it thrilling to venture around without using it. I would look around for the road signs and try to figure out my way back to where I came from. The more I did this blind riding without looking at the GPS, it gave me more confidence to be on the roads of JB. And somehow, I became a better observer of what was around in my vicinity.

3

Life Hints

It was already April 2019. I had saved much of my earnings and rewarded myself with a short vacation to northern Vietnam for the sole purpose to climb up Mount Fansipan (Phan Xi Pang) – the highest mountain in the Indochina peninsula with an elevation of 3,147.3 metres above sea level. I didn't know why, but a sudden aspiration to climb mountains struck me. Actually, the probable reason was to lose some fat as I had been consuming too much good food in JB.

The following day after the summit climb, which was the last day of my stay in Sapa town – a town in northern Vietnam where it's on an elevation of 1,500 metres above sea level, I strolled down the street, shivering frantically, yearning to have a hot bowl of noodle soup. I stopped by just right outside of a restaurant to see a whiteboard with a drawing of a bowl, noodles, and a pair of chopsticks in the bowl. From that drawing, it clearly resonated in my mind that is what I was looking for, and I made my order by pointing at the whiteboard to the cook, and the cook instantly knew what he had to do.

I settled down at a table facing the entrance of the restaurant and was served a hot bowl of beef brisket noodle soup. As I enjoyed my meal, and with a teary eye of mine after inadvertently over-pouring the chilli flakes onto the soup, there came a holy grail sound while I slurped the noodle. A sound of a machine came right to the entrance of the restaurant, which prompted me to tilt up my head to the front, stop my slurping of the noodle, and go on to wipe off my teary eyes to see something worth looking at.

A kapcai bike stopped at the entrance of the restaurant, and the rider got out of his bike to hand over bags containing vegetables to the cook. But that wasn't what intrigued my eyes. I glared at the rider's kapcai bike, which was overloaded with vast stocks of goods on the custom-made rack behind the saddle. Huge boxes of goods stacked up one another, and it was almost twice the height of the rider. The goods were tightly wrapped up by ropes, and it seemed like it was too heavy for the motorcycle to withstand that great amount of weight. But then, the bike was still on its two wheels with the support of a custom-made side stand that prevented the bike from toppling to one side. It really fascinated me how a small motorcycle could carry that amount of load on its back. But strictly through the specification of that kapcai, there's a limit to how much load the motorcycle can hold onto. But then, the law of physics was vague in what I was looking at.

The rider hopped back on the bike and rode off at a steady speed without worrying if his bike would flip over due to the many potholes on the road. But I had worries. Won't that tiny tyres explode? Contemplating how he managed to ride down the slope and up the slope got me to ponder deeply within myself.

As I strolled back to my hotel, shivering frantically, I looked at other similar kapcai bikes going up and down the unpaved and paved roads carrying massive stacks of goods on the back of their motorcycles. There were a variety of different goods loaded up on other bikes, such as wheat grasses, ducks in a cage, and even pigs in the cage. And again, their faces didn't show any sign of worrisome if their bikes were to even break down. It seemed like I had more worries for them than they did. I questioned myself: "These small motorcycles do a pretty good job even at an elevation of 1,500 metres above sea level. I'm riding a similar bike like theirs, and if those people could do wonders with their bike, why can't I make wonders with my bike?"

I wondered to myself, but did nothing about it.

***

Months had passed, and working as a delivery rider made it seem like the days went by so fast. It was 9:15 pm. A delivery order was cancelled while I was about to deliver the last order for the day. The cancelled order had two bags filled with burgers, fries, chicken nuggets, a wrap sandwich, and canned drinks. Having it all to myself was a great pleasure, but I knew I wouldn't be able to finish them all, so I looked around for someone I could share the food with.

Just as when I was contemplating who I should give the food away to, I happened to see a food delivery guy who works at the same food delivery company as me; he was sitting on his bike and using his phone. I walked over to him and offered the food, but he insisted on having them if only I joined him to consume the food with him. I agreed to join him in clearing some food from the bag, and we found a dry spot nearby to consume the food while we chatted about our work.

Since we both couldn't consume much of the food, I asked the fellow rider if his delivery friends were nearby our location. He texted them, and within just 10 minutes, one by one came adding up to five people consuming the food. But to my surprise, those people who he had called over were those people who work at the same delivery zone as me. I knew all of them too, which made it easy to converse with them.

We ate and conversed, and a topic about a road trip to Phuket (an island on the west coast of peninsular Thailand) came up from one of them. Listening to them as I munched the fries, I learned that they were planning on a motorcycle road trip to Phuket with their bikes in few days.

Turning my head left and right as they spoke about the meeting time, when to service their motorcycle and how the ride would be like, I was gradually zoning out from their conversation as usual. But I hear them with enthusiasm and curiousness and turn over to look over at my bike, which was distant away from me and parked illegally on the sidewalk. I stared at the probational sticker or in other word, P-Plate, that was glowing on top of the front mud-guard and smiled as I munched the fries. The fellow to whom I first offered the food to, said to me: "Your bike also can ride far but need to ride slow. If you modify your bike can go faster. But you need to change the exhaust pipe, change the sprocket, change the tyre…." The list was too long. The way he said it sounded like I might as well change to a new bike.

I listened to their conversation until the food eventually disappeared, and then everyone went their own way. I walked back to my bike, staring at it, and thought, "Why can't you ride far too?"

***

Another few months passed. Every day was a copy and pasted from the previous day. Nothing fantastic. Did the same repetitive work cycle. But still had the bi-weekly visits to JB to service the bike. Then came a time the bike needed a thorough cleaning. I noticed a make-shift car and motorcycle wash area along Lorong Bapok. I rode to the wash area and pushed the bike in, handed the bike over to the worker, and then made my way to the waiting bench.

While I was walking towards the bench, my peripheral vision

saw two Chinese men seated at one end of the bench. One of them was wearing a black top with blue riding pants. The other man wore a white top with black riding pants and a red tube scarf covering his hair.

I sat at the other end of the bench, but before I had a sit, I inadvertently made eye contact with the man in black top, for which I had to give a friendly smile before I sat. And there came the conversation from him.

"Come here to service?" he asked.

"Yeah, a usual thing I do," I said while I crossed my arms and leaned against a pillar on my back.

"Your friend still servicing?" he asked.

I gave a bewildered face and said, "No. I came alone."

"Huh? Alone from Singapore?" he gave an astonished look and gave a quick glance at my bike that was being washed.

"Not bad ah, when I was P-Plate, I don't even dare to ride to JB alone," he said and showed me thumbs up and then turned his head to the washing bay, looked at the cleaner spray my bike with the spray gun, then back to me again.

"You not scared get rob?" he asked.

My brain neurons didn't work at that moment, but I just chuckled and said, "Err…I would probably say that I am the son-in-law of the Johor Sultan."

We both chuckled, and the white top guy stood up and walked over to where the worker parked his bike after the wash. It was a white Yamaha FZ1. Its engine displacement is about 1000cc. I turned back to the guy in black top and asked if he had come to JB just to service his bike. The answer that came out of his mouth awakened my brain neurons somehow.

"Soon. Riding back to Singapore. I just came from Phuket. It was tiring but the best ride of my life…." My eyes widened, and he went on talking about the ride, the fall he had, the food he consumed, the things he had done with his friends in Phuket and the many laughable moments. It triggered my mind, and I was fascinated by what he said until I was urged to dig for more answers. He pointed at his bike that was pushed out by the cleaner from the washing bay. "That's my bike," he said. It was a dark-blue Honda CB400. A bike that can be commonly seen in Singapore and is well-loved by most Malay bikers.

Listening to the guy was like hearing a teacher talk about his life story rather than teaching a subject to the class. We kept conversing till his friend gave a sign that he needed to go off soon. Before they set off to ride back to Singapore, the black top guy said, "Bro, if you get the chance to ride over to Phuket, just go man. You won't regret it."

Riding along the highway to get back home after visiting JB, procrastinating on an oddly chilly night in Singapore, I wondered why there were many hints like "Phuket," "road trip," and other enticing life hints that kept coming back-to-back. Is it all coincidence? I had no idea.

"How about I solo ride to Phuket?" I thought.

It was just a thought. And still, I did nothing about it.

4

Game Plan

On 11 June 2019, I sat down restlessly on my desk chair, resting my shoulder blades at the top edge of the back rest, my fingers interlocked and resting the back of my head, and stared up at the 75 cm long black wooden boat that sits on a stand on the top shelf of my desk. I stared at it and wondered what I had done for the first half of the year. I reflected on the ups and downs and the places I've been to and questioned myself a lot.

Was that enough? Will there be any other trips? Will there be a next summit climb to any mountainous peak? Many questions ran in my head. Then, an image of an Island popped up in my head, and a question I've not been answering myself came up.

"What if I ride to Phuket?"

"It's impossible," I muttered. Riding to Phuket isn't like riding to JB. It requires guts, time and the zest to ride that many kilometres to reach Phuket Island.

"Why not try doing something new. So, I won't have to think about the boring life I have."

My mind somehow made this up. Or perhaps, it's just my motivator, my alter ego. But it gave me something to think about. I've been wondering about my boring life and always thought of doing something remarkable for myself. Well, why not try to do something different, right? I thought.

I turned on my laptop and browsed YouTube for people who rode to Phuket. The search results showed that many riders have ridden to Phuket and many of whom were in groups either from Singapore or Malaysia. And to my surprise, many Malaysians have ridden to Phuket with a bike similar to mine, which means that my bike is also possible. This then brought me to another question.

Whom am I going to ride with?

This a tough question to ponder about. Everyone I knew of falls into one of these categories: married, workaholics, or some just lost like error 404. And I'm kind of a random guy who does extemporarily stuff like a sudden aspiration to climb a mountain whenever I feel like it. So, asking someone to ride at an unpredictable time didn't make sense to me.

Apart from that, waiting for someone to ride with wasn't something that I would want to hold myself on. If I were to wait for someone to ride with, and if the trip gets delayed for some reason, then for some reason postponing again would perhaps lead to a never happening trip. And I would be the foolish guy who just relies on someone to travel with, and the waiting game will be an infinite loop.

My mind somehow linked to what the Chinese Singaporean man said when I met him at the washing bay in JB, *"If you get the chance to ride over to Phuket, you should just go."*

It made sense. Looking at what I was doing, there wasn't any obligation that was holding me back. And in fact, I've yet to be called up for reservist. Even if I were to get recalled, I would get six months prior notice before the actual date to book in.

For job wise, where I do food delivery, I can work or not work as I wish. But of course, I wouldn't be making money if I didn't work. And the last thing was that I was still living in my parents' house, which is another positive thing. It all seemed to me that it was, indeed, the right time to go on a road trip where opportunities are aligned perfectly for me to execute them. But then, I just didn't know how to do it.

"Then I have to do something about it. I need to try…"

Again, my mind made this up. I thought about how I could possibly do this ride. The best plan was to explore various states, cities, towns, or even islands along the way. This way, in case something prevents me from getting to Phuket, I'd still be satisfied having visited those places before. And if I make it to Phuket, I shall enjoy the heck out of my time there.

I stared at the black boat on top of my desk and muttered to myself, "Columbus circumnavigated with his ship to see the wider picture of the world. Why not I, circumnavigate with my bike on the land?" I thought.

And so, I made up my mind to give it a try.

***

On 2 September 2019, I embarked my solo ride to Phuket with my stock Yamaha Spark T135. But before reaching Phuket, I did like what I had planned – explore the destination along the way.

I cherry-picked the places that I wanted to explore, and they were Malacca, Kuala Lumpur, Ipoh, Penang and Krabi. In all these destinations, I spent a day or two in each place – which is a relatively short time – which I know, but for the stop in Phuket, I stayed there for five days, enjoying my time there and celebrating my personal accomplishment.

I have to say; I had a great time in Phuket. I did snorkel, Island hopped, tried fishing, hopped from one restaurant to another, went for a massage after another, and also, my eyes were acclimatised to the street full of *wa wa wee ahhh!* But not the ladyboys. My apology.

Before leaving Phuket, I had one final mission: to ride up the steep, curvy road to a hilltop and witness the 45-metre-tall Big Buddha statue in Mueang Phuket District. However, it took me two attempts to do it. The first attempt, a day before leaving Phuket, as I rode halfway up the hill top, dark clouds swiftly rolled in, obscuring the Big Buddha statue and significantly reducing visibility at the summit. Subsequently, strong winds and a heavy downpour ensued simultaneously, forcing me to abort my mission as I was wearing only a T-shirt, shorts, and slippers.

However, I didn't abandon my mission. I made my second attempt the next day, just before leaving Phuket, with full gear on and with all my stuff packed and loaded onto my bike. I rode up the steep road to the hilltop and finally touched down at the peak of Phuket, just to say, "Been there, done that". And that was my final accomplishment for the ride up to Phuket before returning to Singapore.

The total trip duration came up to 18 days. Covered a total of 3000 kilometres plus riding around the cities. Forty-six fuel stops (the fuel tank capacity is only about 4 litres, hence that many), total expenditure came up to $1,500, and few tumbles (locked the front brake disc rotor and forgetting to unlock it before moving off, which led me to flip myself over), few crazy night-riding (with blown off tail light and riding under lightless roads) and two unforeseen incidents. (My phone popped out from the phone holder and dropped on the highway, and unfortunately, my debit card got stuck in the automated teller machine. This made me the first person in line at the bank the very next day to collect my card back – I queued for three hours before the bank opened.)

All and all, I have to say, I've never regretted the ride.

Good thing that I made a move to try.

***

Back in Singapore. Life went on as the same old food delivery rider. However, I was in my *tiny* world as a superstar as some riders that I knew on the road, and on social media, congratulated me for the ride to Phuket as I was still a P-Plate rider which amused them much. But not all were friendly though.

Some knew about it and pretended not to know me when I negotiated a welcome 'hi' to them but to see them walk away as though I was a stranger. Some congratulated me and said that I was inspiring to them, which flabbergasted me as I had never done something before to inspire someone. But some, just the inverse of it.

"You're not the first person who does this kind of trip alone. Others did it before."

It was odd to hear it through my ears as I was only doing it for myself. I wasn't riding for the world. It was a ride to give my life a better story to tell than having a boring life. But it seemed like some people disliked others for doing something good, and I have witnessed it live, apparently.

***

Back to my delivery job, life was going on as usual. The Phuket road trip kept flashing in my mind while I did deliveries. I thought of the impeccable moments of the food I consumed, the dirt-cheap massages I had, the exceptional sceneries I had seen along my ride, and the wonderful people who welcomed me with their cheerful smiles. I was overwhelmed by the experiences, and there wasn't any truly notable thing I had done before that could replace the Phuket road trip.

I even made a montage video of the road trip, which took me almost three weeks to edit and upload on YouTube. By the way, that was my very first YouTube video.

Whenever I had to wait for the order to be prepared by the vendor, I would watch the video I made, and at times, I would smile to myself unconsciously. Not that I was being self-obsessed or what, it's just that I have nothing better to do while waiting for the order to be readied. But the more I watch my video, the more I crave for it. It felt like my mundane life was transforming into something more interesting. But deep down within me, a persistent feeling urge me to pursue something more extraordinary to create *a better life story*. Yet again, I wondered and wondered.

***

On 2 October 2019, I sat by at one of the coffee shops in my work zone, stirring the coffee with a teaspoon while staring at my bike parked across the road. As I was about to daydream, I came back to my conscious mind after a ringtone sound from the delivery application indicating that my shift was about to start soon. However, there was still some time before the shift started. So, I got on to YouTube and watched the video of the road trip I made to see if I could improve on my video edits. As I was watching the video, I happened to see related videos on the right pane of the YouTube user interface, and one of them somehow induced me to have a look at it.

The video was about two guys on their BMW R1200 GS, riding a famous loop called *Mae Hong Son loop* in northern Thailand. This loop isn't an ordinary round loop to speak of. It has numerous hairpin bends and a rough total of 1864 bends around the loop. The total loop distance covers about 600 kilometres long, and it's one of the places where enthusiastic riders would come by to tackle this loop. Besides riding the *Mae Hong Son loop*, the two GS riders rode up to *Doi Inthanon* – the highest peak in Thailand with an elevation of 2,565 metres above sea level. And finally, they rode further up north to *Golden Triangle,* a location where three country borders meet at, and the countries are Laos, Myanmar and Thailand.

I peered up to look at my bike and stared at it momentarily. My alter ego came into action.

"Mae Hong Son loop...Golden Triangle..."

I shook my head and then rolled my eyes to see the P-Plate sticker. An abrupt thought came into my head, hinting me to check on my passing date of the class 2B licence. It stated, 30 November 2018. Two months left to say goodbye to my P-Plate sticker and be part of the normal people on the road of Singapore. My alter ego popped up again:

How would it be like being at Golden Triangle on the day after a year passing of my licence? Since you ride to Phuket, why not go further? Phuket is just a child's play. Too easy. Anyone can do it. Like that donkey who said to you, 'OTHER PEOPLE HAVE DONE IT BEFORE....' Why not ride up Doi Inthanon too? I don't think anyone rode up with their P-Plate bike solo to Doi Inthanon and using a 135cc bike from Singapore.

It would take me, who knows, lots of days for me to reach Golden Triangle. Apart from that, the return trip back to Singapore would take several days, and the total trip duration would take me a long time.

Hold up, hold up. I understood what you were trying to say. Think about this. The 18 days road trip to Phuket, you had a hell lot of fun and had great memories, right? Why not this time round ride to Golden Triangle and complete the Mae Hong Son loop?

Look, it may seem far but look at this picture. What have you achieved in life? Have you ever done something extraordinary for yourself? Phuket is a no-count. So, there's actually - NOTHING!

I've always thought about doing something incredible that would supersede my thoughts on my boring life. Well, the road trip to Phuket was an exceptional one for me. But somehow, deep down in me, it seemed like I could do something much more exceptional.

What if I do this ride up? Will it make my life a better story to tell than a boring life? If I were to do this ride up, I would definitely not be getting paid, nor do I even have cash flow coming in. I'm just not making money, and the trip would take weeks.

Listen, listen. Don't make money as an issue. Do exactly what you did before the road trip to Phuket. You worked extra hours to cover up the non-working days, right? Do the same thing. I know it would be a hectic period, but you get to ride over to Thailand again, and besides that, you're going to make history for yourself. I repeat, FOR YOUR SELF! Ignore what others think of you. Do this ride as though a challenge for yourself.

I have to say; my alter ego is good at convincing me to do something.

"Perhaps, I should give it a try…I would never know this will be the one…." I thought.

I relooked at the licence card again to see my passing date. "30 November 2018… two months left…," I muttered to myself. "How about on the last day, on the 30 November 2019, I end my ride at Golden Triangle?" Soon after this question, I sprouted an idea to do something unique: Within ten days, I have to get my butt up the highest peak in Thailand, complete the Mae Hong Son loop, and finally, reach the Golden Triangle on 30 November 2019. It wholesomely sounded like a real game plan and an endeavour to create a better life story – of course if I make it through.

I peered up to see my bike again, but this time round, I sprouted out an unusual smile of hope.

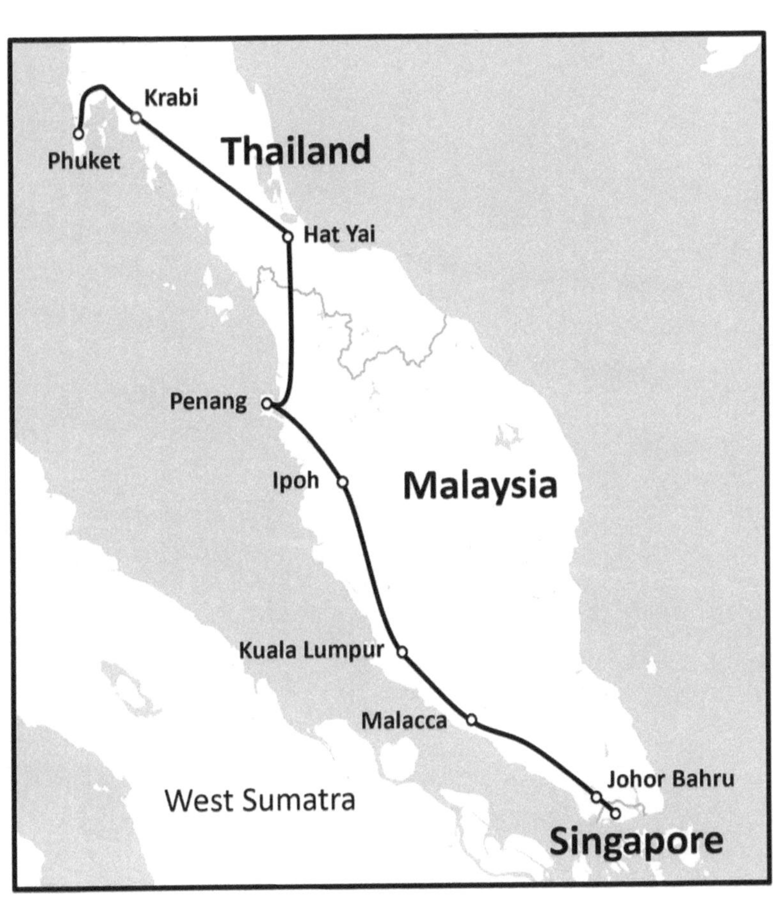
Phuket
Krabi
Thailand
Hat Yai
Penang
Ipoh
Malaysia
Kuala Lumpur
Malacca
Johor Bahru
West Sumatra
Singapore

5

Preparation

Should I even ride up to Golden Triangle with my Yamaha Spark T135? It's twice the distance compared to the ride to Phuket. And not to forget, I have to ride up to the highest peak in Thailand – the Doi Inthanon, and ride 600 kilometres around the Mae Hong Son Loop. I had many sceptics about my bike, but I resulted in having hope with my bike and use what I have.

There was another thing that seemed concerning to me: Will the bike die off halfway through the ride due to the hard push from the last ride to Phuket? I had no idea about that question. And again, I just hoped it would not.

***

Thinking about the time when I rode up to the Big Buddha in Phuket with no apparent problems, will it be the same for the Doi Inthanon summit? It was a question mark to me. The ride up to the Big Buddha in Phuket was mere 400 metres in elevation. Nothing compared to Doi Inthanon, which is six times the elevation of it. However, I thought about those kapcai riders in Sapa, Vietnam, where I had seen the rider ride their heavily loaded bike up the steep hills even at an elevation of 1,500 metres. That inciting thing gave me hope for my bike – or at least just a bit.

I thought about injecting steroids into my bike, but that was impossible. So, I had a different plan. Since there wasn't any modification done to my bike, I thought of replacing the engine top block with a larger piece, alongside replacing the piston and the connecting rod to a larger and longer piece and changing to an exhaust pipe that is loud enough to wake up the whole village. And also, not forgetting to chrome the whee…no…No…NO. It's a NO to all.

I can't do all those stuff. I still had to do my delivery job as normal and get the income to cover the ride up. Apart from that, it's illegal to modify a vehicle in Singapore. If I were to do all those modifications and get busted by the traffic police even before reaching customs in Singapore, then, the road trip can be called "The End". Furthermore, I'm not built like some people who crazily modify their bikes. I'm just a simple and boring dude trying to change his boring life. So, modification is not my kind of thing.

With that said, I left the bike as it was and just hoped that it doesn't fail along the way.

***

There was some stuff had to be replaced and bought: the rear-wheel drum brake shoe, front-wheel brake pad, and saddle (as after sitting for too long on the ride to Phuket, the cushion deflated till I could feel the structure of the seat pressing against my buttocks), spare bulbs, engine oil, oil filter and a spark plug.

I rode over to JB to replace what needed to be replaced. But for the engine oil, oil filter and spark plug, I bought the items and held them till the day before embarking on the journey to service the bike by myself. It's an easy job. I learned most of the basic servicing for my bike by watching the mechanics in JB service my kind of bike and also, watched videos on YouTube for any maintenance related to my bike.

Any other stuff that I had to get, I got them along with my delivery times, where I would rush to shops to get the stuff while waiting for the delivery order to be readied, or I would get the stuff on my off days.

Besides getting the stuff to prepare for the ride, most of my preparation times before nearing the start of the journey, I was riding with fear and as cautious as ever before.

I would ride with extreme caution on roads where there are red-light cameras. Beating one red light could reward me with 12 demerit points and a fine. And since I'm still in the probatory period – which is for 12 months, the max demerit points I could get is 12 demerit points compared to non-probatory, where one can get up to 24 demerit points. But who would want to get demerit points though?

Being rewarded more than 12 demerit points, my licence could be revoked. Not "could" but "confirm" be revoked. So, just getting struck by one red-light camera could make me become a puss in the ball and shoot up my anxiety level to the max. Not sure how others would feel about it, but to me, it's something to me. Even with or without the red-light cameras, I still could get demerit points if I'm unaware of how I ride or do something stupid on the road. Nowadays, so many vehicles in Singapore have cameras in their cars. As such, one could easily report to the relevant authorities if someone does something unusual on the road, and that could lead to being rewarded with demerit points or a fine, or both.

And one thing could definitely cancel off the road trip: getting into an accident. It's taboo to think of, but it's something I was mentally prepared for, but I had much hope that everything would go well.

With that said, as the days got closer and closer to embarking on my journey, I had the scariest rides of my life, even before the start of the trip. (As I type this line, I still think it was).

Part 2: An Endeavour to Create

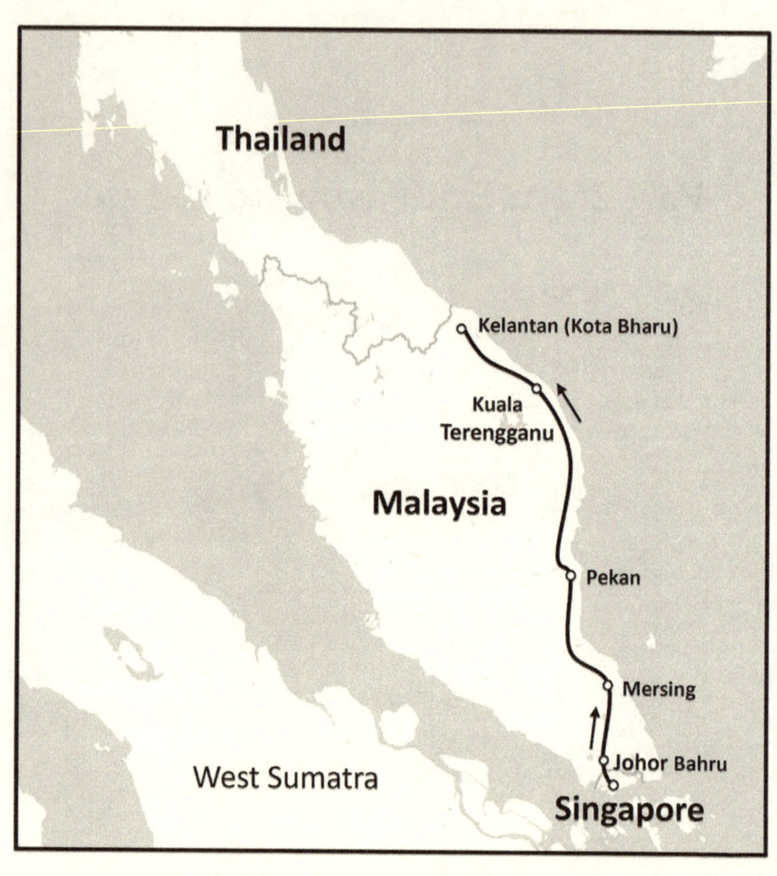

Thailand
Kelantan (Kota Bharu)
Kuala Terengganu
Malaysia
Pekan
Mersing
Johor Bahru
Singapore
West Sumatra

6

Black Figure

I walked out of my housing block elevator with mixed feelings and with racing thoughts. "Should I even do this or should I just get back home and sleep?" Thoughts were ruminating in my mind, but my gut feeling hinted that this opportunity was something I shouldn't miss. That meant that, I have to go.

I was already in my full suit. Starting from the bottom, I wore a three-year-old Nike running shoe with little or no sole to speak of and a new Levi's jeans – somehow, I thought, I might look slightly cool wearing a new pair. My top comprised of a black mesh motorcycle riding jacket, an innerwear of a black dry-fit T-shirt, a turquoise tube scarf that surrounds my neck and last but not least, a new black LS2 helmet to protect my head. Unfortunately, my spectacles were slanted and adjusting them was impossible as I was carrying a pile of stuff around my arms and hands.

The very first mission for the day was to walk to my bike, which was parked 100 metres away from me. I trundled to the parking lot, hugging a fully-filled orange-coloured 40-litre splashproof bag on my left arm. Inside the bag, there was stuff like clothing, electronic stuff, and even another 10-litre haversack bag stuffed inside it. On my right arm, I hugged a blue-coloured 10-litre splashproof bag that had all the necessary maintenance stuff for the bike. My right hand held a zip file that had the paper documents like vehicle registration details and passport-size pictures of myself. In between the orange and the blue bag is the empty jerrycan sandwiched between the bags, and I tried not to let it slip down while I trundled my way to the bike.

The mere 100 metres walk had already made me sweat, and once I reached my bike, I dropped the stuff down to the ground, sighed, and again, wondered if this was even necessary. No answer came to my mind, as it was 7:15 in the morning, and it was the time where I would still be sound asleep.

Helmet off and hung it on the side mirror, then I commenced to load up my stuff on my bike.

Inside the only top box on my bike, there was a tool bag, a chain with a padlock, rain gear wear, motorcycle chain lubrication can, and a picnic mat (a mat that I had wrongly purchased for the Phuket road trip. It ended up looking like a large grey picnic mat that only covers half way down the bike), wet wipes, and few bungee cords. The final item that goes on top of everything is the document zip file before the top box lid closes.

For the 40-litre orange bag, I laid it horizontally on the back of the saddle and made it lean against the top box. On top of the orange bag, I stacked the 10-litre blue bag. After which, I hooked up one end of a bungee cord on the top box rack, then wrapped it around the bags diagonally, and then hooked the other cord end tightly down to the rack. Then repeat the wrap with another bungee cord on the inverse side of the rack. It somehow formed an X-shaped wrap on the bags. I don't know why I chose to wrap up this way, but this wrap did well for the Phuket road trip though.

The empty jerrycan is put in the front basket – which is in between the handlebar and the saddle. However, the jerrycan fail to sit perfectly on the surface of the basket. So, what I did was, I took a black stretchable net with four hooks on its end, wrapped the net on top of the jerrycan, pulled the hooks down to the bottom of the basket to hooked them up.

Much of the space in the basket was used up by the jerrycan. However, there were still small spaces in-between the jerrycan and the basket, for which I used those spaces to place a brake rotor disk lock, a bottle of water, a telescopic selfie stick, and a portable power bank to continuously charge my phone while I'm on my ride.

That was pretty much it. "What do I have left?" I questioned myself. Nothing seemed to appear in my mind. I ran my fingers on the bags, poked them, and mentally visualised the stuff inside them to assure myself I had all the needed stuff. Then opened back the top box and verbally ran through the things to confirm everything.

"Tool-kit check, rain gear check, document file check, check, all checked."

Guess this is it. It's time to leave. My mind sprouted up with some words.

Helmet on, gloves on, and I went pressing the timer button on my phone camera that is attached to a tripod and it was placed metres away from my bike. Then I ran back to my bike to pose for a good shot. Once I was satisfied with the pictures – but after many runs back and forth to get the best pictures, another message came in my mind.

You're about to do the ride. You have one last option to go back home and forget about it. This is your final call.

Looking back at my relentless preparation to prepare for the ride and the days that I survived before this very day, not embarking on this ride can be said as a total loss.

"This will be it. The ride of a life time…" I muttered to myself, but my mind was still sceptical about something.

Maybe there's another ride of a lifetime?

Damn it.

The ignition switched to on, kicked down to gear one, and off I went starting the ride, but a last thought struck my mind abruptly: *Am I really doing this?*

Oh my…What kind of brain I have though…

I rode off slowly, looking up outside my home kitchen window to see no one waving me off, nor was there anyone around to wish me endeavours like how Charley Boorman and Ewen McGregor made a debut for riding across continents. The only thing that made me smile were those clothes that hung on the bamboo poles outside my home kitchen window. The wind flapped the clothes like as though mimicking the flag off for a formula one race. That was more than enough to set me off.

The first destination I planned to stop by for the night is at Kota Bharu, Kelantan. It's in the northeastmost part of Peninsular Malaysia, and it's about 699 kilometres from the move-off point at the parking lot. That was what Google Maps showed me. I have to say, this ride will take a hell lot of time but looking at my rough plan that I had made, it seemed like out of the 10 days, the first day is where I need to take up much distance. So, I had no objections to it and no idea how will the end ride be like in Kota Bharu. However, I had already gone ahead of time to procrastinate my presence at the Golden Triangle, where I creatively plotted people around the vicinity, and they cheered me on while I took off my helmet, shaking my head hair in slow motion like how some movie actors do. And then, posed with my bike, and there came the flashes of camera lights sparkling me up.

What a peculiar imagination I had though.

I ride on like a typical day ride out from my home town but being very cautious on the road. Getting into an accident before crossing the border to Malaysia is sheer bad luck, and there goes the journey. The 10 days to Golden Triangle can be renamed as "no need to go" instead.

"Prevention is better than cure", an old proverb that ruminated in my mind. *"Check over right-shoulder… no vehicle: turn-right."* *"Check over left-shoulder, "no vehicle: turn left…. slow down now!... there's a vehicle at the stop line…. stop at least a bike length away from the vehicle."*

I was that cautious of my movements as I didn't want to get into an accident.

Before heading to Woodlands Checkpoint – one of the land border crossings in Singapore, I rode over to Ang Mo Kio town to withdraw cash from an ATM before riding to the custom.

Cash was withdrawn, and I made my way out of Ang Mo Kio town. But the habits that reside in me easily took over my cautionary ride. Lane splitting to get myself the front of the congested traffic beside the Ang Mo Kio train station, I was horned by some ignorant drivers. I had a presumption that these drivers were those who despise motorcyclist who rides between the lanes. I was about to point my universal middle finger, but my mind brought me back to another old proverb: "Safety starts with me." I rode on and ignored the drivers but thought to myself, why was it necessary to think of the proverbs.

I rode and approached a left filter lane with a zebra crossing. After the zebra crossing, the filter lane would adjoin to a highway that would lead me to the border checkpoint. But before reaching the zebra crossing, I did my pre-checks again: *"Check left-right. No people,"* I rode past the pedestrian crossing and then slowed down to check on the major road on my right for vehicles before merging in.

"No vehicle – check," and I merged into the lane, then checked

back over my left shoulder to say HOLLY SHIT instead of saying other checks.

One of the bungee cords unhooked from the rack, and it was dangling on the tarmac while the orange bag that was supposed to be resting on the back seat wasn't there. It was replaced with the blue bag instead. The missing orange bag was apparently strangling itself against the chain guard – which is on the left side of the bike – and one end of the bag was dragging on the tarmac along with the bungee cord, which made me come to a complete stop at the kerbside.

The set-up for the bags didn't work out well apparently. I removed the blue bag and squeezed it inside the top box without crushing the zip file. Then untangled the orange bag from the chain guard and to see a centimetre hole in the bag.

Good thing that I had checked back. If not, I would have been riding obliviously to the border without any bags behind me.

Not a good start for the day. I thought about the drivers who horned at me earlier. The drivers were horning at me for a noble cause, but my mind misperceived it, saying they were horning at me because I rode between the lanes. Guess that I have been doing food delivery for some time. I had seen many ruthless drivers on the road, leading me to make futile presumptions. Good thing that I didn't show my universal middle finger to them though.

I rewrapped the orange back on the pillion seat again, making sure to wrap it tightly before hooking it back to the rack.

You see! You don't have to do this.

My mind tried to badger me to get back home. The nearest thing to my location was indeed my home, and the furthest thing away from me was the border checkpoint. But I chose the checkpoint as I have already done so much to get to this point. I quickly got on my bike and rode off before my mind created more excuses.

Less than half an hour into the ride, I arrived at the checkpoint and joined the queue along with the other motorists who were crossing the border. But unfortunately, the line moved at a turtle pace that made me paddle with my feet on the ground to move the bike forward instead of using the throttle. However, I didn't mind doing that as there was this unbeknownst person who started to horn while tip-toeing to see why the queue became a standstill. Few others joined the unbeknownst, imitating what he did by tip-toeing to see what was happening in front. They honk like how the first person did it, and quickly, the horns noises accumulated. Then everyone started to honk along together, making it so loud for one ear to bear. It was just hilarious looking at these people doing stuff like this sporadically, and it was more like they were doing it just for the thrill. But I didn't complain much about it. I joined them at some intervals too.

Once my passport was scanned on the biometric machine at the Woodlands Checkpoint, this became the first confirmation that I was for sure embarking on the journey. I rode over to the Johor Bahru border to get my passport stamped. It wasn't busy at the border, and my turn came once I reached the passport stamping booth. The passport was stamped, and this became the final confirmation that I had to do this trip and there was no way out.

I received the passport back from the officer, placed it in a *plastic zip bag,* and kept it inside the left pocket of the riding jacket.

Before starting on the actual long ride to Kelantan, I stopped by a petrol station close to the Johor Bahru border to fuel up both the bike's fuel tank and the jerrycan. But the jerrycan was only filled to half of its capacity – which was just 2.5 litres, as it didn't make sense for me to carry a full jerrycan where there are petrol stations equally segregated along the way. But if I were to miss one, then this 2.5 litres of spare fuel is more than enough to bring me to the next petrol station.

After fuelling up, I took my sweet time to grab breakfast near the petrol station, bringing the time to almost 10 am. There was no sense of worry or urgency eventhough I had 12-hour of ride to deal with. But it was only when I looked up at the sky to see greyish clouds gathering, which nudged me to get going.

Before the big journey commenced, I sleeved up my phone with a waterproof cover and secured it onto the phone holder. Then further securing the phone with elastic rubbers on all four corners of the phone holder. If the rain were to fall, all I had to do was only think about wearing the rain gear and not think about the phone getting wet. Then lastly, the Google Maps set up to Kota Bharu, Kelantan, and the absolute real ride began to turn the ignition key to ON, kick down to gear one, checked back over my shoulders, and off I went to embark on the long ride.

***

I rode along Highway 3, which led me towards the eastern part of the peninsula Malaysia. Low-rise shophouses were mostly seen on both sides of the road, but they slowly changed to greens as I covered more distance.

The possibility for the rain to fall was evident as the roads were already wet, and far ahead of me, grey clouds hovered above the sky. Looking at the side mirrors that reflected the clouds behind me, the clouds appeared even greyer and darker than the clouds in my front view. It's either way, I will get wet. Despite the early warning of the rain to fall, my intuition told me to only wait for the rain to fall first and then wear the rain gear. Probably because of the time when I rode to Phuket, where I was overly prepared wearing my rain gear most of the time, but not much rain poured down.

Forty minutes into the ride, from a few road lanes, it changed between dual and single carriageway. Then after some time, green trees became evident on both sides of the road.

It started to drizzle from the look of the rain droplet that rolled down from the phone's waterproof sleeve. I stopped to wear the rain gear and zipped up the rain jacket zipper till stopping just below the body camera – a body camera that looks like a security camera that is clipped onto the collar of my riding jacket. However, if the rain were to fall hard, the rain jacket zipper would be fully zipped up to cover up the camera as it isn't waterproof.

One hour into the ride, the rain started to pour down. That made me switch the body camera off and zip up the rain jacket fully. The road became fixed to a single carriage road, and my speed fluctuated between 50 to 60 km per hour due to the slippery ground. Not the speed for Malaysian drivers to ride at my speed where I see many vehicles speeding past me on my right. I shifted to the left most of the lane to let other vehicles pass me from my back. However, the unfortunate me sometimes get splashed by puddles of rainwater by the vehicles when passing uneven ground.

The green vegetation on both sides of the road slowly faded away as I entered a small town, and low-rise shophouses appeared on both sides of the road again. The rain subsided and was overtaken by the tiny drizzles, and I went stopping distance away to see a large sign displayed on the overhead bridge. It has a word written: 'MERSING'. My typical activity during the Phuket road trip was to snap pictures of the destination signs in each state or province I entered, with me alongside in the picture. Doing that would give me memories of what I had done during the period. The same rule applied to this trip, but from the look on the skies above, it seemed like there wouldn't be many opportunities to get a good shot on the forthcoming states.

The ride went on, and the time had just touched noon. So

far, the ride was dull as hell. Nothing much to see as the rain continually poured, and much of my view was just dreary green trees on both sides of the road. I stopped at another small town to fill the tank and waited 20 minutes to cool down the engine. Something that I religiously do at every petrol station I stopped at on the prior trip to Phuket. It gave an additional *kick* to the engine for a few kilometres from the start of the ride somehow. The same rule applied to this trip but waiting longer than 20 minutes at every petrol station, I think the road trip can change to 20 days instead.

The ride continued, and I was finally fortunate enough to see something different besides the dull-looking trees. A herd of brown, white and black cattle in varied sizes were crossing to the other side of the road. Vehicles stopped behind me and in the opposing lane. The drivers weren't rushing to move off or horn at the herd of cattle. But instead, waited patiently for these harmless creatures to cross over. I watched them cross over; I watched them wander about plucking the leaves and watched them munch on. Looking at the everyday thing in life soothed my mind as there weren't many animals interspersed along my ride. Probably due to the dreadful weather. I admired their presence and took some pictures of them, but some were just taking their sweet time to cross over the road.

Excuse me, I have to go... I'm late...

The torrential rain poured down sporadically. The one thing I hate about this torrential rain is that it hits me from all different angles. My shoes, which weren't covered up by any waterproof material, had already become wet and my riding jacket collar – which is not waterproof, well the whole jacket itself isn't waterproof – mysteriously became wet although I wore a rain jacket to cover it. Probably it all started when the rain struck at an angle, causing the droplets to wet up the tube scarf first before spreading down to the collar of the riding jacket.

The gloves that I wore weren't fully waterproof to speak of. It became soaking wet and transferred its wetness to the wrist of the riding jacket. And some sneaky rain droplets somehow slipped in through the wrist opening of the rain jacket and slid down, stopping around my elbow area, bulging it up and waiting for more water to be collected. I had to flap my arm down to let the rainwater pour out, but once I placed my hand back on the handlebar grip, the rain droplet still got in somehow.

Not only I had the dilemma of collecting water in my jacket, but riding behind a flatbed truck on a single carriageway, was another dilemma to deal with. Trying to overtake the truck is like an impossible task in this type of dreadful weather. The flatbed truck driver intermittently speeds up at an unvaried timing and then slows down drastically at an unvaried timing too. This made me stay way back from the flatbed, so I don't get into a rear-end collision. However, it further pushed my time back from getting to Kelantan, for which I had to do something about it.

I rode close to the middle of the single carriageway to peep to the front to see if any vehicles were in the front of the flatbed. No vehicles at the front of the flatbed, and the intermittent speeding and braking were absolutely unnecessary.

"Probably the driver is drunk," I thought.

I tried to overtake the flatbed by first sticking my head out to the right to check on the opposing lane. No vehicles approached. So, I rode on the opposing lane, then increased the throttle to get enough speed to overtake the flatbed. However, the truck driver sped up at the same time as I, which made no difference for me to overtake it at all.

I have been intimidated.

I made another attempt again. Peeped over to the opposing lane, rode to the opposing lane, and further throttled again. And there goes the same thing. The driver sped up at the same time as me, and I went back behind it again.

I was intimidated.

Tried several attempts to take over the flatbed, but instead, be overtaken by the other speed demons who sped past me as though I was riding a bicycle and then overtook the flatbed effortlessly.

The ride went on, but I was still behind the flatbed. The rainwater somehow got in through whatever tiny opening on the rain gear that made my riding jacket fully wet. The ride became even more unpleasant when I got splashed by puddles of water from the huge potholes on the opposing lane. And one great big splash came striking me, causing the bike to shift left and almost making me lose control.

Then came one section of the road that appeared to be flooded at the height of the footrest of my bike – which is about a foot height. I rode past it, lifting both my feet in the air and further slowed down to ride past the flooded section. But the unfortunate me wasn't so lucky for the day. The vehicles from opposing lane came speeding through the flood as though it was a normal terrain surface, and I got smacked by the big splashes one after another.

From all these obnoxious splashes, I fully declared that this was the wildest water theme park experience I've ever been on.

***

The time had reached 3:15 pm. The rain subsided as I arrived at a town name Pekan in the province of Pahang. Pekan, to a degree, was my halfway mark for the day-one ride. A total of 300 kilometres had been covered, and here is where my stomach growls for food really bad. I rode over to fuel up the tank and then slowly rode past a stretch of low-rise buildings to look out for any food shops to have a meal. Then I came stopping next to the restaurant that is located at one corner of the low-rise building with a signboard in red and words written in white: *My Mama's*.

After randomly picking one meal on the menu, a tray with my meal came in front of me and it was wrapped up in brown paper. I got back to my table carrying the tray, placing it on the table and as I took off my wet riding jacket, it somehow emanated like tuna – probably the concoction of water types that splashed on me. With some positivity in me still, I ignored the aroma from the jacket but once I sat on the chair, an instant discomfort-ness ignited in me. Apparently, the riding jacket had spread its wetness down to my jeans till the jeans crouch area felt like a soaked-up sponge. Handling the discomfort-ness like a man, I went on to batter down my meal comprised of rice that is splurged with *sambal* (chilli paste), a cutlet chicken that is also splurged around with *sambal*, and finally, on top of the chicken cutlet, a half cut fully boiled salted egg – which is also splurge with *sambal*. An interesting meal perhaps.

The meal was indulged down fast, but I still sat down, staring out the glass door, watching my bike being poured by the rain droplets. I wondered to myself whether the trip was worth the go or not as I was overwhelmed by the exhaustion from the ride. Never felt that exhausted compared to my ride to Phuket, which made me feel like quitting and felt like getting back home to get a long warm bath, then get on my comfortable smooth bed, and then knock off from there. It felt so good thinking about it. But looking at my present circumstance, where I'd already reached the halfway point and had already been soaked up by the many splashes, quitting wasn't the right thing to think of. And so, I got going before my mind creates an alternative game plan.

The farther I rode, the stronger the torrential rain poured down. Riding at the speed of 60 kilometres per hour, it was just pain getting hit by rain droplets. But going any slower than that, it felt like the asphalt and vegetation on both sides of the road kept repeating forever.

A left bend approaches on the right, and I slowed down to negotiate the bend. But once I'd done negotiating the bend, instantly, I became dismayed to see another flatbed in front of me.

Damn it…

I ducked my head close to the handlebar dashboard panel; positioned my body at an arc of 45 degrees – almost; with my chin fully tucked out; and slid my buttock out all the way back till touching the cushion point of the orange bag behind me. And then, I throttled down to speed up and prepared to change to the opposing lane to overtake the flatbed.

Move aside, I'm coming throu…. WHAT THE FUCK IS THAT!!!

A *black figure*, about a metre in height, that looked pretty "buffed up," came running out from the dense green on the right side of the road, using all four of its limbs to pound onto the ground, and it heads straight towards the right side of the flatbed tyres. I instantly sprung up to sit straight, closed the throttle, arm straightened, and went depressing the foot brake together with the hand brake till it let the rear wheel fishtail on the road surface. The *black figure* didn't stop nor became afraid of what was in front of it. It just kept pounding down to the ground heading straight to the flatbed tyres with no mercy. The flatbed driver noticed the *black figure* and made a quick reaction by making the adjoined flatbed fishtail, missing the *black figure* by a hairpin closeness from the tyres on the right. Then quickly recovers the flatbed back to the road lane before its rear tyre skids out from the road surface on the left.

But the *black figure* has yet to cross over to the other side of the road yet. It became my turn to react.

When I got control of my bike after the fishtailing, I hastily lane-changed to the right without even thinking much and missed the black figure wide away from me. But the unfortunate me, I went over a pothole that sprung the bike up violently that almost made me fell off from my bike. I managed to control the bike and recovered back to the ongoing lane – but with much heart palpitations. I looked at the right-side mirror to see the *black figure* run into the greens and disappear from sight.

If I were to fall, oh my, the *black figure* would probably be having an Indian cuisine with marination of whatever I ate from *My Mama's* restaurant earlier.

Everything happened so fast that the flatbed driver rode as normally as though a usual thing. However, I was still in freak mode and pondered much about what had happened and thought of what kind of monkey species it was. I was never a monkey enthusiast nor someone who knew much about monkey species types. But it somehow urged me to figure out what the heck was that. It resembled like a gorilla, but it was much hairier, and it was totally black. Probably the total blackness due to the rain that had darkened its overall hair. I tried to recall whatever monkey species I had seen before, but nothing resembled like what I had seen. Perhaps, one reason for not getting a better look at it is due to the rainwater that pours down the helmet's visor that distorted my vision.

It was a mystery and a waste that I hadn't been able to turn on the body camera. But all I knew was; what had happened was only between me and the flatbed driver. And that was about it. With that said, life goes on as per normal.

The ride went on, and I was still behind the flatbed truck shivering exasperatedly under my wet clothing, and my jeans were already halfway wet through my knees, and my inner dri-fit shirt had already become wet. However, my focus was still on high alert. I added an additional checklist to look out at the dense greens on both sides of the road. With that said, I concluded to stay right behind the flatbed till it exits out of its way and not do any unsophisticated stunts on the road.

The time had already reached 7 in the evening. The lonely ride went on Route 14 and eventually connected to the E8 expressway from Bukit Besi. The portable power bank that I kept in the front basket that continuously charges my phone while I'm on the go, surprised me much that it didn't get short-circuit from the torrential rain. However, the battery had gone flat. The blinking red-light device that is mounted on the fairing of the handlebar is there to tell me if the bike's camera was still functioning, and it's also powered by a portable power bank under the seat. But too bad, there wasn't any red light flashing out from it. Which meant that its battery had gone flat too. My phone battery had come down to 40 per cent, and I had left with 200 kilometres to ride on. However, there's an additional power bank I had brought along, but it's deep inside the orange bag. No way I would want to take that out under this dreadful rain that kept on pouring and pouring.

Three-quarter of the total distance had been covered, and I had reached the state of Terengganu. As heedless as I was, I rode without looking at the instrument panel that brought the fuel indicator needle down to the red zone mark. However, the fuel indicator needle wasn't calibrated correctly. When the fuel indicator needle points at the red zone mark, it means that the fuel capacity is still above the limit. But as I heed to look at the needle position, the needle went *below* the red zone mark. That meant that at any moment, the bike may puff to stop.

Sudden panic struck me as I was still riding on the expressway and feared it would come to a stop. I kept left all the way and looked for the closest exit of the expressway with my mind constantly exclaiming, "GET TO THE PETROL STATION NOW!"

If the bike dies off on the expressway, good luck to me refuelling the tank under the rain. As the fuel tank is under the seat, bringing up the seat itself exposes the 12v battery for the bike and also exposes the bike's camera connection wires. If the rainwater were to enter into the fuel tank, then again, good luck to me. I would have to change the "10 days to Golden Triangle" to "How to fail stupidly on a road trip," perhaps.

Not bad, I am pretty creative in creating failure titles.

I managed to exit the expressway and rode to a small-town named Ajil, to look out for a petrol station. The nearest petrol station shown on the GPS was Petronas station. It was about three kilometres away when I exited the expressway. For every 100 metres I covered, it felt so glorifying, and my apprehensiveness alleviated as I got closer to the petrol station.

A kilometre down, the second kilometre down, and it came down to the last 100 metres. At this point, I no longer feared that the bike might puff to stop. Fortunately, the hopeful me, managed to stop beside the pump gun at Petronas station.

Once done re-fuelling, I sat by on the kerbside at the petrol station, both palms on my jawbone, and stared at my bike that was being wet by rain droplets outside the station. Knowing that there were another 185 kilometres left for Kelantan, felt depressing. Brutally beaten up by the rain, and I could say that I was utterly wet under my rain gear.

From all the negative thoughts ruminating in my head, somehow, I heed towards my passport. My heart beat raised while I unzipped the pocket on the left side of the jacket to take out the zip bag where I last kept the passport before riding off from Johor Bahru border.

As I took out the passport, the zipper bag that secured the passport appeared cloudy inside, and the zipper was half open. My face turned numb, and my eyes were already wide open with shock. Even before unzipping the pouch, my cognitive mind had already presumed that something bad was going to happen.

I unzipped the pouch and retrieved the passport with my wet wrinkled fingers. However, halfway through, I paused to wipe my fingers on the concrete ground attempting to dry them as much as possible. Once I took out the passport to look at it, the passport wasn't the "crisp" feel that I knew of, and it appeared wet. I ran through my fingers on the concrete ground to further dry my fingers, then opened the passport to leaf through the pages. But most of the pages were adhered by the rainwater and the pages flipped in chunks. I further wiped my fingers on the concrete ground and cautiously separated the pages, one by one. But to my horror, I was dismayed to see the previous immigration stamps being smudged out, and some of the stamps had overlapped to either the preceding or the succeeding pages. The smudged stamps had also distorted the travel dates from the prior trips I had been to. It felt so disheartening to look at them, and I instantly perceived that I would be in deep shit.

What if I can't enter Thailand tomorrow? This road trip will just be a joke you know...

Many thoughts plagued my mind, and I just didn't know what to do. I kept the passport back in the same zip bag as I was already feeling numb in my mind and tried not to think about it but just hoped for tomorrow.

The last 185 kilometres of the ride to Kelantan were truly exhausting, but when the distance came down to two digits, it felt so exhilarating. The *Final Countdown by Europe* was running in my head for every kilometre I passed on, and I sang out loud boldly, as if no one was allowed to stop me from singing. But where the endpoint would be, was what I was curious to know as the Google Maps pin-drop directed me to a roundabout on the map.

More infrastructure and shop houses appeared on both sides of the road, but the vicinity looked gloomy as if there weren't many vacant here in this town. But once I was able to see the roundabout from a distance, nothing appeared gloomy to me and the feeling of calling it a day became evident.

As I reached the roundabout and stopped at the kerbside, I see a lit-up clock tower in the middle of the roundabout. I looked at it with much contentment in me, realising that I had ridden over 699 kilometres, and it finally came to an end. But the time had already turned to 11:45 pm.

***

There was one thing left for the day: to find an accommodation. My phone battery left with 8 per cent, and I wasted no time looking out for accommodation on an application that I had downloaded on my phone. From the look on the list of accommodations left in the application, there were plenty of accommodations to choose from. But that wasn't the issue. The real issue was the parking place for my bike.

I looked through the pictures advertised by the properties with parking spots inside the property and with an affordable price tag, but unfortunately, they were all fully booked. This meant that I had to pick the ones that were either expensive accommodations or those with a description of "Street Parking". The latter was something I wanted to avoid. Say, if I were to park my bike on the streets, and it disappears the following day, then it's goodbye to the road trip. But then, I didn't have the luxury of staying in expensive accommodation to avoid what I wanted to avoid. With that said, I have no choice but to pick the accommodation that states "Street

Parking".

I picked a random accommodation on the application, rode over to the property, and stopped next to a few stories' high hotel building. My helmet was off, and I walked over to the glass door to push it open but to realise that the glass door had locked up. I peeped through the glass door, cupping my temples with my hands to see no one behind the receptionist's table or anyone was around in the foyer. I knocked on the glass door to see if any heads pop up, but to see none. I knocked on the glass door slightly harder, thinking someone could hear me. But still, no heads came looking for me.

I leaned my forehead on the glass door frowning to myself, frustrated, and my stomach growled after looking at a shelf adjacent to the glass door that displayed cup noodles on the rack with display lights shining on it. The last proper meal I ate was at the *My Mama's* restaurant. And from there on, I only had a can of coffee from the previous petrol station I had visited.

As I was about to walk away, I heard a voice. I turned back to look through the glass door and see a man walking towards the glass door, hugging onto a pillow. An explosion of euphoria ignited in me, to which I waved at him and mumbled something that I, myself, couldn't comprehend what I said. He came to the glass door and squatted down to unlock it, half opening it, and asked, *"Kenapa abang?* (What's the matter brother?)"

All I thought for the moment was that I had to speak in my unsophisticated Bahasa Malay.

"Ade bilik tak? (Is there a room?)" I asked in solace.

"Ade, masuk abang (Yes, come in brother)," he said in a gentle tone and welcomed me in despite me making the floor wet from my soaking wet clothes.

He went behind the receptionist's desk and instantly asked for my passport, which instantly put a smile on my face. As he flipped my passport pages, he was surprised by its condition and asked me how it came to this state. I told him my dilemma, and he shook his head sympathetically to my story and then said something afterwards. But I couldn't fathom what he had said as his dialect appeared so odd to my ears. I just nodded, but he looked at me as though I had to answer something. I just nodded again, and it was awkward afterwards.

I managed to secure a room but had mixed thoughts after he got out of the hotel to show me where I can park the bike at. He pointed at a walkway, which is beside the steps to the hotel, and tells me that there are close circuit cameras at the hotel premises that could monitor my bike. At my dreaded position, I agreed to park the bike there and took out all the stuff from the bike but left the jerrycan in the front basket. Then, took the chain out from the top box, wrapped the rear wheel with the chain, and padlocked their end rings.

For the front wheel, I used a disc look to lock the brake disc. And finally, I covered up the bike with a picnic mat, but it only covered till halfway down the bike.

Well, at least I tried.

***

Within less than half an hour, the room was already cluttered with whatever stuff that I had brought along. The riding jacket went hanging on the wall hook that is beside the room door. My wet jeans lay on top of the backrest of the one-seater sofa next to the bed. The tube scarf and the gloves were laid spread on the seat of the sofa. My wet inner shirt was thrown to the toilet basin, and it went along with my underwear for hand washing with shower foam that I had brought along.

The long hot shower went on with much procrastination that

made the toilet cloudy and made the mirror fully fogged up. My palm and fingers had become relatively white and wrinkled up, and they appeared soggy like as though I had swum a long time in a pool. My waist had wrinkled print marks which were gotten from the waist of the jeans, and my skin appeared reddish all around which induced me to scratch them. My toenails were pushed inwards, and it caused the peripheral skin around to bloat up, and it looked white. My overall skin became rough, and the supposed-to-be Indian-Malay brownish colour of my skin tone, my true colour had faded off slightly as though I might have the chance to become like Michael Jackson.

Well, this was the result of a prolonged gruelling ride under the rain full of discomfort-ness.

The night didn't end just yet. After plugging in all electronics to charge, I searched for a hairdryer to blow dry the passport, only to find that there wasn't one available in the room. I went back down to the front desk to ask the receptionist for a hairdryer, but to see a dishevelled receptionist who had been awakened by me, and I was told that there wasn't one available in the hotel either. Instead of heading back to my room empty-handed, I bought a curry-flavoured cup noodle. Not much of my energy was left in me, but a little hope from the curry cup noodle would give me some energy to find ways to dry up the passport.

The time had already reached 1:45 in the morning, but still, I couldn't figure out how to dry up the passport. I walked back and forth in the room, contemplating how to get my passport to dry up, but it only drives up my apprehensiveness. I surrendered finding a solution and went over to switch off the lights to get to bed. However, the room became very dark after the lights were switched off. It was something that I disliked whenever I stayed in a hotel. I would always turn on a light that partially lit up a part of the room. Not that I am afraid of the dark, it's just that, in case I need to get up, I need the light to guide me to get my spectacles and to also switch on the room lights. But since there is a window right next to the bed that is blocking the street lights, I partially slide open the curtain to let the street lightings reflect onto the wall in front of me. Just then, my eyes widen to see the lights shine at the air-con in front of the bed. And that was when a not-so-brilliant idea sprung up in my head.

I scrambled to find the air-con's remote controller, maxed out the fan speed, further lowered the temperature, and tried to aim the air-con's outlet's fins at the floor in front of the bed. Then I took the passport and placed it on the floor, opening up the pages of the passport, then took a television controller and put it on the front cover page of the passport and then took the air-con's controller and placed it at the back cover page. It then stuck out like a 3D booklet. The contented me went to bed satisfactorily, hoping the passport would be dried up hours later.

What an unrealistic hope though.

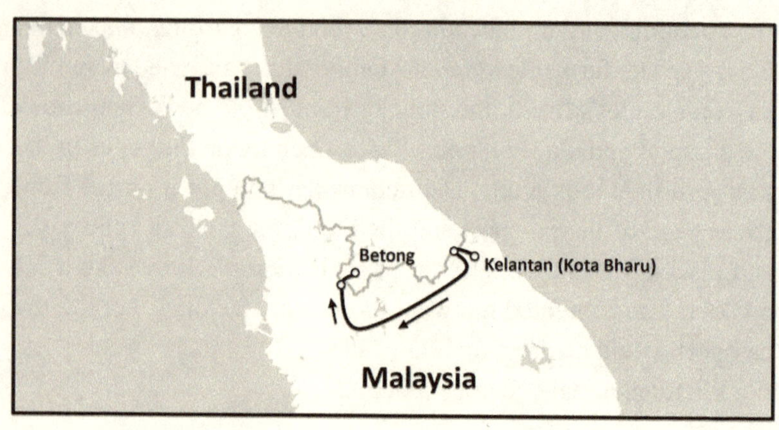

Thailand
Betong
Kelantan (Kota Bharu)
Malaysia

7

What Do You Mean By Enjoy?

I picked up the passport dolefully to see the pages still in a state of dampness. The mere hours of sleep didn't help to dry up the passport pages. And worst, some of the pages where the rainwater spread stopped at, had formed circular cloudy shapes and they turned slightly brown. Flipping through the pages and contemplating at the same time how I could dry up the passport, my mind nudged me to look at the wall clock. The time had already turned to 10:45 am. My check-out time is at 11 am. My pre-trip plan was to get up by 7 in the morning every day and start with my ride as early as 8. But just on the second day itself, things were going haywire and my plans were not going as planned.

Well, not all plans go as planned, right?

Looking back at the wall clock again, staring at the long needle that ticks the seconds, my weary face awakened up further to realise that I didn't have much time before checking out from the hotel.

I scurried around my room, tossing all the stuff that I had poured out onto the floor last night into my bag. Then wore on the filthily wet clothes I had worn the day before but with a new piece of tube scarf, an inner t-shirt, underwear, and a new pair of socks.

Finally, I filled my arms and hands with all my stuff and took the stairs down to the foyer as the elevator was under maintenance.

Thank goodness I had checked out on time. I don't know why, but I just didn't like checking out late. I probably didn't want to trouble the receptionist by informing me that I had to check out on time, or I didn't want to pay additional hours for checking out late. The latter fits me well as I am kind of a parsimony.

The first thing for the day was to check the bike to see if the bike was outside. It was there and untouched as the ugly-looking picnic mat was still there covering half the bike.

Loaded up the stuff to where it was all supposed to be placed and with no change of set up. But as I squatted down to wrap the orange bag with the bungee cord, I felt my back, my shoulders, my quads, and all my body muscles ached abysmally, to which I pondered.

Was it the rain yesterday or the prolonged period of sitting down on the bike? But man, I don't want to have these shitty aches. It's making me feel so restless. This is just the second day, you know... Not even at the mid-point of the journey, and I'm already battered down like this. I tell you what, you end the ride as early as possible. If not, you will, I mean, WE will feel the same feeling again like how we are feeling now.

***

From my location to the Rantau Panjang border was only about 39 kilometres. I rode along Route 3, looking up at the sky to see patches of light grey clouds hovering above, giving me an early sign to get prepared if the rain were to fall, or perhaps, giving me an early warning for 'Round 2' from the prior day's dreadful ride. Even if there were Round 2, I wouldn't be bothered about it as I had already been acclimatised by the torrential rain and the great splashes from the water theme park along my ride yesterday. So, bring it on.

The relatively short distance to the Rantau Panjang border eased my ride. I looked around the vicinity for any roadside vendors to have a quick meal before reaching the border. Not many food vendors were along the way apparently. But as I got closer to the border, there were a few roadside vendors, to which I randomly picked one and stopped by to get a quick brunch before having to see my fate at the border.

The ride continued to the Rantau Panjang border. Upon reaching it, just metres away, I mentally prepared myself as my apprehensiveness grew exponentially. From a distance, I could see the relatively short queue at the passport stamping booth. The longer I waited, my apprehensiveness advanced even further. So, I had to go, and I rode on slowly over to the motorcycle lane and ran through some procedures in my head.

Stop next to the booth; pass the passport to the immigration officer; get a stamp; and then ride over to the Thailand border. Don't do any stupid things. Just ride straight without looking back.

Just as I arrived at the motorcycle lane, only three Malaysian bikes were queuing in front of me. I took off the gloves and prepared my passport with much heart palpitation and watched the queue move fast. My turn came fast, and my hands trembled as I reached next to the immigration booth to get my passport stamped.

There was an officer in his dark blue uniform inside the booth. He smiled at me, and I smiled back but kept a poker face on and passed my passport to him. When he flipped open the passport and leafed through the pages slowly, his face instantly changed. His eyebrows narrowed down, and the concentration on his face was immensely undesirable to look at. My mind was in complete silence, watching him get back to the beginning of the passport pages to reassure what he was seeing. My mouth spewed out some words which I wasn't prepared to say.

"A bit wet."

He muttered something to himself and said, "Go office," with a mysterious expression pointing in a particular direction.

"Where?" I asked without questioning why. I already knew why and to question him may create trouble. So, the best way is to just listen to him.

He points at somewhere that I couldn't see from my current viewpoint. I nodded and asked him where to park the bike. He stood up from his seat and peered out from the window opening of the booth, and pointed at where two other bikes were parked at, and then, he points to a door which represented like an immigration office. I got back the passport with my trembling hands and rode over to park my bike.

Helmets off, phone off from the phone holder, I walked to where the officer had pointed.

Why am I even going there? Is it because foreigners need to get the stamp at the office instead at the booth? I don't know man but hope that I can get my passport stamped at the office.

Knocking on the door and opening it slowly and my half-body holding the door, I see an officer in a blue uniform with a better-looking embroidery decoration on his shoulders, attending to someone on his desk. He stopped whenever he was typing and stared at me, but I was gasping for words to say.

"I, I…the officer at the booth ask me to come here," I stuttered as I spoke and fearfully held on to the door. He looks at me with a baffled look and says, "Got queue?" I looked at him with a baffled look and said, "queue?" after looking around the office for anyone queuing. But to only see one man sitting in front of his desk.

"Sit outside. Wait for your turn," the officer said in a rough tone. Still holding onto the door, I turn back to see two other men, one in a white top and another in an orange top. Let me call the white top as Tom, and the orange top as Jerry for easy reference. They were seated on the bench at one corner and smiled at me when I looked at them. I turned back to the officer on the desk and nodded to him and slowly closed the door, then walked over and sat on the bench.

"*Dari mana*? (From where?)," asked Tom.

"*Dari* Singapore," I replied.

"*Berapa orang datang*? (How many people come here?)," asked Jerry.

I smiled and told them that I had come alone and making my way to Golden Triangle.

"Gold… Go…*Mana tu*? (Where is that?)," asked Jerry.

Trying to figure out how to explain to them, "Er… *tahu* Chiang Mai *kat mana*? (Do you know where Chiang Mai at?)"

"Chi… Chiang…," Tom tried to comprehend what I was trying to say and then turned to the other man to see if he understood what I had said.

They both looked baffled, and they started speaking in Thai and nodded to each other as though they were trying to decipher something. It was then my turn to give them my baffled look, as I had never heard someone switching between speaking Bahasa Malay and Thai language.

"Ohh… *Jauh sangat ni* (very far away)," Tom finally understood me and was surprised by how far it was. "*Moto besar la tu*? (With a big bike from where?)"

"*Tak la. Moto kecil* (No. Small motorcycle)"

"*Boleh tengok moto tu*? (Can see the bike?)," both asked me.

I pointed in the direction of my bike, but they were looking elsewhere other than my bike.

"*Yang mana*? (Which one?)" the white top asked.

Still pointing at my bike and I slowly explained the bike with the orange bag on the seat.

"*Moto tu*? (That motor?)" They asked with their baffled faces, and I wondered why I was seeing too many baffled faces today.

"Ahhhhh," they said in jinx and with much astonishment from them. Then both stretched out their hands to shake my hand and both says, "*Bagus, bagus* (Good, good)" repeatedly to me. I wasn't even sure if I would even get a stamp at the immigration office, but I was already getting praised by them. Well, it was nice to be flattered though.

Then Jerry asks me where am I heading to. I gave a baffled look at Jerry as I had already told them where I was heading to. Then Tom joined along asking me where am I heading also. Thinking that they were asking me where will I be stopping today, I told them I wasn't sure about it. Both nodded and there was a silence for a moment. Then after some moments past, Jerry asked me, "*Pergi mana ni*? (Where are you going?)".

At that very moment, I thought, "Am I becoming crazy, or are they?"

A man came out from the office and then Tom and Jerry went in. Contented that they went in, I sat relaxedly, leaning the back of my head against a pillar behind me and stared at the blue wall which is adjacent to the office door. Doing nothing but to just wait as my phone failed to pick up any signals despite having to subscribe to data roaming from the telecom that I was using. Annoyed and bored me, had no choice but to look around my vicinity.

Twenty-minutes past. I became apprehensive and couldn't wait for my turn. Visualising myself in the office of how I would speak to the officer got me even more anxious. I stopped visualising. It uses much of my mental energy, and it made me ponder about how I could illegally enter the border.

I turn facing the road, hunched forward, resting my forearm

on my quads, and watch the other bikers and vehicles ride past the booth. *Kapcai* bikes were frequently riding past me. Higher capacity bikes did ride past me; however, there weren't many. It became monotonous to see the bikes pass me, to which I turned back to my relaxed position, with my arm crossed, my leg straightened, and stared up at the fluorescent light above the ceiling. Then analysed the structure of the fluorescent light cover with my naked eyes.

Half an hour had passed since the two men went into the office – probably making the officer go crazy too. Frustration and anxiety had erected up in me badly. My palms were sweating, and I patted my palms on my jeans countless times. To keep myself sane, I scanned around with my eyes, whatever was next to the office door on the left, and read whatever I could.

A poster was on the wall, and its three-quarter filled with scribbles of signatures. I focused my eyes to read the words above the scribbled signatures:

NEGA … RAKU … SE … HATI … SEJIWA (NEGARAKU-SEHATI-SEJIWA).

No idea what those words meant, but they should relate to the signatures, I thought. Above the poster, a Malaysian flag is framed up and fixated to the wall. Just next to the poster, on the left, there's a huge board, and I went on to read the words.

PE….JA…BAT (PEJABAT), I…MI…GRESON (IMIGRESEN)… open parenthesis, KA…WALAN (KAWALAN)… close parenthesis.

On the following line, I continued to read, IMMIGRATION OFFICE (CONTROLLER). I face-palm myself as I was dumbfounded to know that the latter words were the translation for the Malay words. Well, at least I had spent some quality time doing something productive.

Forty minutes had passed since I arrived outside the immigration office. I became really restless. Looking all around became really bored. No foreigners came, but some locals came knocking on the door. They went in and out within minutes. I watch them get in and out several times. Are they cutting my queue? It got me on my nerves watching some of them get in but not me.

Looking at my watch, I waited for the digital seconds to restart to zero. Once it restarts the count to zero, I plan to knock on the door and ask the officer if he missed me out.

I mentally counted down to 3…2…1, then I stood up, and the door opened at the same time. Tom and Jerry came out with smiles on their faces and repeatedly said thank you in Malay to the officer behind the desk before leaving.

I walked over, knocked on the door, and opened the door slowly. As I stepped inside, I saw the officer behind the desk who looked up at me, welcomed me, and gestured for me to have a seat.

"Good afternoon, sir," I tried speaking politely to the officer, "the booth officer told me to come here and pass my passport to you." The officer gave a baffled look at me, but I passed over my passport to him anyway. His facial expression was the same as how the booth officer who checked on my passport earlier. He leafed through the pages using the ceiling light to visually help on analysing the details of the prior stamps on the pages, then muttered something and went back to looking at me.

"*Basah* (wet)," he said, then flipped some pages and repeated again, "*basah.*" I was in a still position with only my eyeballs moving and looking at the officer leaf through the pages.

"*Buku basah nie, tak boleh pakai. Tak boleh stamp pon.* (Wet book, cannot be used and be stamp also)," he said unapprovingly and continued, "*Satu orang datang sini ke group?* (You one person come here or in a group?)"

I decided to talk in English after hearing the disheartening words from him. "I, one person, come here. All the way from

Singapore."

He looks at my passport's front page to check my name, then looks back at me. He was probably wondering to himself why I wasn't speaking in Malay.

"Your passport wet, cannot use. This is water damage. Cannot stamp. Where you going to?"

Once he had said those words, I intuitively knew that the road trip had come to an end.

"Huh, sir… I came all the way from Singapore… my plan is to ride to Golden Triangle, in northern Thailand," I said empathetically and continued, "Sir, yesterday, the rain was really bad, sir. All the way from Johor to Kelantan heavy rain until the passport got wet. I even kept the passport inside a plastic zip bag but still it became wet."

He looks at me emphatically and re-looked back at the passport. He shook his head while looking at it and muttered something again to himself, and then stood up from his seat. He then walks over to a door adjacent to his desk and knocks on it, enters the room, then closes the door.

The door opened less than a minute later, and the officer summoned me to see another officer. As I entered the room, I see another officer with more elaborate embroidery on his shoulders, who was holding onto my passport. Presumably, he's a superior officer, I guess. He then welcomed me to have a seat and said my name clearly.

Then, the same words came out from the officer: "*Buku basah* (wet book)", and the same few questions came, like whom I came with and where am I heading to. I told everything that needed to be told. He understood my intention and told me that he's a motorcyclist and loves to tour around Malaysia with his beloved motorcycle. But in my case, he said that he couldn't do anything about it and said that he strictly follows the rules. I just nodded and had little or no words to say after he said that.

The officer looked at my passport again, and I could see his face of how he could possibly help me out.

"I tell you what, you ride up to the Thai immigration and park your bike at one side. Go in their immigration office and show them your passport. If they accept your passport, you come back here, I stamp for you."

I wasn't sure if he was trying to fool me or not, but I had no objection to it.

"Thank you, sir," I gratefully thanked the officer and didn't want to ask any further questions to spoil this hope. He passed me back my passport, and I rushed back to my bike, helmet on, and the officer came out of the office and directed me to the direction of where I should head to.

A sudden scepticism erected in my head that this may not turn out well.

Is he trying to make a prank on me? Or making a fool out of me? I don't know but this looks like the last hope I have. If Thai immigration rejects my passport, then this is the END of my story...

Inside the Thai immigration office, I wandered and wandered around, looking at the many people walking in and out of the immigration office. There was one room cluttered with people queuing up chaotically. Not knowing whom I should speak to nor whom I should approach to, I went into the room and saw two desks separated apart, with one man and a woman occupying each desk. The two were filling up forms for the people queuing, and in return, a small fee was paid to them after the forms were filled up. The nearest desk to me was the woman. I walked towards her, gave a self-conscious smile, and said, "Hello, I came from the Malaysian border. I want to go in Thailand... but my passport a bit wet. The officer at the Malaysian border asked me to come here and show my passport to errr… check my passport…" I tried to speak as reasonably as I could. She gave me a baffled look and turned to the man at the next table on her right. They spoke something in Thai and chuckled for a moment to each other, then returned to filling up the forms. I watched the whole scene like an idiot, and some of the people around stared at me as though what planet I had arrived from.

"Maybe she doesn't know English?" I thought.

She then stops filling the forms unexpectedly, and her head pops up at me, stretching her left arm out, pointing at a door metres away from me.

"Wait a moment," she said.

She indeed understood what I had said. I waited and stood there doing nothing and watched them fill up the forms for the people. It was unpleasant standing there where no one came around me, and it felt as though I was about to report to the discipline master to get punished – well, I have much experience from my younger days in school.

Not long after, two men in their uniforms entered the room and went to another room adjacent to the women's desk. That was where the woman behind the desk pointed at, and she stood up to knock on the door. One of the uniformed men came out, and she explained my dilemma to the officer – I assume she did, in Thai and then pointed at me. The officer then gave me a strange glare at me, to which I already had the instinct of what to do next. I handed over my passport to him, and he took it into the room, disappearing behind the wall without closing the door. In less than a minute, the uniformed man came out of the room, handed me back my passport and beckoned me away while saying something in Thai without looking at me.

The woman looked at me empathetically as if she was powerless to help me in any sort of way, and she carried on to fill up the forms. I had seen everything and understood what had just happened. I was disinclined to ask the woman what the officer had said earlier as I knew the answer from his expression and his action. I looked at my passport hopelessly and felt paralysed inside me with a conclusion in mind that this was the real end of my journey.

Getting back to my bike and staring at my machine right in front of me was exceptionally depressing. I rode back to the Malaysian border and back to the office and told the officer that the passport wasn't accepted. The officer nodded with sympathy and walked me out of the immigration office with his hands in his trousers pockets and told me that he couldn't do anything about it. He then advised me to tour around Malaysia as there is a lot to be seen and done.

But that wasn't my game plan. And I didn't have a plan B or Z. My clear intention was to complete the ride up within 10 days and, on the last day, touch down at Golden Triangle. An achievement I would evidently remember is that I had once made a ride up when I was still a probatory rider in future. That was it. But the idea had diminished away just like that. I even had this vision of seeing myself in Doi Inthanon and triumphantly saying, "Been there, done that." But to conceive that these were all just an imagination, it truly dejected me much.

To create a better life story? Better off creating a bullshit story...

I rode away from the Rantau Panjang border without turning on the GPS. I rode boldly along a single carriage road with no intention of stopping anywhere. I just kept riding and riding as though the fuel tank would refuel by itself.

Dense green forests were on both sides of the road, like the previous day's ride being monotonous all around my surroundings.

Then not long after, the rain started to pour. I stopped at the kerbside where there was a small dilapidated wooden hut on the roadside to take shelter and to wear on my rain gear. A wooden bench was around the hut, but it was sandy, and ants were strolling around the floor, picking up whatever tiny litter was on the floor. I sat on the edge of the bench, facing the road, and watched my bike getting drenched by the heavy droplets of rain.

Droplets of water deflected from the ground to my shoe, but I was careless about it. Not knowing where I should go, back to Singapore or knew what I wanted to do in Malaysia. I didn't have a plan. Nothing ignited in my mind to do something. If I had a plan B, I would intuitively know what I would want to do if something went wrong. But I had no plan, and nothing constructed in my mind as I was still in dejection from the border scene.

I should have kept the passport in the orange bag. You see, now it's too late. One mistake screwed up the whole thing. What a fool I am. I'm just a joke to myself...

Disparaging words were hitting on me. Who am I to blame? But only me.

Looking at the rain droplets and the clouds above, it seemed like it would continually rain for a long time. And so, I zipped up the rain gear, fully covering the body camera and continued with my bold ride to – nowhere.

I was wrong. The rain started to subside after a few kilometres, and the sun began to glow all around the vicinity. However, I wasn't enthralled by it nor obliged to take off my rain gear. I rode on and sped here and there with my unemotional face.

As I rode on, I slowly started to swallow what had happened. I started to think about the futile words that were putting me down. I started realising that I could still change the situation as I am the decision-maker for everything that happens. So why make myself despaired by what had happened? I stopped thinking negatively and focused on this question: Where have I yet to venture in Malaysia and why? I ran through the states I knew of in Malaysia, and just then, a spark ignited in me. I thought of *Penang*.

On the prior road trip to Phuket, one of the stops was at Penang. However, at that point of the trip, I was only there for a day to rest and get going the next day to cross over to Thailand via the Bukit Kayu Hitam border. Since I hadn't spent much time exploring Penang, it made sense to spend some days venturing around before heading back to Singapore. It appeared like a new plan, and also, thinking about what the officer in Rantau Panjang had advised me earlier about touring around Malaysia, well, I could do that too, which was another possibility.

As my mind slowly started to get convinced by my rationalism, I resulted to follow my new plan to ride to Penang.

The new destination set to Penang on Google Maps, and soon I realised that I was on Route 4 all the while – a route that goes across from east to the west or vice versa in the northern peninsula of Malaysia. What a coincidence. It gave me a clear sign that I should indeed head to Penang anyway.

I got going with my new goal in mind and with a new smile on my face. But not long after, my perception changed to *"I don't think so"* when I saw a live view of a falling tree just 30 metres in front of me.

Holly shit...

On the left side of the road, a huge tree snapped from its roots, and it started to fall towards the road. On the opposing lane, a yellow bus approaches and is just shy metres away from getting a direct hit by the falling tree.

The bus brakes hard. I brake hard. And the tree slammed hard on the road giving a loud "BANG" sound. From the hard bang to the road, the tree gave a violent shake for mere seconds before it came to a standstill position. Then the atmosphere became silent afterwards.

My eyes were wide open and well awakened by what I had seen. (Had I sped faster, there wouldn't be a story like this.)

The whole road had been blocked up. There weren't any vehicles coming from my back. I got off my bike and walked to the disaster area without taking anything off from me. Looking over the tree, it appeared like the bus had stopped just shy centimetres away from the fallen tree and there weren't any damages to the bus.

No one seemed to be coming out from the bus. Probably the people on the bus were still ducking their heads down to take cover when the bus driver probably screamed out, "HEADS DOWN", I guess. But the scream should have been in Malay; otherwise, it would probably be odd for the Malaysians ears.

On the extreme left, out of the roadside, there was a road barrier. But it was overlapped by the broken tree trunks and other smaller brunches. On the extreme right side of the road, there is a drainage, and after the drainage, there are dense bushes. There was no way to get over the tree unless I could possibly pile up stuff on the drainage and ride over to the other side.

Looking at the distance I had left to Penang, it came out that I had about 205 kilometres to go. By the time whatever rescue team arrives to remove this tree, I would probably be seeing twilight. The worst case to come probably would be to ride to another major town rather than heading to Penang for the day. I somehow came to think that this road trip was just a complete catastrophe and thought that I shouldn't have even started the trip.

A few minutes later, I hear people disembarking from the bus. But I wasn't able to see them as the branches and the leaves were blocking them. More vehicles arrived and stopped behind my bike.

People start to walk over to the tree with baffled faces and tip-toed to look over the other side of the tree. I was like the star player to reach the crime scene first and explain to the first person who approached me to ask what happened.

As more people arrived at the crime scene, some went on taking pictures of the fallen tree, some walked to one another to chat, and some were talking on their phones – probably to call for help. And there was I, walking back and forth to the crime scene, waiting anxiously to get going with my ride to Penang and not any random places.

Everyone was trying to figure out what to do. Nothing I could do to figure out my way but to watch the people around what they were doing. Negotiating a conversation with someone wasn't that hard. Everyone appeared approachable and keen to talk to one another. But speaking with my broken Malay was tough. So, it was better to zip my mouth and just look around.

Just as I was looking at the people, a man in his grey trousers, beige colour top, and a black bag slung over his right shoulder walked towards the fallen tree with a lit cigarette between his lips. As he approached the tree, he took a few more puffs and looked at the fallen tree before walking back to his vehicle nonchalantly as though he was trying to get a shot for a Bollywood movie.

"What was he up to?" I thought.

I walked back to the extreme right side of the road again to look at the drainage again to see if I could somehow get over to the other side. As I reached to see the drainage, I saw people from the other side of the tree, tossing the smaller broken branches out of the road.

Then there came a bald man with transition spectacles on and was in his full black rain gear. The speciality of him was his goatee which was about five centimetres long or perhaps, longer from my miscalculation. But sadly, his moustache was missing in which it didn't complete the facial hair loop that made it seem odd to look at – at least for me.

The bald man went on to pick up the broken branches and hastily threw them out of the road. He continued doing it until some people joined him along. I was too motivated by it and did it on my side.

Suddenly, cheers erupted behind me. I turned back to see the man in the beige top, who had earlier come to look at the fallen tree, came walking towards the fallen tree. Well, I have to say, he was indeed the true Bollywood star after seeing him hold on to something.

Still with his lit-up cigarette between his lips, he walks towards the tree with a freaking *chainsaw* in his right hand. It was a well-needed tool for this dilemma, and he got the exact right tool. I cheered with other fellow people, and smiles sprouted on everyone's faces.

Back looking at the front, the bald man somehow managed to jump past the drainage, then onto a small section of the grass patch beside the drainage, and then hops to the road on my side.

Everyone watched the Bollywood star chainsaw the branches effortlessly as though it was his usual job. Just as the branches were being cut, I heard someone calling *abang* (big brother). As I turned to my right, the bald guy came next to me and realised that he was actually calling me.

Big brother? Me? I like being called that.

The first thing he asked was if the bike parked on the side of the road was mine. I agreed with his saying, and then asks me where I came from and where I was heading to. Somehow, just to feel good about myself, I lied to him that I was heading to Bukit Kayu Hitam border instead of Penang. (Bukit Kaya Hitam border is located at northwest of peninsular Malaysia.)

As I was the only person who wore gloves, I volunteered to pick up the rough textured branches and threw them out of the road. Eventually, the people around helped each other to carry the bigger branches out of the road. While picking up the branches, the bald guy asks me, "Where are you going after Bukit Kayu Hitam border?"

"To Thailand," I lied again.

"From there?" He asks.

I fumbled my words, saying, "Chi-ang…Mai," (a city before Golden Triangle). He probably wouldn't know where Golden Triangle be at, so I said the state name closest to it.

He looked at me with stun look, then gave a thumbs up and continued to pick up the cut branches.

Shit, he knows the place...

"Err…slowly, slowly I will get there," I told him, but deep down in me, I knew the Golden Triangle ride was already dead. Anyway, this type of conversation will end fast, and we will part ways soon. So, making up a story was a better option, I thought.

I continued picking up the cut branches and tossed them out of the road. The bald man then continued to tell me that he came from Songkhla – a city in Songkhla province in southern Thailand, and he was on his way back home to Terengganu.

We both carried a bigger branch and threw it out of the road, and he went on to ask me if I was crossing the border to Thailand today. The question made me edgy as I wasn't even crossing the border at all. It made me ponder whether he might head back to Thailand again, or perhaps, he might want to join me. I didn't know what to say, but I had to answer him somehow.

"Er… later. Then from there, Hat Yai…Phatthalung… Bangkok…Chiang Mai." I added additional provinces and cities so that he might not follow me and may think that it's too far for him. He nodded and gave me a thumbs up, and continued to pick up the branches.

The fallen tree was cut to one lane width, and the road was almost readied for commute again. My hope of getting to Penang came to life again, but only after tossing all the bigger branches out of the road.

Once the branches were all kicked and tossed out of the road, it was all good to go. The entire process, from the tree fall to complete clearing of the road, took less than half an hour. Well, when everyone puts their hands to help, things get done faster.

Tapping my gloves to clear the wood dust off while walking back to my bike, I hear a bike rev behind me. I turned to my right to see the bald man on his bike, slow throttling and came right next to me. His bike was the same model as mine, but his bike's fairings were all white. He came next to me and asked me where I came from before arriving here. It was either I say I came from Kelantan, or I say that I came from Singapore then ride to Kelantan and then ride to Bukit Kayu Hitam. But the latter one seemed senseless. Why would someone do a number seven on the map of Peninsula Malaysia before crossing the border to Thailand? Wouldn't that be asinine?

I should just say what happened earlier. There's no point making up stories. Maybe, there's still hope and he could give me ideas.

I told him what had happened earlier on at Rantau Panjang and the torrential rain. He hears me with empathy, and he nods at every sentence I said. He understood my resentment and talked about the hassle of the paperwork that has to be done at the Thai border. I nod as he speaks, and he then pauses for a moment to look down the tarmac and brushes his goatee. He then looks up at me again with a serious look on his face, raising his right arm, fully straightened, points to a direction, and then says, "You try Betong," he nods with full confirmation and repeats, "Betong, try Betong."

I had heard about Betong before and had also seen some riders in Singapore wearing design t-shirts with Betong's name imprinted on it. But it has never been brought to my attention after this man told me to try Betong. I re-configured the Google Maps route to Betong, and it showed me that I have about 132 kilometres to the border. However, I thought about the rejection I had from the immigration officials at Rantau Panjang. What makes me think that I can get my passport stamped at Betong? I thought. Besides that, the time had already turned to 3:20 pm. I have roughly less than three hours to reach the Betong border, get the immigration forms filled up, and most importantly, get two stamps before the sky turns dark.

"You should try. If you can't go in Betong, you try other borders. Total seven land borders to Thailand." I nod slowly and hear him continue, "You went Rantau Panjang just now, so that one out. You have six more to go." He then named all seven borders and insisted I try the Betong border first. Then he asked me if I had standby fuel. I nodded and said yes. And then he continued saying the direction to the border and explained to me what the checkpoint looked like. As I listened, I pondered to myself:

Am I riding there? I just don't know man. What if I get rejected by the border officer there? I probably need to ride in the dark as I don't think there would be that much road lighting around, and I still have to look out for accommodation... But wait, he's helping me out... not trying is like a waste, you know... maybe I should just go ahead and try Betong. I never know if I could get in or not unless I try... Most to most if I get kicked out, I just YOLO ride and find accommodation somewhere near the border... Alright. Let's fucking do this!

I made up my mind to ride to Betong and thanked him for his great ideas. I took a picture with him before he got back on his bike, and he went off sounding a horn "beep" – it's usually a friendly horn gesture done by bikers who happened to pass by other bikers.

There was no time to waste. I rumbled off soon after, and I rode between 60 to 80 km/h on a single carriage road.

The roads to Betong had lots of bends apparently. Frequent gear changing was done, but most of the time, while I was riding, I was looking up at the poles on the roadside. These poles only carry land-line cables, and there weren't any road lightings to speak of. If I were to be rejected at the border, then I would probably be riding back on the same road again. With that fear in me, I truly hoped not to get kicked out.

After an extensive ride, I reached the Bukit Berapit immigration complex at the Malaysian border, but stopped 100 metres away from it just to mentally prepare on how to present myself to the officer and what to say:

Ok, here's the plan. Stop right beside the immigration booth, smile at the officer at the booth, take out the passport and pass it to the officer. Whatever happened earlier – just shut up, don't think about it. Just think that this is a new place and a new me. Picture me coming from Singapore to this border. I repeat, don't say anything about the rain or whatever nonsense.

Slow throttling in the border, I see few motorcycle lanes, but unsure which one to ride on. I chose the leftmost lane and slowly rode over, stopping next to the booth on my right. Then I hear a voice, "*Lane tutop. Datang sini* (Lane closed, come over here)." An officer from another booth calls me over.

WTF. You just screwed up the start of the plan!

I backpedalled the bike and gave a light throttle to the next booth, and stopped at the booth on the right.

"*Dari mana ni*? (Where you came from?)." The officers ask in a friendly tone.

"Singapore," I said while taking out the passport from the zip-lock bag and then passing it to him. He then said something and smiled. I looked at him and said, "oh," but pretended to know what he had said. He flips through the pages and concurrently asks which land checkpoint in Singapore I had exited from. When I was about to speak, his facial expression changed when he flipped the passport pages. I instantly replied, "Woodlands Checkpoint."

He kept looking at the pages and then said, "*basah* boss (Wet boss)."

Here it goes again. Wait, did he just call me boss?

"*Alamak*," I said with a fake expression of dismay and worry on my face. His eyebrow narrowed, and he ask me when I entered Malaysia.

"Yesterday, 21…" He observed the Malaysia inboard stamp date and then looked at me again, but I was quick enough to look forward. Then a complete silence in the air. My heart palpitates. To break the silence, I turned back to him and asked where is the nearest petrol station. His face still appeared unsatisfied, but he eventually spoke out and said that there isn't any nearby, but in Betong town. I nodded and gave a surprised look. And there came another complete silence.

The officer then asked me to place my both index fingers on the biometric fingerprint scanner.

At that very moment, I felt like jumping up to scream, but I still maintained my poker face on. I immediately placed both my index fingers on the machine before he took back his words. The machine scans my fingerprints, and the one thing that I'd been waiting for came, and that was the sound of stamp punching onto a passport page.

I got back my passport and thanked the officer before I rode off, passing the speed bumps and out of the Malaysian border. I kept my poker face on and did not become complacent as I could still be kicked out from Thai border, like how I got kicked out from the prior border.

After a short ride to the Betong border which is the Thailand border, I stopped right next to a kerbside to see a woman seated on a plastic chair under a shade. I waved at her and asked her the direction to park my bike. She pointed at a location, and I precisely followed what she said, and I tried not to screw up my final try here on this border.

As I take my helmet off and hang it on the side mirror, I hear a loud revving sound that resembles a higher-capacity motorcycle. I turned back to see two Indians on their Harley Davidson motorcycles ride past me and ride further forward up to park their bikes.

I took my document file, climbed a flight of stairs, and looked around like a lost child. An immigration woman approached me, forming the shape of an A4-sized paper with her hands, and asked, "You, have TM2 and TM6?" (The forms that are required to be submitted to the officials and they can be taken and filled up in the immigration itself.)

"Where to get them?" I asked.

She points at the two women seated on a separate long table, metres away from me, and says, "You bring log card?" (Log card refers to vehicle particulars.)

"Yes, I have," I said.

"Go there, go, go faster," she said cheerfully and beckoned me away to get it done fast. Probably her shift was about to end soon.

I walked to the table, and I had the recollection of the Thailand border where I went earlier and remembered the two staff in a room helping out the people to fill up the forms. It was the same here, and people were helping to fill out the forms too. But here in Betong immigration, at the hour that I came at, only two people were queuing up.

The woman at a table automatically asked me to pass my passport and the vehicle's particular information once my turn came. Then there came the two Indians who were on their Harleys – one of them was a head taller than the other man – who came to the other table next to me. Trying not to screw up my process, I kept silent and waited patiently for the papers to be filled up.

It was too awkward just to be silent as there wasn't anyone queuing up. Somehow, I broke the awkward moment by fire starting a conversation with the Indians while I waited for the forms to be filled up. The conversation then was in Tamil.

Usual questions were asked. Where are you from? Where are you going? How many people are in your group? But the expression I received after telling them where I came from, gave them a good surprise on their faces. Eventually, I told them that this was my very first time here in this border but didn't say anything about the wet passport. They advised me what to do with the forms after the forms have been filled up, where to pass the forms to, and what forms to keep with me. I then mentally thought to myself: *It's a good thing that I had opened my mouth though.*

I followed them, and they showed me the queue to get the passport stamped. Only two people were in the queue, and the two were the Indians in front of me which raised up my anxiety. The queue moved fast, and I was internally freaking out from it. Not only that, I couldn't even see the immigration officer as the desk façade was covered with reflective glass with only a small semi-circle opening there to pass through my documents.

When my turn came, I handed my passport and the forms

through the opening and inconspicuously watched the officer's reactions through the opening. His face appeared normal as he checked through the forms. But when he started to leaf through the pages of the passport, I saw his eyebrows narrow down slowly. He regressed the pages, and his face wasn't like how I first saw him earlier. My heart gave a faint beat, and his looks became more intense.

"I'm going back to Singapore," I muttered and stopped looking at the officer and instead looked up at the ceiling.

"BANG!" I heard the stamping sound. I duck down back to look through the opening. He closes the passport sandwiching it with the forms, and passes it back to me. I took them and walked away, controlling my facial expression, while my mind screamed, *10 DAYS TO GOLDEN TRIANGLE HAS OFFICIALLY RE-BEGUN!*

***

Nonchalantly rode off the border with euphoria in me, having no words to describe how contented I was. Hadn't the tree fall, I would have gone to Penang without trying out other borders, and there wouldn't be a story like this. I considered these two borders crossing an incredibly lucky get-through and will always remember this day and tell myself that I was once a very lucky man when I was unlucky – I hope that made sense.

***

Not long after I got off the border, the two Indians stopped at the kerbside on the left. By the time I stopped to chat with them, both were having a mini party of having a beer in their hands and a cigarette to the tall man.

"Hat Yai far from here?" I asked and switched off the ignition. Hat Yai was where I initially thought of riding to. And from there, head up north to northern Thailand.

"Far away," said the tall man and took a puff of the cigarette.

"You come here to *enjoy* or just stop by here?" the short man asked.

Enjoy? What do they mean? I thought.

"No, I want to go to Chiang Mai," I said.

"Oh, the thousand corners? With this bike?" asked the tall man with disbelief.

They refer to the Mae Hong Son loop as thousand corners.

"Yes, yes. Using this bike."

They were uncertain when I said that.

"You, want to ride to Hat Yai, right? You shouldn't come to this border. You should cross through Bukit Kayu Hitam border, then from there, straight up to Hat Yai," the short guy says and continues, "From here to Hat Yai very far away."

I nodded and paused for a moment, then the short man asked, "But why you come here?"

As I was about to answer, I watched the tall man gulp down the beer fast as though he was drinking water, then crushing the can and tossing it across the kerbside.

I told them where I wanted to head to and the ten days plan, but to see a sceptical look on them. The tall guy takes another can of beer from his bike's side pannier box and offers it to me, but I waved off and thanked him.

"How many leaves did you take from work? Your trip looks like a long one," the short man asked.

I create my own leaves. What should I say?

"Er…14…15 days," I said unsurely, then continued, "It will be like 10 days up then 4 to 5 days down. Maybe taking the railway back."

"Oh…then the bike?" asks the short guy.

"Er, load up the train. Still not sure about it. If not, I will ride back to Singapore."

"So, you're not here to *enjoy*?" the tall man asks and then heads up again to gulp down the beer.

"Eh…Just two months ago, I rode to Phuket…I enjoy there a lot…err…yeah…," I said unsurely and wondered what do they meant by *enjoy*.

Both nodded slowly, and there was silence for a moment.

"So, you come here to …… or going to Hat Yai?" asked the tall man, but I didn't get what the first thing he said. Guess the beer was kicking in fast.

"Yea…I want to ride to Hat Yai," I said unsurely.

"HAT YAI YAAA," both said in jinx and shook their heads in disapproving way.

"It's really far away from here bro," the short man said, and the tall man supported it by nodding his head.

"So, you come from Rantau Panjang Highway?" asked the short man, which I did tell him earlier when we were queuing up at the immigration.

"No. It's like forested road. I use the GPS and it brought me here."

The short guy came beside me and explains the route to me using the Google Maps of how I should've crossed the border.

"…If you exit from this border, you can ride up to Bukit Kayu Hitam… and from there… cross over and ride up straight…," the short guy explains.

"I could go up north from here to Yala then from there I head West?" I asked.

"You can, but the road to Yala is old road. Like the roads where you came from Rantau Panjang till here. Both sides of the road forested, right? Only with two lanes, right? Is the exact same along Yala," he says and continues, "Are you going to ride now?"

"Er…No choice," I said, then told them about the wet passport at

Rantau Panjang as it was like the missing link for the conversation with them. They both shook their head with empathy after I told them what had happened.

"Like that Yala is the route for you," said the short man. "How about you stay in Betong today and then leave early morning tomorrow? It's too dark for you to ride to Yala now."

I nodded and agreed with their saying, then asked, "Is it easy to get a room at Betong?"

"Oh, you can get it easily. Everything is here…," the tall man said and continued saying what are there in Betong town, but some words he spoke were slurred and incomprehensible.

As they were about to get going, they gave well wishes to me with a big handshake before they rode off. But before they rode off, the tall man said, "Watch out for the pick-up trucks and enjoy bro."

Enjoy again?

***

The Betong town was a distance away from Betong Border. When I reached Betong town, the roads were busy with commuters and many motorists weren't wearing helmets. An interesting town, I guess.

The traffic light turned red, and I came to a halt behind an orange *songthaew* – a passenger vehicle that looks like a pick-up truck uses its bed to ferry passengers. To get to the front of the traffic stop, I checked back on my right and tried to overtake the songthaew. But when I was about to move off, I heard someone holler at me from the songthaew bed, but I couldn't see the passengers properly as the canopy that shelters the passengers made the bed appear dark.

"From Singapore?!" Someone shouted out from the songthaew.

"Yes! Singapore!" I hollered back and looked in between them, not knowing who asked. But there are two Indian men inside. One wore a blue top and the other person wore a black top. The blue top then asks, "You travelled from Singapore all the way here?!"

"Ya!" I hollered back proudly.

"Woahhh! Good, good!" The blue top praised me and gave me a thumbs up to me.

The traffic light turned green, and the songthaew moved off, and I tailgated behind the vehicle.

"You Indian?!" Asked the blue top.

"I'm mix!" I replied while being very wary of the vehicle's tail light in case it brakes hard.

"I first time here!" I hollered.

"Enjoy ah! This place very nice!" the blue top hollered out. Then the other guy in the vehicle hollered, "Follow!" then the blue top joined in hollering at me, "Follow! Follow!" with their hand beckoning me to follow the vehicle.

Being sceptical and unsure of where they were heading to, I hollered back, "I am looking for a hotel!".

The black top hollers, "you come stay at our hotel! Very clean!" The blue top then joins in, "come my hotel! We going there now! Very nice, very clean!"

"How far away?!" I hollered before entering the roundabout.

"Very near! Few minutes!" then a truck cuts me on the right in front of me just before the roundabout, and the songthaew drove away.

The roads were busy apparently. I waited for the right time, got into the roundabout, exited where the songthaew exited, and caught up with it. The songthaew then came to a stop next to a hotel, and both the Indians got down the vehicle carrying shopping bags. Both smiled as I arrived, and the blue top guy directed me to an alley to park my bike where the other bikes were parked at.

As I entered the alley, there were three men in white tops at one corner of the hotel – who looked like employees of the hotel – and they were chatting among themselves as I entered the alley. I stopped metres away from the start of the alley, just opposite the hotel, where there was a row of scooters parked on the pavement neatly, and all were close to one another. There was a small space in-between them, and it could fit my bike in perfectly. I turned to ask the three men if I could park there as I was unsure if that area was someone's property. Then a loud holler came from my back but a distance away: "Park your bike there!" Then two of the three men in white tops scrambled to action and guided me to park in the space. From the familiar voice I had heard earlier, it was definitely the blue top man.

Once the bike was parked, there came the blue top Indian man walking towards me from a distance. And now I have a better image of how he looks like. He wore a black slip-on shoes, with white shorts on, and the blue top with print text of, "Hot Tuna, Let's go surfing". Interesting, but I was doubtful if he is a surfer as I could see the oval-ness of his belly protruding out from his shirt. His hair was short and curly, but he sported a thick manly-looking moustache that is accompanied by a big smile on his face.

"You are mister?" He asked with his hand out to shake my hand.

"You can call me Khai," I said, and I shook his hand.

"I'm Vishnu."

"I met other Indians earlier when crossing the border, and they jokingly recommended coming here to enjoy also." I said while unstrapping the helmet's chin strap.

Vishnu gave a manly laugh and then pointed at the hotel, "This place very nice, very cheap."

"Look like a nice hotel… Thanks for recommending this hotel anyway. Is today your last day?" I asked and then hung my helmet on the side mirror. He smiled and said, "Yes, so enjoy ah!" Then he continued, "From here, go to the next road, all the way straight, you will see one junction, and on the left side, there's Indian pub, restaurants and everything there. You will like it. Go there."

"Don't worry. We are just here. If anything, come join us."

Never had I come to a place where visitors were so contented of the place where they even welcomed other new visitors as though they were native citizens.

Strange.

***

The atmosphere had turned twilight when I got myself changed and back down to the streets. There were two things I had to get them done fast: Get a SIM card – since my telco SIM card became useless despite subscribing to data roaming – and have a palatable meal. I went on to fulfil the latter one first, as I was starving.

Sitting next to the window of my dining table, I waited for my food to be served and watched life pass in Betong town. Switching on my phone camera to take a picture of the life outside, my phone camera frame shook violently. I pondered and closed the camera application, and re-opened it again. The frame shook again. Looking at the camera lens with my naked eyes, there were no visible damages. I brought the phone closer to my ear and heard a buzzing sound from the back camera. I wondered if it was due to the rain damage from the yesterday's ride. The upset me tapped the phone's edge to my palm and tried to retake a picture. But still, the frame vibrates violently. I knocked it on the table, it still didn't help but to see patrons' eyes on me. I knocked it on the concrete floor; it somehow worked like a charm, but after a few seconds, the frame shook again. The critically important thing for this trip was to take as many pictures as possible. But just on the second day of the journey, I had to face this dilemma. What frustrated me was that the phone was only a month old since I bought it.

A damn it to me.

Two meat steaks were on the plate, and each one was about the size of my palm, and it was spread with barbecue sauce all over it. There was also a small portion of fries on the side, mixed salad on the side, and the final toppings of mustard on top of the mixed salad. And last but not least, a quarter-cut toasted bread came on the side of the plate. Not having to start the meal by first sipping a tall cup of Thai ice milk tea. But then, once I sipped it, it felt like I could get diabetes anytime soon.

Nevertheless, the meal overwhelmed me, but what even overwhelmed more was the price tag – it cost me 114 Baht. To convert to Singapre dollars, the meal costs less than five dollars. What a worthy meal to have on a crazy day.

Once the meal was done, I went over to get a SIM card and bought a bag of chips and roamed about looking at what was there around the streets. By the time I had started to walk, the street shops appeared to be closing early, in which it seemed as though the town is under curfew. Well, it was just me who came to the town late. It was already turning to 9 in the evening, so there wasn't much I could possibly see.

However, I just roamed about and happened to see a clock tower that's in the middle of the roundabout. But the intriguing thing wasn't about the clock tower, but the thousands of tiny birds that were on the streets cable lines around the roundabout. All the birds were spaced out evenly like how soldiers evenly space themselves among each other in a contingent. Interesting.

I further walked and munched, bringing my curiosity towards what Vishnu had earlier said to me. I chanced upon a street where there was a stretch of pubs, and I could hear the loud bass sound whenever someone opened the door of any pub. And outside the pubs, I see people dancing with beer bottles in their hands and trying to flirt with the bar girls. I smiled to myself as I happened to see the tall Indian Harley Davidson rider I had earlier chatted with, enjoying his time there outside the pub. Well, I understood what his term of *enjoy* meant.

Since pubs and clubs aren't something for me, and I was exhausted from the crazy day, I walked back to my hotel. As I reached my hotel, a few men were loitering about right outside my hotel stay, and there were tables and chairs right outside the hotel where a few women were sat on. The men that were around were flirting with the girls, and I see a man choosing a woman as though choosing what food to eat on a buffet line.

When I took the elevator to my room level and walked on the corridor towards my room, I saw a man with two other women behind him. The man then was knocking on someone's room door, and when I walked past next to them, both the woman catcalled me seductively, saying, "hey baby", "I want you", "You look naughty". I sheepishly continued walking to my room door thinking what hotel the Indians brought me to with my eyes wide open. Then the man who was knocking on someone's door, whistled at me and hollered surreptitiously from a distance, saying, *"Abang, I later bring ladies to you."*

"What in the world have I got myself into," I thought.

I have finally understood what the Indians were trying to tell me earlier and what 'enjoy' actually meant now.

Oh my…

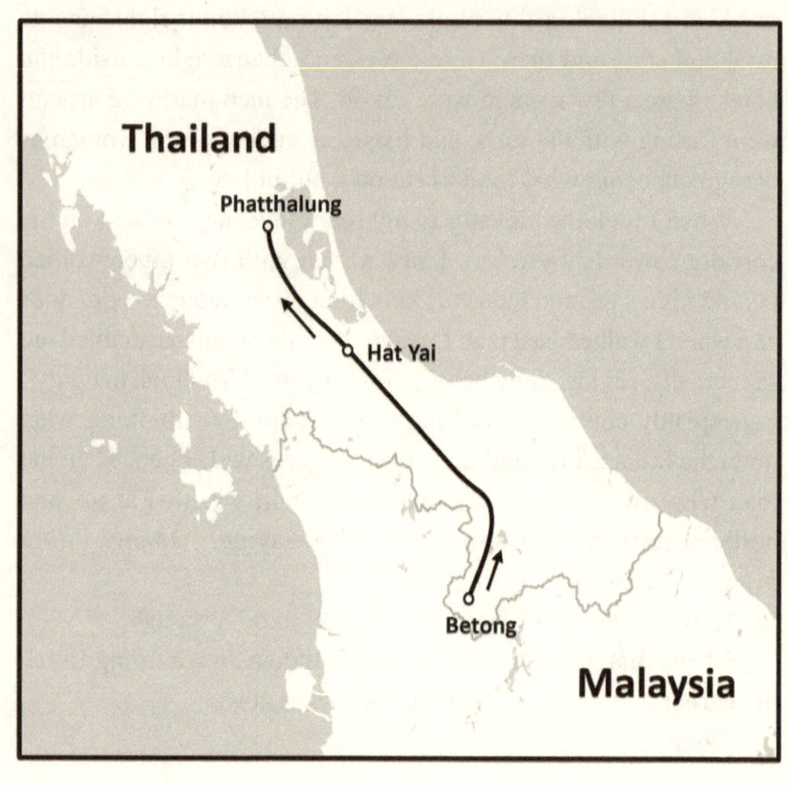

Thailand
Phatthalung
Hat Yai
Betong
Malaysia

8

Cowboy Town

It was 7:30 am when I checked out from the hotel with the motivation to cover the lost distance that I was supposed to cover from yesterday's ride. As I walked towards the soi (it meant 'alley' in Thai) where my bike was parked, I noticed the same tuk-tuk from yesterday where hotel employees were chilling at. However, there wasn't anyone flocking around the tuk-tuk at this early hour. As I entered the soi, one of the men approached me from a distance and hollered, "*Abang nak pijat* (Brother you want massage)? Three ladies ...Very beautiful!"

I knew what he meant, but man, it's freaking early in the morning. Even yesterday, when I was in my hotel room, I heard knocks on my room door and heard a man speaking through the door to offer me a woman. I remained silent in the room till the man left. Despite my intrusive mind urging me not to be a wimp, I thought about the consequences and getting myself into any unnecessary trouble which could possibly decimate the story I want to create. With that said, I stayed sane and silent in my room much of my time there – but with slight regrets, of course.

Back to the man who asked me if I wanted to get a massage, I smiled back at the man and told him that I was going to ride off

99

soon. He nods and shows me thumbs-up, and walks back to the tuk-tuk.

The usual day started for me to get the stuff in the top box and wrap the orange bag down the seat. As I squat down to wrap the bag with the bungee cord onto the rack, an older man rides on a bicycle, stops next to my bike, and watches me wrap my bag down. I looked at him and gave a smile. He returned it with a huge smile, revealing a few missing teeth against the dark background of his mouth. Then, he let out a wicket laughter, and in that moment, I had a feeling that I might be dealing with someone special.

As I continued to wrap, he read the route stickers that were pasted on the top box from the prior road trip.

"Hat Yai…Krabi…Phuket…you go?"

"Yes sir. Last two months ago." I said, and he gave a comical look at me and then looked down at my bike with astonishment. He then abruptly started to cycle away immediately and said 'giler' without looking at me. I knew what the word meant but didn't get offended by it. *Giler* is a Malay word that means 'crazy' in English.

Well, he wasn't wrong after all.

The purported plan for the day-two ride was actually from Kelantan to Phatthalung. But unfortunately, it didn't happen thanks to the border rejection. And the purported plan for day-three, which is for this day, is to Phatthalung to Hua Hin. And that wasn't happening too. Say, if I were to cover the distance till reaching Hua Hin, it would take me a thousand kilometres from my current location. That's never going to happen with this bike, and I don't need to have second thoughts about it.

However, I resolved to ride as much distance as I could for the day, and the likely city I would probably stop by to call it a day seemed like a city named Surat Thani. It's about 315 kilometres from my location, and it seemed like an ideal distance to ride for me. Or perhaps, another option would be taking on more distance and stopping at Chumphon town, which is about 484 kilometres away. Well, it all depends on how the ride will be like and what obstacles I will encounter.

Helmet on, gloves on, and off I started on with my ride and the man who tried to offer me ladies earlier, appeared again and waved at me from a distance. But this time round, he massages his left arm up and down with his right hand and says something surreptitiously to which, of course, I comprehended what he was trying to say: *"Massage, massage."*

I chuckled at the way he said that and off I started my ride for the day.

***

Before leaving Betong town, I made my way to see the largest mailbox in Thailand, which apparently situated in Betong town, and it was something I didn't want to miss.

The ride to the mailbox wasn't far off. Upon reaching the mailbox, it didn't quite look like what I had seen from the pictures on Google. Looking from the bottom till up the structure of the mailbox – which is about a few stories high – then looking at somewhere around the centre, there was this 'paper plane' logo, and that was it. It supposedly should be in bright red; however, it appeared pink instead. And somehow, it looks like a furnace to me. Guess the colour had faded off after going through many weather changes. Anyway, since I was there, I snapped some pictures of it and rode off to find something to eat before starting with the real ride.

There weren't many vehicles on the road in the early hours of Betong town. Turning my head left and right to see where I should stop by to have breakfast wasn't easy. Most of the shops that were around were still closed – I mean, of course, it was early in the morning. I continued the slow ride looking around, and in serenity, I chanced upon a food vendor that was opened up. However, the shop next to the food vendor, caught my attention more to which I made my way to check it out first.

There's this pristine-looking milestone just right at the front of a shop. The milestone has inscriptions of BETONG 0 KM on it and a logo that says BETONG ROUTE 410. But it seemed peculiar to me having to see the milestone in front of a shop. I further looked around the entrance of the shop, many small-sized country flags were hanging above the walls, posters with hundreds of signatures, and motorcycle club stickers were pasted on the walls. They all meant that I had to get my butt in the shop somehow if not it might be a waste.

Peeking into the shop, there were a few women in their hijab wear, seated on a carpet and chatting with each other at the back of the store. One of the women saw me keenly looking around the shop, to which she immediately stood up to welcome me in.

"Hello, *dari mane* (from where)?" She asks me with a smile on her face.

"Singapore."

"*Bagus. Satu orang* (Good. One person)?"

"I came here alone."

"Where your motorbike?"

Alright, she understands English.

I went out and pointed at my bike, and she continued, "bring your bike here. I want to take picture of you."

I wondered why but it seems like I'm famous for no reason.

I pushed the bike to the front of the shop, in front of the milestone, and she snapped a picture using her phone. Once she was done, I quickly jogged to her and whacked the phone on my palm hard before passing it to her to get another picture with my phone.

"Is this the actual 0 km mark for Betong?" I asked.

"No. This stone is our shop 0 km," she says and continues, "the actual 0 km stone at the roundabout."

I nod to her saying, and she says, "Come in, come in. Outside hot."

She welcomed me in, and my head turned all around the shop. There were myriad types of route logo stickers, t-shirts, and souvenirs. Almost all have the imprints of the 'Betong 410' name on them.

I sat on a high chair, and she went behind the display rack and asked me where I'm headed to. I told her the location, but in return, she gave me an amused face.

"You are a brave…very brave man," she said in a way like she meant what she had said. I was flattered internally but didn't express myself but to thank her and thought about how cowardly I was when I stayed silent in my hotel room yesterday night. Then I told her the probable places I would be stopping at, and she asked, "Are you riding to Bangkok?"

"Eh…Yes."

"Bangkok, the roads very confusing. I scared you get lost there."

I nodded but said nothing about it as I hadn't seen the situation in person, nor had I ridden there before. But the way she said it like it won't be a good ride there.

"Best time is to go before the peak hour. Or you don't go in the centre. Take another way outside Bangkok."

"Ah, I see. Will take note of that. I will check on the routes."

"Where are you going after this?"

"Er… I plan to ride far but still not sure where I want to stop at. Maybe at Surat Thani, if not, Chumphon."

She looked down at her watch and looked back at me. "Maybe you cannot reach before the sun goes down. I don't advise you to ride at night also. Some roads very dark," I slow nod and she continued, "How about stop by at Phatthalung for a day? You can look for my friend at Route 41 Phatthalung."

I nodded and mentally knew the rough distance from here to Phatthalung. But the distance was just too short. The plan for the day is to cover more distance. But if I don't, then, other days I would need to cover more distance.

"That place really nice. They have restaurant, souvenirs shop, coffee saloon shop, and also have rooms to sleep over."

"Where is it at again?"

"Route 41 Phatthalung."

Isn't that the highway number?

"O…k..." I ask again. "So where is this place at?"

"It's at the highway 41. The name of the place is Route 41 Phatthalung."

"Ohhhhh…." I got what she was trying to say but wondered why naming the place as a route number though.

I did a quick search on Google, and it was indeed named as what she had said. But from the pictures on Google, the place looked like a cowboy town.

"You can look for Mrs. Jirajit. She's a very friendly person. She and her husband are there most of the time."

"Long distance friend?"

She giggled and said, "She is my very good friend."

"Er…I will think about it. If I happen to stop at Phatthalung, I will go over to that place. So, its Mrs. Ji…"

"Let me write down for you."

She took a sticky note, wrote down the details, and handed it to me, saying, "Send my regards if you stop there, ok?"

I nodded and kept that sticky note inside the phone's protective cover.

She then took a logo sticker from a shelf behind her and turned back to me, "This is a gift from me. You come a long way from Singapore and you come alone, you are a brave man." I took the sticker with much appreciation and with much contentment in me.

"I wish you all the best for your ride."

I thanked her and took a picture with her before rumbling off with a thought of: "Dude, someone just called me brave!"

***

Patches of white clouds hover above the sky, and the evidently seen blue atmosphere intuitively made me think that it would never rain for the day. Riding on a dual-lane asphalt road and turning to a right sharp bend, then negotiating the bend, several stunning-looking green hills appeared a distance away on my left. Then turning to a left sharp bend, there were too, stunning looking green hills which made it seem like copy and paste hills all around my vicinity. It appeared like it's the start of my journey to experience the beautiful landscapes after overcoming my dreaded experience on day-one ride.

Passing by some rural sites, the houses around were abundantly made up of corrugated rooftops, and some looked as though it was soon to collapse. The people I had seen along the way, many faces sprouted exuberant smiles especially the children walking on the roadside with backpacks bigger than their body size. But they all appeared joyful and cheerfully running on the side of the road. I mean, who wouldn't be happy living in a placid environment out of the noisy and bustling city, right?

I get waves from kids who walk along the roadsides and also from the locals who are on their kapcai bikes. Not one, not two, but four people cramped themselves up sitting close to one another to share a ride on a bike. None of them wore helmets on their head, but they were carrying huge smiles on their faces. As they neared me, they hollered out the usual Thai greetings to me alongside with much hand waves.

I hollered back *KAP KHUN KAAA* (thank you in English) cheerfully and waved back at them, and the proud me was contented that at least I knew something in Thai and was able to make full use of it. It would have been better if I knew hello in Thai as it doesn't make sense to say thank you in Thai without a purpose.

I liked their cheerful waves, but these people aren't adults to speak of. They appeared like they were in their teens.

A few more kapcai bikes came along, and some looked like they aged below 12. Not bad, at this young age, they are already riding motorcycles despite the danger of not wearing proper gear to protect them. But what can I say? If I were to live in this rural life, I would indeed do the stuff like them and ride nonchalantly.

Less than an hour's ride from Betong town, I came to a stop at a bridge called New Bang Lang. On both sides of the bridge, both have an exceptional panoramic view that makes it seem like it's a must for every road tripper to stop by to have a look at the vicinity. Hills staggered left and right, and in between them is where the running river flows. The river water looked green from the reflection of the body of the green hills, but it made it appear calm to look at it. What made this view so appealing to me was the perfect atmosphere's background colour of blue and the patches of white clouds hovering above. It's a view that people would take a picture and make it as their computer background image. I guess I need to change to a new one too.

The time had already reached 1:30 in the afternoon, but I was still in Yala province. I rode into a new town to see more bricked buildings and shophouses than from other small towns I had passed by, which made me want to stop around for a while. Not that I wanted to look around the town, but rain droplets started to trickle down, which made me want to look for shelter and have a meal before moving on.

"Payom burger" was what the banner depicted, and the vendor is located on the roadside. I stopped at the kerbside and went over to check the menu, but it was written in Thai. However, the fortunate me was grateful to hear the staff speak in English which saved the trouble of using Google Translate on my phone.

I ordered a double petty beef burger with green Thai ice milk tea but remembered to tell the staff to make it less sweetened, then went over to sit on the wooden chair just in front of the shop vendor to consume my meal.

Taking a large bite of that double patty beef burger and sipping the green Thai ice milk tea saved my stomach while I watched the rain fall hard on my bike. Then there came a stubby kid and a skinny kid. They ran out from one vendor to another, one trying to catch another, and then they ran out to the road to get themselves drenched by the rain. They ran back into the shop vendors making the vendor's floors wet, but no one stopped them as there weren't anyone around at the moment. All I saw was a man, who served me my meal, and he was in full concentration on cutting the tomatoes.

The kids ran back out to the road and played in the rain. Not only kicking the puddle of water to each other, but they did something I did when I was a kid too. They both tilted their head up to the sky, opened their mouths, and started to collect rainwater. Then when the rainwater reaches a certain level in their mouth, they gurgle it. Then compete with each other of who could make the gurgling sound louder. It was hilarious and entertaining to watch them while having my meal. But then, they went to the next level, where I did not do what they did when I was a kid.

As the rain droplets slide down the canopy edge on the side and fall to the drainage, the stubby kid breaks the flow by getting in between and opening his mouth wide to collect the rainwater. The skinny kid looked at what his buddy was doing, then ran over to join next to him. When the rain droplets reach a certain level in their mouth, they compete among themselves again by making loud gurgling sounds and even made songs from gurgling. "Magnificent!" I said, watching their entertainment. Then once they had enough fun gurgling, they spat the rainwater to the ground and stared at me while I took a bite from the burger. The stubby kid then said "yummy" and continued staring at my burger.

"You want some?" I asked and started to split the burger in half, but the two just shook their head not wanting it but kept on staring at my burger. The stubby kid said "yummy" again, and then he went back to his mission by opening his mouth to collect rainwater and gurgle again. I shook my head, chuckling at their actions and continued having my burger. But I hoped to hear a screaming sound from a mother though. I truly hoped.

It had already turned 2:45 pm. Three hours left before the sun goes down. "Three hours to Surat Thani? That's over 300 kilometres from here!" I exclaimed as I checked on Google Maps. I wasn't even close to Hat Yai yet. Looking at the distance left to ride on, it seemed like I had to forgo the thought of stopping at Surat Thani and should instead head to where the woman in Betong 410 had recommended to stop by at Route 41 Phatthalung.

Riding between 90 to 100 km/h on a straight road was just butt-paining, and watching a pick-up truck pass me fast on my right, felt as though I was riding on a bicycle. Good thing there's a road shoulder that I can tag along on and watch the speedster pass me on the main lane. But one thing I had noticed from the many vehicles that had passed me, many of the vehicles were pick-up trucks. But it seemed like an excellent vehicle to have in Thailand to store a myriad of stuff on the truck's bed. Some pick-ups carried cages with chickens in them, some carried dried wheat grass tied up like square cubes, some carried pigs inside large cages, and there's even a pick-up rode passed me carrying a life-size horse. Interesting.

The ride kept going, and I finally reached the southern part of Hat Yai town. Then I connected to Highway 43, and then continued towards Route 4. This Route 4 is where the single route leads up close to Bangkok, and it's unlikely for someone to get lost when there's only one prominent route that can be seen clearly on a map.

After much enduring the needle-poking-sensation on my butt from the prolonged riding, my ride had brought me close to a new province called Phatthalung. I set the pin-drop to the city's centre on Google Maps instead of the Route 41 Phatthalung destination as I wanted to see what were there in the centre of Phatthalung. The pin-drop showed me a roundabout again, like how I had seen from the day-one ride to the Kelantan roundabout.

Reaching close to the pin-drop point, I see a small temple near the roundabout, and there is a running track adjacent to the roundabout on the left. The running track had a single large lane that looked like a combination of 8 lanes, and there were lots of people jogging on the track with the song of *Ra Ra Rasputin by Boney M*, blasting out from the speakers at the grandstand.

Some cyclists were cycling past the roundabout in their full tight clothing and with number tags on their chests. It appeared like an event was happening, but I couldn't figure out what it was about. But I have to say, the vibes here felt so energetic and lively in which it felt nice being around, nodding to the rhythm of the song, while I watch the bright orange bulb across the track set down slowly.

The ride went on to find the location of Route 41 Phatthalung.

Somehow, I find it odd to say the extended form of the name of the place. So, R41P seemed like a better thing to hear and speak.

Locating the place itself was tough as the GPS pin-drop pointed directly in the middle of the highway which made no sense to me. That meant that it was either on the left side of the highway else it was on the opposite side of the highway. The only way to find the R41P is to slow down and look at the opposite side of the highway and also the way I'm riding at.

I rode slowly, looking anxiously to the left and right, but I couldn't find where it was. I made several detours at a U-turn point to locate where the R41P at, but still, I didn't get to see a pinch of it. I further slowed down to look for any signs along the highway. Fortunately, there was a sign on the roadside that stated: "Route 41 Phatthalung - 100m away." I followed it and finally managed to come to what I was described by the woman in Betong Route 410 about the place I should head to. Like what she had said, and like what I had seen on Google, it did appear like a cowboy town.

My eyes widened up, looking at the place with profound interest while I rode in slowly on the gravel ground that also appeared like a parking area. On one side, there were wooden built housing structures with names on their façade like, "COFFEE SALOON", "STEAK HOUSE", "SOUVENIR SHOP," and "DORMITORY", and they were all inline next to each other. Perpendicular to the inline wooden houses, oddly to see, there was even a retired train carriage.

Riding slowly on the gravel ground, squinting my eyes to see anyone coming out of the wooden house doors to welcome me, but to see no one. I got off my bike and went over to the door of the STEAK HOUSE, but to see the façade front of the door and the wooden walls around it were hijacked by thousands of motorcycle club stickers all around the walls. Even the window pane in the middle of the wooden door wasn't given any sympathy for the invasion of the stickers.

Looking through the small spaces between the stickers from the windowpane to see if there was anyone in, I saw one person. A woman talking to someone right at the back of the house that looked like a kitchen. I opened the door and said hello. One woman came peeping out of the kitchen and came to me saying, *sawadee kaaa.*

"I'm looking for Mrs. Jirajit," I said, "I was recommended by a woman in Betong 41 to come over here for a stay. By the way, is Mrs. Jirajit here?"

"Ahhhhh, Jirajit at *Trang*, she come back at night."

"I call boss," she said with her strong Thai accent. While she tried to get in line with Jirajit, I Google searched different words associated with the word *Trang*. Then I came to know that *Trang* is a city located about 50 kilometres west of Phatthalung province.

She got into the line with Jirajit and handed the phone to me. I wasn't sure what I wanted to say, but after Jirajit welcomed me on the phone with her fine and friendly tone, I told her where I came from and told her that I was looking for a place to stay for the night.

After speaking on the phone, I handed over the phone back to the staff, and she then walked me to all the individual wooden houses, explained the amenities around, and even brought me over to a retired train carriage. I was told that the interior of the train carriage was still under renovation and it would be used for accommodating in future. I was amused to hear that and it seemed cool to accommodate in a train carriage with hotel style amenities.

As I went from one house to another, I noticed that there wasn't anyone around to speak of. And it seemed like I was the only person here for the day. However, I was told by the staff that it's usually busy every day with other riders coming in and out. Not sure if I was lucky or not, but I have to say; I really liked this place.

I got myself a bed in the DORMITORY house – where the bed frames were made up of wood too – that still had the scent of wood. I didn't like it, but once I was told that I was the first 10 to ever accommodate here in the newly built bunk beds house, I somehow liked the scent of the wood.

***

I roamed around the cowboy town as though I had booked this whole town to myself. However, I wasn't wearing a cowboy clothing with a wide-brimmed hat on, nor clothes that would make me look like one. I'm just a simple guy who wore on a red army singlet, shorts, and slippers. That was more than enough.

I roamed around, taking pictures and video recording myself opening each house door to video record what was around. When I slurred a word while recording, I would get out again, closing the door and open the door again to start over whatever nonsense I wanted to say to the video. I did it many times, and I could do it as many times as I wanted as there wasn't anyone around who might be annoyed by what I was doing. But an exception to the staff that kept watching me getting in and out of the houses.

Then once all the fun video recording was done, I got into the STEAK HOUSE to have a meal and had the restaurant to myself. I had a hearty meal of fried rice, French fries, and hot Thai milk tea and was pleasantly treated with in-the-house tea by the staff.

I got back to my bed early like 10 pm as I promised myself to get up early the next day to start the ride as early as possible. Just when I was about to doze off, I heard the gravel sound outside, indicating that a vehicle entered the premises. Then moments later, a few knocks came on my house door and the door opened. I peeked out from my blanket curiously to see who was there; I saw a silhouette shape of a woman that didn't resemble any staff I had seen earlier. As the woman was about to close the door, I got out of bed hurriedly and opened back the door.

"Hello, is this Mrs. Jirajit?" I said with an overwhelming smile, but it should be impossible for her to see me in the dark.

"Sorry to disturb you," she said and continued, "You can rest."

"It's alright," I said and continued, "I was in Betong 410 earlier and a woman recommended me to have a stay here for the night." Then I switched on the house lights and went back to my bed to take the phone out as I had earlier placed the sticky note behind my phone cover, then passed it to Jirajit.

"Wow. Thank you," she said with a big smile, looking at the note enthusiastically.

We conversed for a while, and along the chat, Jirajit's husband came in and shook my hand and welcomed me to the place. As we converse, I got to know that her family is actually living in a tiny wooden house just next to the dormitory house and also, I learned that she started from just a coffee shop at a petrol station and made it all the way here with her husband, which amused me to hear her humble endeavours. As we chatted and when our conversation was heading to an end, she told me that there would be another person coming in tonight to accommodate, and the person is also a Singaporean man.

Just before midnight, while I was in the midst of my sleep, I woke up to hear a familiar motorcycle sound. After some minutes pass, Jirajit's husband opens the door and welcomes the person in. There came a man wearing a full overall of blue-grey BMW riding gear, with a red tube scarf covering his hair, and was carrying a large duffel bag in his right hand. I eventually sat up on my bed and said hello to him. He then sees me and asks, "Hey, you came in alone?"

"Ya, came from Betong. I came in like 6."

"Ah, that's early," he said and shook my hand, "I'm Jauhari."

I got off my bed and went out to see Jauhari's bike while he went back and forth to take things out of his bike. It was a BMW GS1200, and it was parked just a few metres away from my bike under a porch on the other wooden house.

After Jauhari got his stuff in the house, we went over to the smoking area to have a chat, and I watched him smoke one cigarette after another as we conversed. Hearing his past road trip stories with his group riding in Africa, from north to south, just WOW-ed the heck out of me. The current road trip he was heading to was to Vietnam and ending the ride in the southern end of Vietnam. From there, he would ship the bike back to Singapore which intrigued me to hear more as I may never know if I might ship my bike elsewhere in future.

I asked one question after another, and he explained with a story after another like listening to an older man talking about his nostalgic days. And somehow, I got to know he was already in his fifties, but he seemed like a man who has the energy of someone in his twenties.

Apart from that, after many conversations, I got to know that he was the left-out person among his group that had come in here yesterday. The group had left to ride north earlier today after having a night stay here. That made sense as the staff earlier told me that I was the first 10 to accommodate here in this dormitory house. And the other few of the 10 were the ones who had been accommodated here in this dorm house a day ago. But unfortunately for Jauhari, he didn't feel well on the day before his road trip commenced, for which he told his group to head on first and would do the catching up after he got better. So now, his group was a day ahead of Jauhari, and he was doing the catching up.

There was another dilemma that Jauhari had encountered. He

had trouble getting signals on his phone after crossing the border to Thailand, and I had the same issue with my phone when I crossed the border to Thailand too. However, he still managed to find this location without using his phone's GPS, which fascinated me. Anyway, it's still possible to ride without the use of GPS if one is sure to ride only up north. And also, the majority of the road signboards in Thailand have English letters printed on them, which is even better for non-Thai commuters on the road. But still to me, I prefer to use the GPS as I don't have to look at the signboards to navigate around.

As we converse, somehow, something popped up in my mind that I got to do something about it. I realised that I didn't have Thai insurance for the bike and myself. I was riding all the while without being conscious of the danger on the roads despite seeing the pick-up truck zoom past me dangerously, bumping into potholes that made my bike lose control, and even near miss a stray dog that ran across the road, causing me to do emergency braking that almost got myself rear-end to a vehicle in front of me. I thought about the elderly man I spoke to while wrapping my bag in the morning who called me 'giler.' Well, he should be a smart man perhaps.

I asked Jauhari if he knew any place I could get insurance from, but he was clueless as he got his insurance together with his group from an agent in Singapore.

"Later in the morning, try asking Jirajit. She might know one," he said.

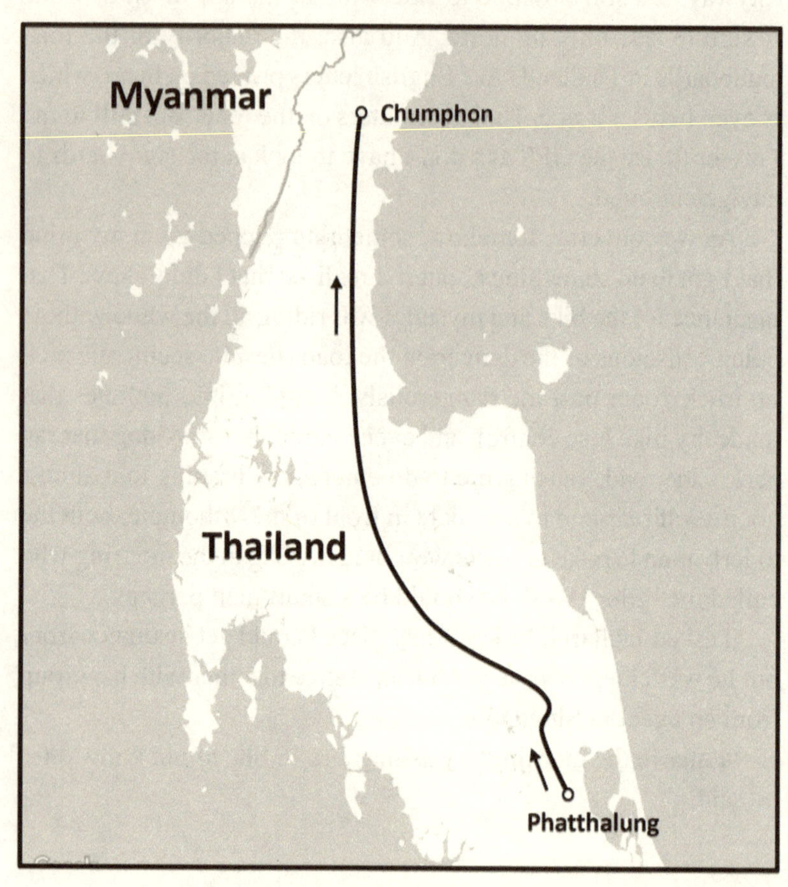

Myanmar
Thailand
Chumphon
Phatthalung

9

When Plans Don't Go as Planned

I took a peek from the porch outside the dormitory house to have a view of the cowboy town, which appeared tranquil yet was visibly misty all around. The first objective for the day was to check on my bike to see if it was still there on the other house's porch. Yes, it was, and it gave me the first delightful smile of the day.

It was too early to do anything, as no one was awake. I walked about on the porch thinking what I could do in this early hour of the day while I listened to the loud snores from Jauhari which could even be heard from the porch. As I walked and walked, I sprouted an idea to service the bike.

As the bike had reached 1200 kilometres since the start of my ride from Singapore, the time had come for me to service the bike which I would religiously do on time. But where would I be doing the servicing at? It is a question I pondered much about while walking back and forth on the porch. But looking at the open spaces on the gravel ground in front of the wooden houses, it seemed like an excellent place to do servicing here where there's no one around to bother me. But then, doing servicing on someone's property felt wrong to me.

"I can keep the area clean while doing servicing, right?" I

thought.

Well, I can do that.

I pushed the bike out of the porch to a spot on the gravel ground and put the bike into the mainstand position. The tool bag and the maintenance stuff like engine oil, oil filter, and rugs were taken out from the top box, but I didn't have an important item before working on changing the engine oil. I didn't have a bucket or a container to let the dirty engine oil drain out from the engine. But I had an idea. I took a spare zip lock bag from my orange bag and rolled the mouth of the zip bag outwards, then made it shaped like a small bucket.

Sometimes, I am amazed by my intellectualness as I always get things done wrongly.

But wait, the dirty oil may splatter out spilling off from the bag, right? I took a spare plastic bag, tore it apart to get a wider surface area, ironed it flat on the ground using my palm, and then the makeshift bucket went on top of it.

The drain plug is unscrewed at the bottom of the engine using a wrench, then the dirty oil drips down, and a spring and a metal oil filter drop down to the makeshift bucket. I removed them from the bucket and used a rug to clean them. Then moved over to the other side of the engine to unscrew the three small screws to remove the oil filter cover. Then drips the dirty black oil from the engine housing as I take off the cover. Then pulled out the dirty oil filter from the housing and dropped it into the makeshift bucket.

Rocking the bike side-to-side to let out the excess dirty oil inside the engine to drip down while I admire the train carriage just metres away from me, then wipe clean the oil filter cover and the housing of the oil filter. After which, a new piece of oil filter goes in the housing, and last but not least, the oil filter cover goes back to its position and the three small screws were screwed back with a wrench.

Jauhari came out from the dormitory house, walked to my maintenance site and squatted next to my bike to watch me do the maintenance.

"One bottle of engine oil enough?" Jauhari asked while picking up the engine oil bottle to have a look at it.

"Ya. The engine only needs one litre," I said.

"Ah…how many oil bottles you bring?"

"Just two. Should be enough for the trip."

"When will you be changing again?"

"For that… still not sure about it. Maybe half-way before the return trip?"

He nodded, then put the bottle back down, and there was silence for a moment.

"Did you see Jirajit?"

"Oh, not yet."

He nodded and then introspected about something, probably about his phone SIM card that couldn't get a signal since yesterday.

I fit back the metal filter and spring onto the drain plug cover and screwed back the drain plug under the engine, and then further tightened it with a wrench.

The final thing I had to do was unscrew the dipstick out from the engine, then fit a funnel into the orifice, then fill it with new engine oil. Once the engine oil bottle is fully emptied, the funnel goes out, and the dipstick is screwed back into the engine. Mission accomplished.

Jirajit walked out from her wooden house that was adjacent to the dormitory house, waved at us with a smile on her face and made her way to the Steak House. Somehow, I felt guilty about what I was doing, for which I hurried to get things done fast. And for Jauhari, he stood up and walked over to Jirajit before she got into the Steak House.

I kept the tools back, unrolled the makeshift bucket, and zipped up the bag. Then overlapped the zip bag with another plastic bag, threw the dirty rug inside the plastic bag and then stared at the bag.

Where the heck to throw this? I can't just throw it anywhere I want...

Guess that I am too self-conscious about this kind of stuff. As in Singapore, throwing engine oil in housing block dustbins, one could get into serious trouble with the law if one were to get caught.

"Khai! You want to have breakfast!" Jauhari hollered from the Steak House porch.

"Yaaa!" I hollered back.

"What do you want to get!" Jauhari hollered back.

"I will get the same breakfast as you!" I hollered and saw Jirajit with the same prominent smile still intact on her face that could be seen from a distance. My guilty conscious elevated further looking at her. Then Jauhari returned to the dormitory house and Jirajit went into the Steak House.

I pushed the bike back to the porch and walked out of the porch with the dirty oil bag. As Jirajit then walked out of the Steak House, I walked to her with my full guilty consciousness stopping in front of her to ask her embarrassingly where I could throw the bag. She takes it without hesitation and says, "Oh, I throw it for you. It's ok." I thanked her profusely but felt bad inside me. (I still felt guilty when I type this paragraph)

Jauhari and I had our breakfast outside the Steak House porch and conversed as we ate breakfast. Munching while hearing Jauhari's past road trip stories still fascinated me a lot. During our conversation, Jirajit brought a tray to our table and asked about our breakfast. We nodded and flattered her with praises of the delectable meal and she then put down hot tea on the table and a small plate with sweet potato balls.

"The tea and sweet potatoes are on us," she said. We thank her and just before she walks away, my hesitant mouth opens up: "Do you know… where… I can get Thai insurance for my bike? I totally forgotten to get it when I entered Thailand."

She pauses for a moment to think, then replies, "what I know is at Danok. There have many insurance shops." (Danok is a town close to Thailand's Sadao border, which I had crossed over from the Malaysia border during the Phuket road trip.)

"Ah, That's far… It's like over 150 kilometres from here."

Just then, she remembered an insurance agent's contact number and went to get her phone. While waiting, Jauhari recommended the type of insurance I should get as I knew nuts about insurance. On the prior trip to Phuket, I obtained insurance from an outlet a few kilometres before the Bukit Kayu Hitam border. Around that vicinity, there were many insurance shops around. I randomly picked one and went over, and the insurance seller did the insurance forms for me and also helped to fill up the forms for border crossing. It was frivolous back then, and I didn't have to do anything.

Jirajit came with her phone and sent the agent number to me. I dialled up on my phone and got in line with the agent. Upon hearing the agent's voice, his voice sounded a Thai person and his accent appeared strong for my ears. Despite it, I still explained my dilemma to him but had trouble understanding what he was trying to say and the only thing that I comprehended was that he was far away from my location. So, I passed my phone over to Jauhari to help me with what the agent was trying to say.

A few nods came from Jauhari and also an astonished look from him. Jauhari learned that he got his insurance from this agent's colleague – a Singaporean, and they both were partners who does the insurance for the overlanders. "What a lucky ass I am," I thought. Jauhari then explains what I need for my insurance to the agent, and I just nod like a kid listening to him.

I got back in line with the agent, and he recommended me the appropriate insurance for my trip duration and told me that I could transfer him via online banking transfer. But then, I was sceptical about transferring money through online banking as I don't usually do online transfers to someone I don't know.

I asked the agent for any alternate ways to transfer the payment. He paused for a moment and told me to pass the payment over to Jirajit and said that he would collect it from her. That's when I felt like a troublemaker to Jirajit. But since the agent is a frequent traveller here, it shouldn't be a problem for Jirajit, right? I thought. But I told myself that this would be the last time that I would want to hassle Jirajit. And so, I agreed to pass the payment to Jirajit. Before the agent ended the call, he told me that he would call me back once the insurance is finalised.

I went back to my bunk bed to get the cash and back out passing it to Jirajit and thanked her much. The same prominent smile came on her face. Somehow, I still felt like a troublemaker to her, even though she was just too kind to me.

Back carrying on with the breakfast, Jirajit tells us that she's heading out to the market and will be back later and left with her vehicle with her husband.

It was already 15 minutes past noon. No calls came from the agent. My supposedly promised plan to leave early in the morning to cover much distance didn't happen. I had packed up all my stuff and had already placed the orange bag on my bike and even wrapped the bag up. My usual riding gear was already on – except for the riding jacket, and Jauhari was already in his full gear but without his riding jacket on. I felt like I was holding him back as I told him yesterday night that I would accompany him to a 7-Eleven store to help him get a tourist SIM card. But looking at the dilemma I was in, I didn't know when the agent would call me back or what time I would even be leaving for my ride. I told Jauhari to go on with his ride first, but he insisted that it was alright and told me that he wasn't in a rush to move off. However, I intuitively knew that I was indeed holding him back from catching up with his group. What a troublemaker I was though.

My phone rang. The insurance agent called me back and said, "Bro, I busy at the moment… I pass you my partner number… he will do the paperwork… he's from Singapore also… easier to communicate with you… please transfer the payment to him."

I somehow understood his saying now and agreed to it with nothing much to say. I got the new agent's number and called the other agent, and he verbally went through the paperwork with me. Once it was finalised and the copy of the insurance was sent to my email – I don't know what I was thinking at that moment – I transferred the quoted fee to the agent via online banking transfer without realising that I had passed the cash to Jirajit. What a fool I was!

Then I realised that I had created another dilemma, I had to collect the cash back from Jirajit but I didn't know what time Jirajit would be back from the market. And that brings me to another problem: I have to hold Jauhari back longer!

I could just ask Jirajit to transfer me the cash, right? The thing was, I didn't want to trouble her anymore and explaining the situation to her on the phone would make me look like a crook rather than a visitor here. So, it was better off waiting for her to return and then collect the cash back.

I mingled around anxiously and watched every minute pass waiting for Jirajit's arrival. During the waiting time, Jauhari and I conversed more, and we went into the Souvenir House to purchase some stuff. Jauhari got himself a designed t-shirt that has imprints of R41P and a tube scarf. I got myself a designed t-shirt too, and alongside bought some route stickers to paste on the top box but left the sticker pasting for the later part of the journey.

Some visitors came into the premises and one of the visitors knew who Jauhari was. They conversed, and somehow, I became an impromptu photographer for them. Even after taking the pictures for them, they continued to converse – which I really liked because it could keep Jauhari busy and prevent him from worrying about when Jirajit would arrive. I just stood on one side, watched them chat, and wished they would converse until Jirajit arrives.

And yes, they did, and Jirajit arrived. But it was already 1:25 pm. I received my cash back, and I thanked her profusely again for the inconvenience I had caused but was denied by my apology. She said, "It's OK. I will try to help as much as I can. Even if I can't, I will still try. I tell my staff the same thing to help people who need help."

***

We rode to the nearest petrol station with a 7-Eleven store. When we found one and got to speak to the cashier, we had difficulty communicating due to a language barrier. We resorted on doing up some sign language, and I used Google Translate to communicate with the cashier. Although the cashier understood the message, the reply we received was surprising. We were told that the SIM cards were only for locals and not for tourists. I was baffled to hear that as I got mine from a 7-Eleven store on my road trip to Phuket.

We rode farther to the next petrol station where there's a convenience store. And again, we received similar answers from the cashier, saying that they didn't have SIM cards for tourists.

It was hard luck finding one. We continued looking for convenience stores along the route, stopping at a few that seemed promising to try our luck. We tried each one, but still had no luck. However, I managed to create as many hand signals as though I could take up an interpreter job.

We continued to look around as we rode. I was well ahead of Jauhari and zealously looked for the next petrol station or any convenience store as I felt like a burden to make Jauhari wait for a long time.

Many kilometres passed, and we stopped over at one of the petrol stations again that has a 7-Eleven store to try our luck. Using Google Translate again and then showing it to the cashier, some words of wisdom came from the cashier's mouth: "Have! Have!"

That was more than enough for the day. But I was still baffled about why the other 7-Eleven stores didn't let us purchase the SIM card from them though.

It was already 2:30 pm. By then, Jauhari had his tourist SIM card and configured it to his phone. I bought a hot coffee for him as a token of appreciation for all the thoughtful experiences he had shared with me and tips for the road trip, which I greatly appreciated. After enjoying our coffee and having a brief chat, it was time to bid our final farewall to each other.

We got back on our bikes, exchanged a fist bump, and we rode off tackling our respective missions.

***

The whole vicinity was well lit up by the midday sun. Within less than an hour of the ride, I was already sweating under my jacket. Distance ahead, I could see the simmering heat waves dancing in mid-air, making me well aware that I was the one that is going to bash it and absorb the heat waves.

With only three hours and thirty minutes of daylight left for the ride, it was too little to cover much distance as I still had consider the usual engine cooling breaks that I would wait for after refuelling. The only way to cover more distance was to continue riding even when the sun had gone down, which is something that I didn't like doing. But well, to visually see myself at the endpoint at Golden Triangle, I have to make some sacrifices.

The speed at 90 kilometres per hour was still slow for local commuters as I was overtaken from my right and pushed to the side like a feather easily blown away. I pretty much preferred to stick to the road shoulder and enjoy my time looking at the green field plantation on my left and whatever came ahead. But still, I couldn't stay out of trouble with those people who blatantly rode off the human-created path through the grass fields or land and recklessly connected to the road shoulder. These people abruptly merged in fast onto the road shoulder without checking for the incoming vehicle or checking the road traffic, to which I had to steer to the main lane quickly and hope not to get sideswiped by the vehicles.

Short breaks for the engine to cool down were still necessary, but taking longer than 20 minutes wasn't the game plan for the day as the main goal was to cover as much distance as possible. But at one petrol station, I took a longer break as I had been looking at this coffee shop sign named Café Amazon in most of the PTT petrol stations that aroused my curiosity to get a drink there before continuing with my ride.

Tank refuelled, and I got in the café and got an Iced Americano which is something that I didn't like having. But for the sake of keeping myself going and for the sake of getting cooled by the air-conditioning in the café, it was all good for me.

It was 5:30 pm, and I was still in the café sipping my Iced Americano. The Google Maps showed me that I had about 121 kilometres to reach Chumphon town. The distance seemed like a doable distance and most to most, I would probably reach the town before 8 pm. That seemed like alright to me. But the atmosphere would gradually turn dark after 6 pm, and the inevitable me, have no choice but to ride on to cover much distance. However, I do have the choice not to ride after the sun goes down, right? But the thing was, I just couldn't foresee what the next day would bring me, or who knows, I might get held back for whatever reason like how I was held back in R41P. I just couldn't predict, and it wasn't easy to predict my movements. So, when there's any given opportunity to ride, I have to grab that opportunity and just go with it.

I went on riding and riding targeting Chumphon town as the stop point, and watched the orange bulb that lit up the atmosphere go down the horizon till the atmosphere switched to dark mode. As I had said earlier, there weren't many road lightings that could be seen along the road, and yes, certain roads along my ride there weren't any lights to speak of and the road shoulders became more dangerous to ride compared to the main road lanes. I could barely see what was ahead on the road shoulder, as my bike's headlight was too weak to illuminate what was on the front. And also, thanks to myself for not having to mount any auxiliary lightings to which it made my ride as dangerous as hell.

The first main danger of riding on the road shoulder in the dark atmosphere is the road shoulder's width being inconsistent throughout. It would put me in fear that I might get off-tracked out of the shoulder and bash myself into the bushes, or perhaps fall into a drainage.

The second main danger of riding on the road shoulder is when the road converges whenever getting close to the bridges or river bridges. Even riding at a speed between 50 to 60 kilometres per hour, it's hard to visually see the convergence from a distance especially when there's no vehicle on the road to help to lit up the road with their powerful auxiliary lights.

Just imagine focusing only on the road shoulder and not paying attention to the front; I could get myself smashed directly into the bushes or collide into the cemented walls that comes ahead when the road converges.

Hence, for night riding, sticking prominently on the main lane and adhering to the road traffic speed, would increase the chances of staying alive while riding on unlit roads. However, it's advisable not to ride in a dark atmosphere where there are no road lights.

A pick-up truck overtook me, not on the lane next to me but a mere hairpin close to my right. It created a gash of wind turbulence for which my bike wobbled perilously. However, I didn't feel dreaded about what had happened but instead got back quickly to the centre of the lane and focused my sight on the pick-up ahead of me that brightened up the road with its bright fog lights. But it won't be long after the pick-up disappears out of sight. Then I had to slow down and wait for the next vehicle to pass me.

Riding under the dark roads, I realised that I didn't have to check back to see the traffic behind. Since my vision is mainly focused on the front, it was still obvious to know how near a vehicle approached me from my back. The first sign of a vehicle approaching from the back will be the bright light shining on the side mirrors, which depicts that the vehicle is approaching my rear. But this is slightly hard to justify if it's a 4-wheeler or a motorcycle. It may not be a 4-wheeler but rather a motorcycle changing lanes from right to left or the inverse way. So, what I did was, I kept on riding along the centre of the lane until the ground around me brightened up brightly. Then I would wait till I visibly see my lean shadow and the shadow of my bike in front of me, then I would signal left and slowly shift to the left-most of the lane – but not to the road shoulder, to let whatever vehicle behind me overtake me from my right.

Once the vehicle on my back overtakes me, I would still hold on to my position as I would intuitively know that some reckless drivers will speed past me eventually. If it was all good to be back on the centre of the main lane, there wouldn't be any light shining on my side mirrors, nor my surroundings be lit up – unless an ignorant who rides without any headlights. I would then slowly shift myself back to the centre of the lane and ride as normal.

The ride kept on going and passing several potholes or whatever that I had bumped onto. The one that didn't feel like a pothole; I pondered about it, and hoped that I didn't knock onto any live animals there were crossing the road.

The time had already turned 7 in the evening, yet it felt like I was riding past midnight. Thankfully, there were road lights on certain roads, and I was truly grateful for that. The intense focus I had on the road, constantly watching the front and mentally hearing the vehicles that passed by me, left me exhausted. The thought of bed was quietly whispering in my head. However, where would my bed be? I just couldn't prophecy it.

The time had reached 7:30 pm, and I reached Chumphon, but I was still riding on the highway. The centre of the Chumphon apparently wasn't close to the highway. I had to get off the highway and follow a route that would lead me to the centre. So, I followed the GPS, and after a few kilometres of riding looking for the U-turn point, I finally found a U-turn point, then negotiated the U-turn bend, and then steered to the leftmost lane to prepare to turn left to a route that would lead me to the centre of Chumphon town.

As I got closer to the point where I needed to make a left turn, the tarmac appeared sandy. Then after some distance, the tarmac transited to gravel textured ground. And then metres away, I see construction barricades with long tubes of coloured fluorescence lights sticking up the barricades on the left side of the road. The supposed left turn that I had to make was closed apparently due to ongoing road construction, and there was a road marshaller whistling and beckoning away vehicles from entering the route.

I rode further up to find another left turn, but to see another left turn that didn't seem like a ridable path. Even though the GPS re-routed my path to a new route to Chumphon centre, there wasn't any road lighting along to speak of. And from the look on the route at the entrance, the route looked creepy as though the flying creature from *Jeepers Creepers* movie would just drop by to snap my head off. I have wild imagination though.

I rode even farther up the highway, but unfortunately, there weren't any more left turn ahead to Chumphon. It frustrated the heck out of me as I was already exhausted and wanted to call it a day quickly. I had to make a detour kilometres away, then ride another few kilometres away, to make another U-turn to get back to look for a left turn to Chumphon town.

Back on the road shoulder, riding slowly, there was one route on the left with road lighting that could be seen along the entrance of the route. I stopped at the entrance, but after one look at the route, I could mentally count the number of street lamps on the right side of the road. But I was unsure if the street lamps would continually go on along the route as I look further ahead, it appeared to be dark. I sat on my bike and waited for someone to ride in the route so that I could follow behind.

I waited for a while, but no one came from the highway. But one sleepy-looking man came from the route with his dilapidated-looking kapcai bike and continued on with his ride to the highway.

Since he came from the route, it's a ridable route, right? I thought.

And so, I got back on my bike, and light throttled in slowly. As I continued on light throttling in the route, I noticed that I was counting down on the remaining road lamp posts as I further got in the route. Not a good sign, but I continued. Then as I covered slightly more distance, there weren't any more street lamps afterwards. From there on, my front slowly became dark, and after a few metres of ride, it turned utterly dark to which, I couldn't see what was on my left or on my right. But I saw a bright circular light shining in front of me, a distance ahead, like a glowing white ball, and it increased its size as I got closer to it.

Taking reference from the glowing white ball in front, I continued riding and watched the light becomes brighter and broader in its size. Then the light ball splits into two glowing balls and levels horizontally apart from each other. I intuitively knew that it was a 4-wheeler, and when the 4-wheeler got closer to me, I finally had a better picture of my surroundings. I was riding on cemented ground, and tall green grass was on both sides of my path that was about the height of my bike – about a metre in height from the ground.

WHOOSH! The vehicle passed me on my right, and my front became completely dark. The brightest thing around was my phone screen and the instrument panel lights. That was when I reached my plateau and could no longer ride any farther. At least, on the highways, when there isn't any road lighting, I could still be able to see the reflective arrow signs on the roadsides and also the headlight of the oncoming vehicles on the opposing side of the road, which it is still possible for me to ride on. But for this route, it became a complete NO-GO to me.

To make matters worse, I thought of the flying creature in the *Jeepers Creepers* movie again that was coming to eat me up any time soon. I made a U-turn hurriedly and slowly got myself back to the entrance of the route and not wanting to go back in again.

I rode up the highway to detour again with an exhausted face of mine to try to find a possible route to the centre of Chumphon.

But once I had detoured from a U-turn point, I noticed something on the left side of the road. There was an evenly cut grass patch with several globe lamps sticking out from the grass, and some deer-carved stones were around on the grass patch. As I got closer, I saw a yellow illuminating arrow sign pointing towards a premise with the motel's name next to it.

I scraped my plan to ride to the centre of Chumphon town, and I rode into the premises and stopped next to the receptionist's desk. But it was strange having to stop next to a receptionist desk that was close to the highway outside. Probably it was my very first time having to arrive at a motel next to a highway, I guess.

"Hello, got room?"

I asked the receptionist, and he nodded without saying anything and showed me his open palm with his five fingers fully stretched out. Which probably meant that it's 500 baht.

"I…one…person," I said.

He nodded again and showed his five fingers again.

"What room is that?" I asked.

He didn't reply but typed something on a calculator and then showed the display screen to me. It displayed "500" on the screen. Guess he couldn't comprehend English, but that wasn't his problem. It was my problem for not learning how to speak the basic Thai language.

"How…big…the room?" I said with the support of my hand gestures.

He first gave a confused look, but after I made the hand gesture, he pointed at a room at one corner.

The room was close to the highway, but I hadn't had a second thought to say no to it as I was too exhausted to look for another accommodation, and the plus point was that there was a private parking lot just right beside the room.

Well, that is more than enough.

***

The day hadn't ended till I got something to eat. I changed up and left the premises to a restaurant next to the hotel. But unfortunately, as I got closer to the restaurant, it was on the verge of closing as the staff were busy cleaning up the area.

There wasn't any restaurant besides the one next to the motel. I got back to the motel and asked the receptionist about any food vendors nearby – of course, with the help of Google Translate. He walked me out to the entrance and directed me in a direction along the highway, telling me that there is one 7-Eleven ahead.

The walk to the 7-Eleven was about 500 metres away from the motel. But walking next to the highway was a peculiar thing to me. There wasn't a paved walkway for which I happened to be on an obstacle course where I stepped on the mud ground, slipping myself on a slippery area and getting my toes knocked on whatever-was-that on the ground. From whatever I had knocked on; I truly hoped it wasn't anything that was related to animal dropping.

Once I got to the 7-Eleven store, I got myself an instant Tom Yam cup noodle and a small bag of barbeque chips, and I sat in the dining area to consume them. As I munched on, I stared out of the glass window of the store and watched the vehicles on the highway pass by. But as I kept watching the vehicle on the highway, some vehicles were so deafening to hear, even from inside the 7-Eleven store. Then came another loud cacophony sound from a motorcycle exhaust pipe that zoomed passed the highway.

And that was when I knew, as I munched on, that I had another dilemma to tackle: I have to hear this in my room.

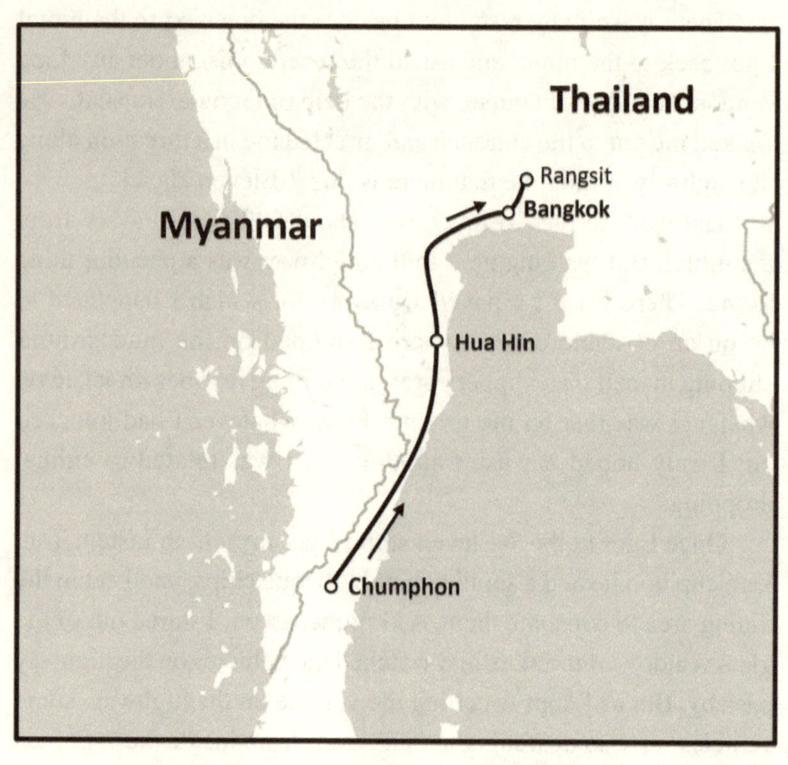

Thailand
Myanmar
Rangsit
Bangkok
Hua Hin
Chumphon

10

Crazy Traffic

Eeeeeeeerrrrrrrrrrrrrrrr! That's what ran through my mind for a light sleeper like me, and I hope it accurately translates the cacophonous sound emanating from a modified exhaust pipe. In some instances, it was silent enough for me to hear the sound of the air-conditioner's cold air blowing out from the outlet. But at some moments, I could hear the loud cacophonous sound of speeding vehicles on the highway, penetrating through all four walls of the room. From all those dreaded sounds, I had achieved my personal best for the most significant number of turns on the bed so far, and by far, in my lifetime. What an unusual accomplishment that can be though.

My phone alarm rang off at 7:15 am, and I got out of bed to take my pocket-sized notebook from my riding jacket pocket that is secured in a zip bag. In the notebook, I had written down the game plan for each day's ride. I leafed through the pages and stopped at where I had written the game plan for the day-five ride, and once I had read the plan, I came to my realisation that taking the game plan trivially may not bring me to the endpoint. I was way too far behind the supposed distance I should cover for each day. Today, the purported plan for the day-five ride was to stop at a town called

"Tak". It was a random location I picked to stop at as there's a prominent cross junction that can be seen clearly on Google Maps. As I checked the distance between my current location and Tak, the GPS showed me that I was 880 kilometres away from Chumphon, and that's a crazy amount of distance to ride for a person like me and a bike like mine.

For someone to ride that number in a day with my type of motorcycle – without any modification, that person can be given a gold medal or perhaps a cookie or perhaps a treat of Thai ice milk tea. Probably someone had already done that long ride before or bygone days ago, but I wasn't that person who was up to it. After the day-one ride to Kelantan, covering over 700 kilometres, I came with peace with my bike and decided not to ride any longer than that. It was tough and butt-paining to speak of. Then where will I be stopping at? It was apparently a tough question to answer.

***

After a quick breakfast at the motel and after filling up the tank at a PTT petrol station, I rode off to start my ride at 9:15 am taking on the highway and watching the patchy clouds above that looked like giant cotton balls hovering close to each other.

The roads weren't busy with commuters. I weaved in and out from the road shoulder to the main road lanes to overtake the goods trucks that took up much of the space on the lanes. Then after passing the goods trucks and riding farther up, a pick-up came behind me and started tailgating me.

"PEEP PEEp PEep Peep peeeeeeeeeep," the pick-up that tailgated me, horns behind me and then switched over to the rightmost lane. Then it sped past me, and a man on the passenger seat wound down the window, stuck his arm out and pointed down to the tarmac. I wondered what he was trying to do and thought he was trying to intimidate me by showing a thumbs down. However, from the look of his hand, it didn't seem like he was intimidating me. He was pointing down the tarmac with his index finger, and it seemed like he was referring to me as there weren't any vehicles behind me.

I checked back to my right to see the orange bag. The bag was still there. Then I turned back to the front to look at the hand again. The man kept pointing down the tarmac while the pick-up got farther from me. I checked back on my right again to see if any bungee cords dangling on the ground. Nothing was dangling. All cords were intact, and the usual cross wrap I usually do, was still there tightly holding onto the bag. Then I drew my eyes to the engine area to check for any liquid dripping. There weren't any drips to be seen, nor anything that amused me. I turned back to the front to see the pick-up even farther away from me, and the passenger then stuck his head out of the window with his arm out still and exasperatedly pointed down to the tarmac.

What the hell is he trying to say? I thought.

I slowed down drastically and halted at the road shoulder to inspect the bike while still on my seat. I checked back on my left, looking at the back of the bike till drawing my eyes to the centre of the bike; I realised what the issue was. It was a foolish mistake. The side-stand was sticking out and has yet to be retracted. It may seem like a minor issue, but it could lead to a grievous mistake. I thought about what I did earlier by weaving in and out of the lanes nonchalantly without knowing that the side-stand was out. It could have hooked onto whatever stuff on the road or perhaps hooked onto something that could make the bike flip over. Or, worse, hooking onto something that could get me into serious injury. And from the unfortunate injury, maybe, who knows, my scene might have a chance to be nominated for the future sequel of the *Final Destination* movie franchise.

Sometimes, I ponder to myself from my wild imagination.

***

Back to my ride, while observing what was around my vicinity, I sang frivolously out in the space as though no one was allowed to judge me on how I sang. I sang out loud and did some arm movement dance with my left arm, following the song's melody while my right hand held onto the throttle grip. Not knowing the lyrics of a song wasn't an issue. The lyrics that I didn't know of, I would replace it with "na, na, na." It was simple and easy. It helped a lot with the melody, and not knowing a song's complete lyrics wasn't an issue.

It felt so good to be on the road with no real obligation but a goal to complete what I have set. But I have to say, the ride was getting really tough now.

I had seen videos on YouTube of people riding long distances with broad smiles on their faces. But in reality, the truth from experiencing from my ride, it wasn't as easy as it seemed. It was tough, and never have I thought that it would be that arduous and bodily pain. I could feel my foot arch rest on the foot-pegs, became inflamed from the prolonged period of resting my feet on the pegs; my butt felt like it had lost much weight from much vibration from the bike's engine and my butt felt like it became rock solid; my hip felt like I was carrying a ton of weight on my shoulders in which I struggled to keep myself upright; my back muscles ached much, and I felt the muscle fibre vibrates as I ride; my shoulder and neck strained much as I have to hold on to the weight of the helmet for a long time and keeping it balanced was challenging. In addition to all the strains and pains, having my body to fight against the headwind, had mentally drained much of my energy.

That brought me to create a vague philosophical quote in my mind as I realised what was happening.

To achieve something challenging, the mind and the body have to somehow go through physical stress or mental pressure. The one who endures the stoicism long enough to accomplish something is the one who truly feels the game and remembers the story vividly.

I'm no philosopher, and I don't read anything related to philosophy. But the random quote I made, it somehow made sense to me.

As I covered much distance, there's always something interesting to see as I rode further up the direction of north. Beautiful lucid green hills can be seen near, and mountains can be seen afar. On some hilltops, I came to notice several statues above hill summits. Some statues are in gold, some in white, and some in black. Many of them were statues of Buddha, but some were monk-figured statues in traditional robes. All the statues were intricately carved out, and some were huge enough to be seen even from kilometres away.

Not only religious statues or monk figure statues were the only huge ones; I came to a point where I had to stop for a picture as it was unusual to my eyes and something new to me. On the roadside, I looked up to a giant gold rooster that had features of Thai traditional embodiment design on it, and it was a few stories high.

I kept riding, and the Route 4 that I was riding on, the road splits up into two routes. One is Route 37, which diverges out to the left, and the other route on the right is still Route 4, which heads towards the coast and leads to Hua Hin city. Both routes will eventually converge back to a single route after 50 kilometres. Still, I chose to ride on the Hua Hin city route as I had researched about the city back when I was at home and got to know that it has similar beach sides like Phuket – but has lesser crowd compared to Phuket, which captivated me to check it out.

"Hua Hin - 4km". That's what the information signboard on the roadside says. Riding on a dual carriage road of Route 4 nearing Hua Hin, there were many parked cars on the road shoulder as I rode farther into the centre of Hua Hin. The road increased in vehicle volume, and more low-level buildings came popping up, and there was a decent number of tourists walking about in the vicinity. But the atmosphere here in Hua Hin wasn't as bustling and noisy as when I was riding on the road to, and on, the populous beach in Phuket named 'Patong,' where the roads were polluted with the sound of the vehicle and horns. Or perhaps I came at a time when it wasn't the peak season for Hua Hin? I don't know, but the roads here seemed to be much noiseless and less touristy, which suited my taste as I dislike being around touristy areas.

There's another reason why I like it better in non-touristy places. I have a better chance of upgrading to a better hotel room for the same price I paid for. Yes, I'm kind of a cheap guy, but I always get a good deal. Always.

I came stopping at a kerbside, just stopping in front of a white-painted bus stop to have a better look around the area. "Market Village", large green words on the white overhead bridge in front of me. On my left is another infrastructure with a sign on the façade of the building that says, "Hua Hin Market Village." It's a modern shopping mall with a contemporary exterior design, and it's white too. On the sidewalks, there were several garden arches along the sidewalk which looked like they were for decorative purposes, and they were also white. The condo or hotel that's on my right, a distance away, was also in white. There are many other things around my vicinity which somehow have white features on them that make it seem like the customer persona for this place should be made all white. Interesting.

I continued to slow throttle and looked to my far right, where the coast should be at. But unfortunately, the coast was 300 metres away from the road I was riding on and buildings on my right were blocking my view. Despite my view being blocked, I still could smell the sea breeze travelling past my nostrils, making me feel like running to the beach shore and deluging myself with the ocean water. It then made me have thoughts of staying a night here in Hua Hin. But as I looked at my watch, the time had reached 1:30 pm. The day was still young. But something nudges me to keep on going.

I stopped by one of the roadside food vendors along the road of Hua Hin to have a meal and cool myself from the dreaded heat that was barbecuing me. Tall-skinny-chilled-glass of Coca-Cola came along with an aluminium tin cup with ice cubes in it, and a white plate came with cup-shaped rice on the centre of the plate, black pepper beef on the side of the plate, and on top of the rice, a sunny egg took its place.

I devoured the simple meal and thought about where to stop for the day. I checked on Google Maps for the next prominent destination and the next appealing one showed me a place I always wanted to ride on: Bangkok.

It wasn't far off from my current location, and it was just about 172 kilometres away. The estimated time to reach Bangkok was roughly 3 hours, including a break in-between. But the 3 hours is planned according to the pin-drop pointing directly to Bangkok's centre. Will I even be able to get to the centre easily? That was a big question mark to me, and I couldn't imagine myself riding there, nor I knew what the traffic be like. That brought me another dilemma of what the woman in the Betong 410 had said to me: *"I scared you get lost in Bangkok... It's not so easy to find your way..."*

I sent a text message to Jauhari regarding the route he took since he was way ahead of me and should have passed Bangkok.

Luckily, I received the message quickly as he was also having his break at the same time as I. He then recommended taking Route 9 – a route on the outskirts of Bangkok, and told me it should be fine. But the thing is, by the time I reached Bangkok, wouldn't it be the peak period when the roads become busy with many commuters? A flashback of words came into my mind again: *"I scared you get lost…"*

Well, the only way to find out the traffic situation in Bangkok is to get myself there and experience it live.

***

The ride went on to find a place to end my ride. My view was open, and I could see what was on my far left, far front, and on my far right. Everything looked wide open, and the blue sky filled up much of my view but less of what was on the land. The rays of sunlight overly cast my surrounding, and I was heating up faster than the bike's engine normally heats up. Even bringing down the sun visor from my helmet, it looked as though I hadn't brought it down, as my vision was crystal-clear with no shades of tint to be seen. What it actually meant was: it was freaking hot.

Unsure of the exact temperature, but it felt as though I was continuously bashing through the simmering heat waves along my ride. And yes, that's the fact, and that is why it is more logical for me to look forward to the PTT station – not only to fuel up the tank but to get an ice coffee from Café Amazon and cool the heck out of myself.

The ride was smooth, with moderate traffic after the quick quench at Café Amazon. The lanes got wider and the road changed between two to three lanes. Just after Samut Sakhon district, the traffic on the road started to increase fast, and just before reaching Bang Khun Thian district, the traffic increased exponentially. Then another few more kilometres, the traffic came to a still position. Lane splitting was the best option to get forward. Then lane changing became detrimental as I got closer to the outskirt of Bangkok. The GPS had trouble reading the road I was on, in which I had a tough time keeping up with where I wanted to go.

Some roads have many lanes, but it was packed like sardines. Changing lanes to where the GPS instructed me to go seemed impossible. Other vehicles do change lanes too, but when they do, some drivers would deliberately stick the nose of the vehicle in-between the lane, to get in position before changing lanes. When they do this, they're unaware that they are blocking the motorcyclists from lane splitting, making the road even more packed like a sardine. With that said, the motorcyclists had no choice but to wait and smell the unfavourable smell of the exhaust fumes that choking up the vicinity. And yes, I was one of them.

But the Thai bikers are smart people. They backpedalled the bike whenever an obstruction occurred between the lanes in front of them. And with the help from their pillion passenger, the pillion passenger would be the helping buddy to wave to the drivers on the other lanes to get their way unblocked and then get to another lane fast and continue to lane split.

I did try like what the Thai bikers did: sticking my hand out and waving at the driver on the next lane to let me pass to the next lane. But it didn't go like what I had perceived, and it frustrated me much. The driver waved back at me and smiled through the windscreen as though I was just giving a friendly wave.

Well, the driver wasn't wrong. Isn't it welcome to the land of smiles?

I continued riding on the wrong route until I got to a U-turn point, then made a U-turn, and then found another U-turn point that would lead me to the correct route I intended to take. Once I found the U-turn point and was done with the U-turn, I would look at the GPS, and if the GPS tells me that I must stick to the leftmost lane, I would stick to the left no matter what and be a dramatic guy on the road. I would make peculiar waves to the drivers to let me change lanes, or when the drivers don't let me cut into their lane, I would abruptly cut into their lanes and not look at the drivers but give a thumbs up to them.

I know it may seem like I'm an a-hole rider who abruptly cut into other lanes. But the thing was, the traffic was going at a turtle pace and almost every driver was cutting each other lanes.

So, why not?

I kept doing what I had to do, and somehow, I survived changing lanes and then continued to lane split following the Thai bikers behind since they very well know how to zig-zag between lanes without getting caught in a dead stop. It did work out well, but lane splitting on a tight between lanes and breaking through dancing heat waves, and the smell of the exhaust fumes, truly battered the heck out of me.

I rode farther up north, and on one area where the traffic subsides to some extent, I came to a stop at a kerbside to take a break.

Gloves off, helmet off, a headliner off, tube scarf off, unzipped the jacket, and then sat on the kerbside leaning against a lamppost behind me, and exhaustedly watched the raucous road in front. Never have I fought myself through so many lanes to get where I wanted to be, and never have I done so many waves to drivers ever since I started to ride a motorcycle. That includes the total number of flags off for a taxi in my lifetime. It was a crazy experience and exhausting to do what I did.

I just sat there and continue to watch the road and introspected whether I should even get into the centre of Bangkok. It was my mistake that I came to Bangkok at the wrong time, and it seemed senseless for me to head to the centre of Bangkok, where I didn't have any purpose. What resounded in me well was to ride farther north of Bangkok and find accommodation there instead of heading to the centre so that I could easily get on going with my northern ride the next day.

But wouldn't I want to be in the centre of Bangkok with my bike since I came from Singapore? I thought about that, but I came to a resolution that I will return to Bangkok with my bike on the return trip to Singapore – if everything goes well of course.

Everything on, and off I went back to the raucous roads again doing some U-turns; getting horned by some; I horned at some; annoyed by the driver that suddenly breaks hard in front of me, and eventually getting far off from the centre of Bangkok.

The sun had set down and overtaken by the dark atmosphere. But the good thing is, I have reached Bangkok. And the majority of the roads had street lights. But the intended plan was for me to take Route 9, a highway situated on the western side of Bangkok. However, I ended up riding on Sirat Expressway, then connected the ride to Udon Ratthaya Expressway, and then eventually reaching a city called Rangsit in the Pathum Thani province just above Bangkok.

As I continued riding, distance ahead along Leab Klong Rangsit Road, I noticed bright white bulbs lining the street under a series of canopies. As I got closer, I better understood what those white bulbs were all about. There was an array of street vendors, and it was fairly crowded with people walking past the vendors and making purchases. And on the other side of the street nearby, there were also similar markets that could be seen from a distance too. I need not have a second thought of what all those were – it's a night market. Not having to find a place to accommodate nearby the market is just pure asinine. And so, I went on looking for one;

found one; satisfied to have a parking place for my bike; and settled to accommodate in the hotel.

***

I walked up and down the night market, looking at the variety of shops and vendors both on the street and in the shophouses. However, not long after the walk, I concluded to have a meal at a restaurant instead as I could just sit and enjoy a meal than having to walk and eat.

A white squared plate came with delicacy on it. A perfect cup-shaped rice stands still on the plate with stir-fried cube-cut chicken mixed with spicy sauce. And right next to it was mixed salad that has zig-zagged lines of mayonnaise poured on top of it. Then, another thing came to the table too. Classic cut French fries that lay on an oval rattan basket. I don't know why; French fries is like a must for any trips I do.

After the satisfying meal, I had a wonderful foot massage, but somewhere in between the foot massage, I dozed off and then abruptly woke up to hear the last lyrics of my snore. I have never slept while getting a foot massage before – never – and always envied those people who do. When I woke up with a flabbergasted look, I first rushed to check on my wallet and phone. Everything was there, but the masseuse who pressed on my foot and the Chinese national man who was also having a foot massage on the other chair beside me, chuckled at my reaction.

"Bro, you sleep relax…." said the Chinese national man in his strong Chinese accent. I smiled, stared at the ceiling, and wondered how loud I snored.

***

The last shuttle service to the hotel had ended when I reached the entrance of the soi, and it was where the shuttle vehicle would wait at. There were motorbike taxis just at the entrance of the soi

146

and I was offered a ride for mere few baht to the hotel. However, I resorted in walking back instead and contemplate about what I had done since the start of the day.

I walked and pondered to myself if the ride was even worth doing. Just five days on the road, it felt like I had been on the road for years – although I have never been on the roads for years – which made me feel dreadfully exhausted and felt like I had many days of short night sleeps.

After enduring several short nights, all I hoped for tonight was to get good sleep and recuperate from the sleep deprivation of the past nights. That was all I wanted for the night, and I truly hoped for it.

Arriving back at the hotel front, I took a last peek at my bike to check if it was still there. And that was a yes to it. But there were other things on the soi as well. Two stray dogs roamed about in front of the hotel. I wondered why though.

Myanmar
Laos
Chiang Mai
Lampang
Tak
Thailand
Rangsit

11

A Bottle of Good Memory

The culprits who disturbed my sleep were out of my sight when I looked out from my room window to the soi. It all started with a rooster that began to crow at 5 am, and sound of clamour came from the stray dogs that barked along with the rooster's crow. Then out of sudden, the barking sound intensified and sound of nail-scratching on the tarmac came. And after some seconds past, it was all silence. From my subconscious mind, while I was partially awake but still on my bed, I could mentally create the scene of what was happening at the soi.

That nail-scratching sound seemed like the stray dogs were chasing each other. Then at one moment, the rooster's crow stopped abruptly as though it had been run over by one of the dogs which should have probably made the rooster succumbed to its death. And that was when I got out of my bed to look out the window to see no animals at the soi.

"Probably the dogs were fighting with each other to get the rooster?" I thought but with much annoyance on my face.

Another day, another nonsense.

***

It was just 7:30 in the morning, and I was already down to the foyer with all my stuff in hand to check out early. As I walked out of the hotel to my bike parking area, I was finally able to see the two culprits clearly in front of me, who had disturbed my sleep. The two stray dogs that look like Thai Ridgeback – one in brown and the other in black were roaming about in front of the hotel building while I walked to my bike to unlock the locks. Unfortunately, I didn't see the rooster. Probably, it indeed succumbed to its death.

The chain and the locks were unlocked, and I pushed the bike to the hotel front to load up the bags and stuff back into the top box. Once done loading up, I sat on my bike and flipped my pocket notebook to the page where I had written my game plan. I initially planned that I would be riding to Mae Hong Son loop today. But too bad, I wasn't anywhere near there which suddenly elevated my apprehensiveness. Looking at the days I had left and mentally doing some quick math, I learned that I had only five days left to reach Golden Triangle. That meant I must somehow get to Chiang Mai by this day, then have at least three days to ride Mae Hong Son loop, and the very last day would be to Golden Triangle.

Since I have never done the Mae Hong Son loop, I couldn't envisage how difficult the bends would be and if the three days were enough to complete the loop. But any lower than three days, it seemed senseless to ride the loop. With that said, the days I had left were all fixed, and I couldn't tinker with my days nor be complacent on my ride.

From my current location to Chiang Mai, the GPS showed me that I had to ride a whopping 666 kilometres. A nice number, but not fun to ride that long. And if I were to do that many kilometres, then that would be the second longest single-day ride compared to the day-one ride from Singapore to Kelantan.

I shook my head looking at the distance, and it made me ponder while I watched the brown dog walk towards me and sniff on my right shoe.

"Didn't I make a deal with my bike that I won't ride any long distance again?" I thought and looked down at my bike. But the deal was not to ride beyond 700 kilometres. The ride to Chiang Mai from my current location was about 666 kilometres. And that was below the deal I made with my bike. I pondered for a moment while I gave a quick glance at the brown dog to see if it was staring at me or looking at other things around me, as it was hard to determine from its dark eyes.

I looked at my watch; it was reaching 8. It seemed like a perfect time to start my ride, but I had this sudden reluctance to ride that many kilometres. Then, out of the blue, the brown dog started barking at me as though I needed to get off his territory. I stomped my feet down to intimidate it, but nothing happened. The brown dog then gave me an even more nasty look at me, and the barks became even louder. Then the other black dog came and joined along with it. Then both looked at me like they were going to put an end to me, like how the rooster abruptly stopped crowing earlier in the morning. By then, my reluctance changed to full of willingness to pursue the ride oddly.

And at that very moment, I knew I must go. And I did. It was the fastest move off by far since the start of the road trip.

***

It was still early in the morning, but the entire vicinity was overly cast. The sun brightened up everything on the land, making me squint my eyes while I rode on. I intuitively knew that it was going to be a sweltering ride by just looking at the shadows on the tarmac. The shadows of the cars and motorcycles that appeared on the tarmac were dark, and the contour of the shadow seemed so well-defined.

As I rode farther and got to Route 32 – a route that leads

north, the infrastructures, buildings, and shop houses that were around eventually faded away and then back to the usual view of the greens on both sides of the road with buildings occasionally popping up. The whole scenery repeats like a broken recorder, but from the broken recorder; I have to say, the sky was unique to me. No clouds hovered above, and it was just a pure blue sky. Although the heat was burning me up, having to ride in this type of weather and looking at the blues above, it was all I needed, and it was way much better than riding under the rain. However, I still hoped for cooler weather though.

My thoughts diverted to finding something to eat as my stomach growled for food. But looking at where I was riding, which was on a highway, it can be concerning as it was tough looking for a roadside food vendor where it isn't abundantly found.

There were lots of highway billboard infrastructures along the highway. Most of them were advertisements for automobile brands, petroleum brands, and other brands that I had never seen before. And when the billboards appear on the roadside, there will be a path to exit out from the highway, and it will lead to the venue of the advertised brands. But as I rode on and on, it was tough to find an advertisement that gave me the intuition to stop by to have a meal.

Fortunately, after some kilometres of ride looking at the variety of billboards along the highway, one of the billboards struck my mind that put a smile on my face: the portrait picture of that white-figured guy with his cloudy hair and the red background colour that surrounds the white figured guy. Well, that's the *Kentucky Fried Chicken*.

Breakfast was served after a tough battle communicating with the staff from the language barrier. Not their fault, but my fault for not knowing basic sentences to communicate in Thai. However, the breakfast was served to my stomach but having a commonly known fast-food meal where it could be found ubiquitously around the world; wasn't what I would want to have when travelling to someone's country. It was for the sake of getting a quick meal and to keep me going with the ride and not wandering about thinking about what to eat.

Back on the road, just less than three kilometres away from where I had my meal, a large bottle structure appeared a distance away from the roadside, and it resembled a large beer bottle. It was as tall as a 4-story high building, and at the tip of the bottle structure, a flag pole with a Thai flag fluttered freely by the wind. As I have mentioned before, there is always something interesting to see along the ride on the roads of Thailand, and this is one of the many out there.

But oddly enough, from looking at the bottle structure, it somehow linked to a memory in my mind back when I was in Phuket, where I met a group of five young Malaysian tourists. But then, it wasn't a touristy thing for them though. It was hell for them in Phuket.

On one of my days in Phuket, I bought a tour ticket to do an island-hopping trip via a shared boat with other tourists. Onboard the boat shares many interracial tourists such as Egyptians, Russians, Europeans, Indians, and a Bangladesh man – who thought I was one of his countrymen. But when I told him that I wasn't, he thought I was bluffing him, and he kept speaking to me in his dialect. Oh, man. Also, there were a group of Malaysians, and there was one Singaporean man on the boat – and that was me.

The island-hopping was to Maya, Phi-Phi, and to Khai island, where we can stroll about on the beach, snorkel, and also do some swimming. As the boat went to one destination after another, I got along speaking with some of the groups who I shared on the boat with. I'm kind of an introvert; however, I convinced myself to lean towards ambivert to get myself out to talk to people. That was one of the reasons why I went on the island-hopping trip.

Firstly, I spoke with the Egyptian couple while heading to one of the islands. I learned that they were newlywed and on their honeymoon in Phuket. I congratulate them and get to know that the man, who is a motorcycle enthusiast, tells me about riding a motorcycle on sand and dunes and enthusiastically talks about a popular event called *Dakar rally* (it's an off-road endurance event using an off-road vehicle or motorcycle to ride on terrains such as dunes, mud, rocks, and other rugged terrains.) I heed the conversation, but all of which I couldn't possibly create in my mind of how it's like riding a motorcycle on the sand. All I could remember and conceive of was a popular TV show where Bear Grylls does his survival in the Sahara Desert and eats strange insects in different episodes – but some look tasty, and that was about it.

But that tells me that I do not know much of what is out there in the world. I only knew all this new stuff hearing from the Egyptian man about what '*Dakar rally*' and '*dunes*' *was*. That is one good reason why talking to people is important even if one is an introvert like me. One could probably learn something noteworthy, and that may lead to something else in future.

I listened enthusiastically to the Egyptian man, who said, *"Egypt has many biker groups and many love to ride on sand. You should come over to Egypt one day. You will love it."* I nodded and somehow envisaged riding on the sand with my Yamaha Spark T135. It didn't end well though. I cart-wheeled somehow in my imagination.

Here and there, I slide in to speak to other groups of people on the boat while riding to the subsequent islands. On one of the island's stops, the boat halts on an open sea to let us swim. I somehow became an unofficial photographer helping the people to take pictures of them swimming, and I did get a shot for myself too – floating on the open sea with an orange life vest on. But somehow, I spent much of my time taking pictures for the Bangladesh man who kept hollering at me: "One more! One more!" And doing different swimming poses as though he was planning to send his pictures to *Vogue* magazine. I just smiled and took many shots of him and tried to ignore my intrusive mind that was pestering me to throw his phone into the open sea.

Wait, but all these didn't relate to the bottle structure I had seen on the highway, right? Please continue.

Almost everyone had jumped into the sea; however, few didn't want to jump in, and they were the young Malaysian men. Most of the Malaysian had bandages on their arm or legs, and one had bandages on his chin. There was this scent of despair look on them that can be seen on their faces, in which I wanted to know why, as it's unusual to see people who go on trips like this be on bandages.

The boat stopped at the last island. Some went on to snorkel, some wandered about at the beach sight, but the Malaysians and I, loitered near a table where the boat crew took out a large food container that has full of cut pineapples and watermelons and dropped it on a table for our boat group to consume. We walloped the fruits and chatted along, and I learned that they were all 20 years old and below. But I was curious to know why they were in bandages though.

We walked and talked and sat on a wooden boardwalk on one part of the coast. I got to know them more, and they told me to visit a *bar* and specifically directed me on how to get to the bar. I heed the conversation like a new kid in town – which I was – but somehow diverted the subject to why they were on bandages. Then slowly, one spoke out, and the rest joined in, telling me the dilemma they had gone through that costed lots of tears and money.

All came here to have an *eye-cleansing* trip and to enjoy their holiday on the island of Phuket. Interestingly, Phuket was their very first destination out of Malaysia to try out what a beer tastes like, and not only that, but some had their first-ever flight out from their home country.

On the second day of their three days trips in Phuket, they rented scooters, and they were in pairs on each scooter. But unfortunately, calamity struck on the day they rented the scooters.

It was raining heavily while they were riding, and from the misjudgement from the first bike at the front, the rider depressed the brakes too hard which caused the bike to slip and self-skid on the road bringing down the rider and the pillion to the ground. The bike behind them, which was also the other Malaysians, had a head-on collision with the bike at the front, which made them fall and skid too. Only the third bike – ridden by a lone Malaysian rider – had a near miss with the two bikes in front. But somehow, he did sustain injury too.

All sustained some kind of injuries on their limps, and the scooters that dropped and skidded had the fairings damaged and scratched. When they returned the bike to the rental shop, they were demanded to pay an exorbitant sum for the damages. As their passports were collateral for the motorcycle, the renter kept the passports till they paid up the amount, and the Malaysians had no choice but to pay up for the damages. They tried to haggle down the exorbitant sum but only managed to bring it down a mere little. They only brought enough cash for themselves and had all-in whatever they had to pay the renter. But still, it didn't amount to what the rental shop asked for. And worst, no one had a debit card, credit card, or safety cash set aside if anything were to go wrong on their trip.

They walked to one shop after another on the streets, asking for help and to borrow money, but were rejected one after another. They even cried and pleaded, but no help came. They even tried to get a refund for the purchased tickets for the island-hopping trip (the island-hopping trip I was in), but they couldn't get the tickets refunded. They were broken down, and two of the group had university interviews back in their country after their Phuket trip. Anxiety was running high, but luck somehow came to save their day.

They found a Muslim store vendor and told them about their tragedy. The owner sympathised with them and borrowed what they asked for and exchanged contacts to repay the owner once they arrived back in their country. They got back their passport after paying the exorbitant sum to the renter and left the shop with mere nothing. They only had enough to buy cup noodles and had an apartment arranged for them by the Muslim store owner as the hotels they booked were cash-on-arrival which became futile to them.

From what had happened the Malaysians were devastated by what had happened, and the island-hopping boat trip was somewhat meaningless to them.

Listening to their story was so intriguing but not in a good way, and there's lots to take back from their experience. No one would ever want to go through this type of dreaded circumstance – literally no one. But when it happens, the well-prepared one gets to tackle the issue dexterously, and perhaps, it may not hurt much on their pockets or whatsoever that could lead to a loss. That is why researching only where to go, what tour to book, and what to eat isn't enough for a trip. There is still a need to ask: "What if it goes wrong," "What if the plan doesn't go as planned," and all the other what-if questions have to be asked before the trip so that when things go wrong, there's still a way.

***

Out of curiosity, I walked along a stretch of go-go bars the night after meeting with the group of Malaysians. I recollected the directions that the Malaysians told me to walk to, and I arrived at a bar that was right at the end of a walkway. There were several salespeople beckoning people to get in their bar, and they were holding on to a laminated menu that had the prices of the alcohol beverages. I picked the cheapest beer on the menu, and I got the beer even before entering the what-the-heck-is-this-place.

It was smoky when I walked past the entrance, and it felt as though I was a WWE wrestler walking out of the entrance. But once my eyes acclimatised from the white smoke, and saw what was inside the bar, then looking up a stage…oh my…

I see humans with nothing on.

Lesson learned: Talk to people. One may hear something one has never heard before, and sometimes, it can be an eye-opener.

***

Kilometres went by, and I came to a stop at a petrol station in a town called Thoen. While I wrapped the cords down to the rack after refuelling the tank, the pump attendant came next to me and tried to say something to me. She was saying something in Thai and made some hand gestures showing me her eight fingers, then changed to ten fingers, then changed to eight fingers again, and finally ten fingers. Then she made another hand gesture where she pointed straight ahead at the front. I pondered for a moment and tried to decipher what she meant.

8…10…8…10… something at the front…

I shook my head, not knowing what she meant; then she pointed at the petrol pump gun and then pointed to the road that goes north.

Pump gun…direction to the north…

I paused for a while, and then my face lit up with amusement like I had deciphered the Da Vinci code. What she was trying to say was that the next petrol station is about 80 to 100 kilometres away!

I pointed at the pump gun and then made my hand gesture that meant 'far away.' She laughed and nodded excitedly, confirming that I was right. Well, that was a good charade.

The ride kept going on and on. My mind had fixed on only covering distance and getting to Chiang Mai. As I rode on, the view changed drastically in which it felt like I wasn't riding in Thailand.

The full greenery on both sides of the road slowly fades away and turns into a spread of brownish-skinny trees. The leaves had fallen, the trunk of the trees looked dried up, and the grass appeared light brown. Perhaps it was due to the burning season, where the farmer burns down the land to start a new season for loosening the soil before seeding. Unsure about that, but the brownish-skinny-trees, the light brown grasses, the smooth highway road, the backdrop of curvy waves of the mountains' ridges that can be seen afar, and last but not least, the sun gave out its delicate rays of orange light to the atmosphere that made the whole scenery exceptionally beautiful to look at. I have to say; it was just stunning to see.

I had seen this type of scenery before on Discovery Channel when I was a kid. At that point in time, I had never once thought that I would be looking at it in the future. And the day had come for me to see it live. It was a magnificent moment, and somehow, I thought I had made the best choice to do a road trip.

As I reached Lampang, the third largest city in northern Thailand, the GPS somehow led me out of the highway to ride on some tight alley to take a shortcut. The GPS brought me to a narrow alley, and it felt odd to me as the houses on both sides were just right next to the alley, and the alley was mere less than two metres wide. I rode passed the houses watching the locals standing at their door front with their baffled looks on them, and some kids stuck their hands out to hi-five me as though I was a superstar. But it felt good, and there were lots of smiles around, and it sprouted out a big smile on my face. I gladly hi-fived the kids back and cautiously dodged the potholes, dodged the kids playing in the alley, and dodged some women hand-washing their clothes. The whole scene felt like I had seen this type of view in a movie before, but unsure which movie it was. But the more I rode further up north of Thailand, whatever I had seen on Discovery Channel when I was a kid, it all slowly came alive to my eyes, and I was out of words about how surreal it was.

I watch the orange bulb spew out light to the atmosphere, slowly going down below the horizon while I pick up more speed to cover the distance before the atmosphere light dims. Then after taking a shortcut, I got back on the highway again and came to a stop at a Shell station to fuel up and grab a small bite at a store adjacent to the Shell station before I set off for the last 88 kilometres to Chiang Mai.

I got an ice coffee and two glazed doughnuts to fuel myself but pondered whether the ice coffee was worth the purchase. Probably because when I came to a stop at the Shell station earlier, the weather felt chilly.

The sun was almost down when I got out of the store, and like what I had perceived, the environment temperature had dipped down to a degree where I could see my breath clouds as I exhaled out. Well, a battle of cold just started.

I rode with my eyes wide open and shivered pathetically, like having the spasm when I had to pee in the toilet. The warm air that I was exhaling out from my nose; made the visor fog up internally, in which I had to bring up the visor and get blasted by the cold chilly headwind on my face continually. I wondered why the temperature had dipped so much, but as I looked on the Google Maps, I realised I was riding on a highway where a national park surrounded me.

There was no stopping. Not even having thoughts to stop to wear a layer of cloth to keep me slightly warm. I kept on riding and mentally spoke to myself, "almost there, almost there," but the almost there seemed like it wasn't coming at all. The faster I rode, it felt like putting my face into a freezer. The slower I go, nope, I didn't want to think about that. I just wanted to get my butt to Chiang Mai as soon as possible.

Passing by Lamphun town before Chiang Mai city, the ambient temperature got back up to the normal night temperature that I conceive of, but the ambient air felt much cooler than those past evenings when I was still on the road. The transition from a hot and humid day ride to chilly weather had made my face oiled up, and my body felt sticky inside my clothing. Craving for a bath was more appreciable than finding food. That's when I knew that I got one more job to do before the day ends: to find a room.

The usual automotive brand infrastructure popped up as usual whenever I neared a town or a city. And for the streets and the roads, better lightings started to illuminate the vicinity, and there were more commuters on the road as I got closer to the city. I rode on and came to the final stretch, where I stopped at a traffic light surrounded by other local Thai motorists around me.

"Hello, welcome to Chiang Mai," said a fellow motorist next to me and waved at me.

I smiled with my exhausted face and thought, *I'm done with all these long rides.*

The traffic light turned green, and I continued to ride on the roads of Chiang Mai to see the road busy with commuters. Slow zooming and un-zooming the GPS map to have a better look at Chiang Mai, there's an obvious 'square' on the map of Chiang Mai. The 'square' is actually moat that runs along the perimeter of the square. The moat seemed well maintained and there were even fountains with lights lighting up the fountain and it looked beautiful at night. At the inner side of the moat, runs the ancient bricked wall, but didn't fully surround the perimeter of the moat. Only patches of bricked walls were still standing tall but the walls on the sides of the 'large gates', looked grandeur and had that ancient wall look on them. But looking at the moat and the bricked walls while riding, wasn't the right thing to do as I kept doing emergency braking just behind a vehicle that kept braking hard.

Leaving the sight-seeing of Chiang Mai to another day, I randomly picked an accommodation and rode over to look at the parking area for the bike. Luck came in for the first try as there were parking areas for my bike in the accommodation premises, but I had two options: to either pick a room for myself or get a bed in a dormitory room. I chose the dormitory room instead as the receptionist told me that no one had taken up the dormitory beds for the day. I happily got the dormitory room to myself, but I truly hoped no animals loitering around the hotel premises.

My very first road trip to Phuket, Thailand.

A near-miss with a falling tree and a close call for
the double-decker bus.

What a coincidence to encounter a man with a
chainsaw!

View of Bang Lang Dam reservoir from the bridge.

Above left: An unexpected arrival at Betong Route 410 store.
Above right: Posing with Jauhari at the Lucky Gate on the premises of Route 41 Phatthalung.

An unknown path I rode into, thinking that I would reach
the centre of Chumphon town.

Just after a short ride, oh my...

Thailand always surprises me.

Tough time overtaking goods truck along Mae Hong Son loop.

Bua Tong hill known for its wild sunflowers at Mae Hong Son Province.

One of the many scenic spots to stop by to indulge the beauty of the nature.

Somehow, I managed to ride up this high. (Doi Inthanon)

At the summit of Doi Inthanon which is 2,565 metres above sea level.

Beautiful royal pagoda close to the summit of Doi Inthanon.

The Chamber of Commerce in Mae Hong Son had been hijacked by thousands of road tripper's stickers!

An unexpected off-roading along Chiang Mai that went on for over 30 kilometres!

Touchdown at the Golden Triangle on the very 10th day of my road trip. I could finally say:

BEEN THERE, DONE THAT.

Longtail boat ride to Don Sao Island (Laos).

Is that crocodile meat? (Chiang Mai Night Market)

Loading the bike onto the cargo carriage of the train.

A long-dreaded train ride from Chiang Mai to Bangkok.

At Patpong night Bazaar. (Bangkok)

Bottom left: The bike was pulled out from the bushes by the locals after a self-skid.

Bottom right: Getting my bike fixed in Penang.

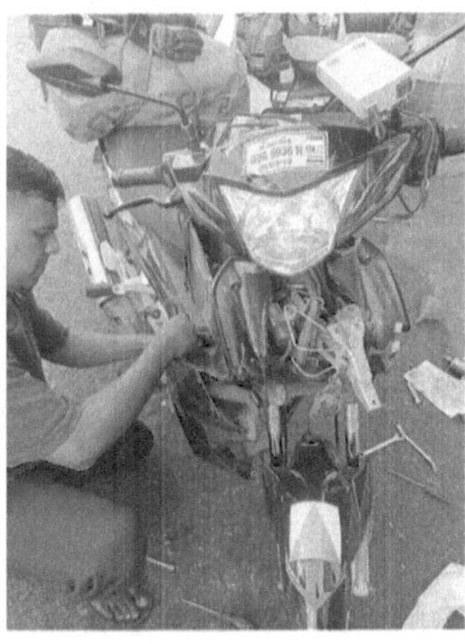

Bike fixed at Ragu Motors in Penang.

Invited to the Sepang International Circuit to catch cub bike races.

A well deserved bike wash at Johor Bahru before ending my ride in Singapore.

The aftermath of the water damage to my passport.

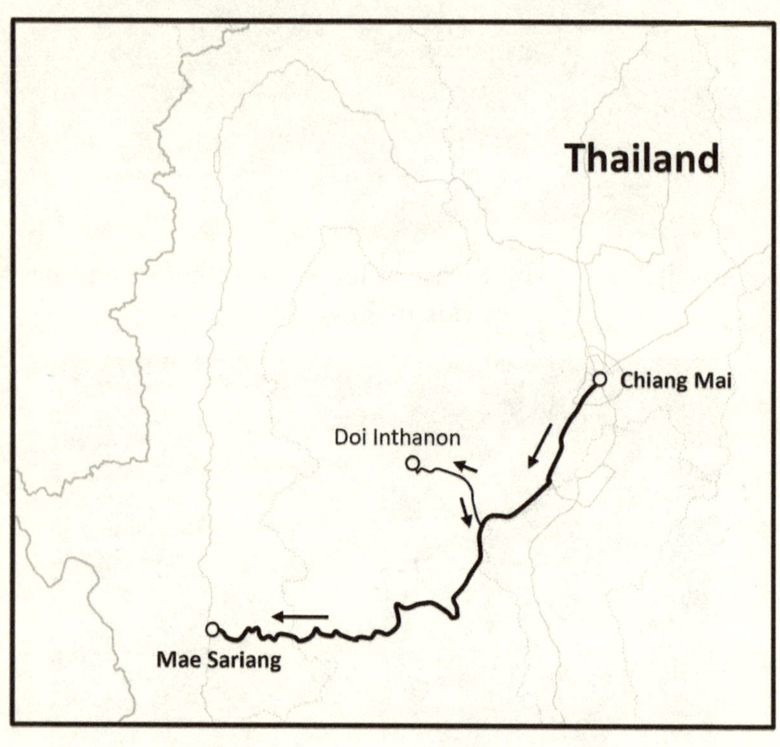

Thailand
Chiang Mai
Doi Inthanon
Mae Sariang

12

Teeth Chattering Ride

No rooster crowed early in the morning nor sound of dogs barking, or nails scratching on the tarmac. And there wasn't any cacophonous sound of loud vehicles zooming past the road. Sleep deprivation had been sub-eliminated, but not entirely. I was still experiencing lethargies in my body, and getting out of bed was a trouble to me.

Actually, it was more of laziness.

The dormitory room was silent, and I was still in a daze sitting up on my bed. As I slowly came to my consciousness, I became really aware that I was far away from home. A sudden fear shoots up in me that awakened me further. I got out of bed and walked back and forth on the aisle between the double-decker beds to ponder not about the plan for the day, but instead, ponder about how to get back home.

Answering the question was too tough at the moment as it was tough to think I had a long ride back to Singapore. I dreaded thinking about it, and tried to face the fact that I was already far away from home. And so, I tried to look at the bright side. I told myself that I was already here in Chiang Mai and beaten my personal best ride by riding twice the total distance from my prior road trip to Phuket, which I should rather be contented about it than thinking about anything that is negative. Then I thought of how amazing I was, and flattered myself by bellowing words like, "IM RIGHT HERE BABY!" "IM INCREDIBLE!" "IM EXCEPTIONAL!" It helped to change what I was thinking, and it slightly eased up my apprehensiveness.

There were more words that I had bellowed out in the room, but I had to stop once someone shouted, "OI", outside the dormitory room.

It may seem odd that I boast myself with self-praising words. But when there's only one person to motivate himself, he shall motivate himself however he wants.

***

I did the usual stuff by loading up the bike and getting myself ready to start the actual ride of the day. Once the bike was set up, I sat on my bike and took out the pocket notebook to look at my game plan. On the page where I had written the game plan for the Mae Hong Son loop, I hand-drew the loop, divided into three parts and approximately gauged where I should stop for each day. On this day, the plan for the day was to stop at a town called Mae Sariang. Why I chose that town, I had no idea. It was easy to divide the loop into three parts and plot a dot indicating where I wanted to stop. However, I just hoped it would be a good place for the night.

The distance came up to be 190 kilometres to the town, but I have yet to add the distance that I would be riding up the highest peak in Doi Inthanon, which is approximately 47 kilometres ride up to the summit and the same distance back down to the main route. In total, it would be roughly less than 290 kilometres. It seemed like an unintimidating distance to tackle for the day; however, I cautioned myself as this wouldn't be like an ordinary ride like riding on a highway. This is the very start of the day where I need to tackle the countless numbers of bends and it would definitely take a lot of time compared to all the past days of ride. So, watching the time closely is crucially important, and I have to somehow reach my planned destination to call it a day – not any other town before – since the time I had in hand before reaching the Golden Triangle are all fixed.

***

The ride started off by riding past shop houses on both sides of the road and alongside dodging people who walked across the road as though wanting to get themselves knocked down by my bike. Getting knocked down by a Lamborghini or a Bugatti, at least one can be proud of themselves, but why my bike?

Glancing at the shop houses stores that were already open at an early hour of the day, I see shops like hardware stores, stationery stores, plasticware stores, and fabric stores; the one that captured my attention was the homeware store that had a string of flags of the South-East Asian countries hanging above the entrance of the store. These flags are just sized at 21cm by 14cm, and it's a few times smaller than the standard-sized flags. All I wanted was just the Singapore flag so I could clip one end of the flag to the mouth of the top box and show off to the people around that I came from Singapore. Well, I'm not a die-hard patriotic type of guy. I'm an all-country lover type of guy who welcomes me with their open arms, and the flag is just there to make my bike look cooler. And so, I got one, clipped onto the mouth of the top box, and off I went to start the real ride.

Real ride? There isn't any start points for the Mae Hong Son loop nor a sign that says, "Start Here." All I got to do was to just start the ride anywhere in Chiang Mai. So, following my game plan, I headed towards the south of Chiang Mai to ride the loop in an anti-clockwise direction.

***

Riding kilometres after kilometres, I observed the urban city with an abundance of low-rise-buildings, gradually transforming into a suburban living society around me. I glance at the cluttered green trees lining the roadsides, admire the far-flung mountains exposing their exceptional green hues to the atmosphere, and notice green fields occasionally popping up here and there. As I ride on, I also encountered groups of foreigners riding pass me with their rented mopeds, dressed in flip-flops, shorts, and unbutton shirts. It makes me wonder if I came overly prepared or if their riding attire was more than enough.

Of all those, I waited eagerly for the hairpin bends to tackle on, but none had come yet. Only a slight degree turn from my handlebar was negotiated to tackle adorable bends. I pondered if the over a thousand bends were legit or just a marketed thing. But I have to say, the road conditions were pretty decent in which I didn't have anything to criticise about. However, I have to push the blame on the hot and humid weather that had already made me sweat under my clothes at the very early start of the day. Anyway, it's way better than riding in the rain. Definitely.

After riding about 55 kilometres down from the south of Chiang Mai, I neared a specific junction where I had to make a right turn to Route 1009 that would lead me up to the national park of Doi Inthanon and the peak. And that's where the real deal is on. But I was concerned about something before making the right turn: it was about the weather.

If it rains like how it rained on the day when I was riding up a hilltop in Phuket to see the Big Buddha statue, which made me cancel my ride up, then too bad for me. I don't have another luxurious day where I can afford to ride to the summit of Doi Inthanon. There's no backup day nor an additional day for me. I have to get to Golden Triangle on the 30th of November no matter what. That was what I had set, and I have to somehow achieve that. So, if it does rain, then I have to get down like a man and just continue with the ride, and accept that the summit climb will not be in the story that I want to create. With that said, my fingers crossed.

The right-turn has been made. Just riding a few kilometres on the smooth terrain, the hot and humid weather transited to chilly weather. The exact state of how I felt can be said like this: after a long ride under the scorching hot sun, then stopping by at a convenience store to get cooled by air-conditioner that instantly relieves the soaked-up heat in me. That was what I felt when the weather changed unexpectedly. But it was too much of coldness for which I had thoughts of getting back down to absorb back the warm air.

As I rode on, I could feel the temperature get lower, and the bends that I was looking forward to tackle on, still yet to come by. Not long after, I reached the 1st checkpoint post of the Doi Inthanon national park, where military uniform men waved at me when I arrived and marshalled me over to one side of the road. I parked and walked over to the post and was told to purchase the entrance fee of 300 baht for the entry ticket and 20 baht for the motorbike entrance fee. I paid the sum, and the man handed me the ticket and told me to show it to the next checkpoint post. I nodded and got to my bike and off I went on riding with a slight bitterness in me. I didn't realise that I had to pay the entrance fee while I was researching the national park back home. Well, what can I say? Nothing is really free in this world, right?

Once I had passed the first checkpoint, both sides of the road changed to tall green trees, and there wasn't any infrastructure afterwards. The temperature further dipped, and it baffled me much as I could see the vicinity lit up by the sun's light evidently, but it oddly felt cold.

As I covered more distance, I shivered uncontrollably like a madman as I was too novice for this type of weather. And the jacket I wore isn't built to withstand cold weather. It's just a basic riding jacket that protects the shoulder, elbow and a thin layer cushion pad on the dorsal area. Furthermore, it's a mash type of jacket. Whatever the temperature of the air in the environment, I was absorbing that heat too. But what can I say, I bought it for mere 50 sing-dollars from a previous owner for the sake of serving the purpose of the Phuket road trip, and to make full use of it for this trip. But thank goodness to myself, I brought along a pullover top that could give me slight warmth and brought some heat packs that come in small sachets where I could place them in my gloves and under my feet. But I hold on to the thought of putting them on till I reach the 2nd checkpoint.

There are several waterfall sites in this Doi Inthanon national park, and I had passed by a few of them but didn't have the zest to stop by any of the waterfalls to have a look. The problem was me. I was shivering terribly on my bike, and I didn't want to stop anywhere but to keep going until I reached the 2nd checkpoint.

As I kept on going, I started to notice at certain parts of the road, the inclination of the road increased gradually, to which I had to change the gears between one and two; to get more power before riding up the steep slopes. Then there came the bends. And more bends came subsequently. I was all ready to tackle the bends as I had been waiting for them for a long time. But then, some bends appeared really intimidating: it was all the sharp left bends.

Riding close to the centre of the road is a no-go thing, especially when negotiating a sharp left bend. I couldn't possibly see what is after the bend, and it was hard to justify what will there be.

But I have found the main danger when riding in the centre of the roads lane when approaching a sharp left bend.

Some pick-up trucks negotiate the sharp bends – their right bend – like no one is riding in the opposing lane. The pick-ups would ride in between the lanes, if not dive into the opposite lane with half its vehicle body in or its entire body into the lane. I could have been knockdown by the pick-ups, but after just one near miss, I was already sticking close to the left most of the lane all the time.

Vehicles piled up behind me although I was riding close to the road's edge. Whenever possible, I slow down drastically and beckon the drivers behind to overtake me. But the good thing was that the drivers weren't horning at me, but rather waiting for the right moment to overtake me swiftly when a long straight road approaches.

Since the roads are mountain roads, there aren't many straight roads to speak of, but more bends to be ridden on. And the downside of the straight roads was that there aren't many long straight roads in which the drivers have to be prepared if they want to overtake when a straight road approaches. And it's only possible if no vehicles are in the opposing lane. And that's challenging.

It was getting really cold as I covered more distance. My hands under the glove felt like it was frosting up; my teeth chattered uncontrollably like I could crack many nuts at once; and my body shivered as though I was intentionally exaggerating. But nope. The obnoxious shivers came in autonomously. And the faster I rode, it felt like the temperature dropped twice as low. The slower I rode, erm, not much of a difference.

The road started to get even steeper on certain area. Meeting up with a goods truck – in front of me, made my ride even more challenging. On steep bends, the goods truck struggles to move up and it climbs at a speed below 20 kilometres per hour. And the unfortunate me, the one behind it, it became even harder to control my bike at that low speed. It felt like the bike might roll back, and I feared getting the bike stalled. And that would probably be someone's nightmare too.

My right foot was all prepared on the brake pedal if the truck did roll back. But at any moment of the climb, depression of any breaks wasn't on my mind. An inadvertent depression of any brakes could spoil the momentum of the climb, and my arduous work would become a waste. I will then have to back down to an even ground to get back the speed and power to continue with the turtle sprint climb, which can be hassling job to do.

I tried to take over the goods truck, but it seemed impossible to do from the tight road that could only fit one vehicle on a lane. I got out of the road and stopped at a grass patch, and waited for the truck to cover much distance. It's better that way to let the truck go ahead to cover much distance as I could catch up with it sooner or later and not struggle myself. Then soon after, as I looked around, I realised that I was pretty high up in elevation after looking across the road.

On the other side of the road, two grown trees stood about about two metres apart from each other. But in between the trees, I saw a view that startled me of what I was looking at. I see a view of green mountains interconnecting with many other mountains and they look like green patches of humps and bumps protruding up nonuniformly. The nearer humps and bumps, I see tiny green trees close to one another till they fill up the contour of the mountains. The tiny green trees aren't tiny, it's just that I was at an elevation where I see the trees like tiny plants to me. I consciously comprehended that I was at such a high elevation, and it left me gasp for words of how contented I was after looking at them.

I had caught up with a goods truck, but I was rather the fifth vehicle waiting in line to overtake it. After a bend, a straight road approach. The first three vehicles behind the goods truck managed to overtake the truck by riding on the opposing lane when there weren't any vehicles. Then another bend came. The vehicle in front of me and I, waited for the upcoming straight road to overtake the truck. The straight road came, and the last vehicle in front of me made a move by driving in between the lanes. The unconscionable me tagged along with the vehicle by tailgating the vehicle behind, as I was a novice in overtaking in this type of road context. Let me call the vehicle in front of me the *daredevil*.

I peeped out to the right to see a pick-up truck exiting a bend far ahead at the front. An instant sense came into my mind that the pick-up isn't going to ride slow. It's going to speed up. My heartbeat raised as I feared I might get squashed in between the goods vehicle and the pick-up truck if the daredevil in front of me doesn't take over the goods truck fast.

"HURRY UP!" My mind screamed. I tailgated close to the daredevil watching the pick-up speed up. *"HURRY THE FUCK UP!!!"* My mind screamed more legitimately. The daredevil sped up till its rear bumper passed the goods truck front – a few metres away from the truck front – and quickly made a sharp left veer back to the lane. But I intuitively knew it was impossible to veer left to the small space between the daredevil's bumper and the truck front. But I managed to speed up fast and get next to the daredevil, but I was still in the middle of the two lanes, and there was nothing I could do about it but do this: I locked my elbows in tight to my pelvis and hoped not to get squashed.

WOSHHHH! The pick-up passed me on my right. And I found out that I was still alive a second later.

The daredevil sped up, and I got back in the lane with a heart that felt like it could fail from overly pumping.

Fucking hell! What the hell am I doing?! I almost get

sandwiched by the cars you know!

From there on, I was a puss in a boot and promised myself to not overtake again. But not bad that I have a clever situational analysis mind. But still – nope. It was better off riding slowly behind a vehicle.

Far ahead, the same look-alike checkpoint appeared like the first one. That's the 2nd checkpoint. I stopped beside a booth and handed over the ticket to the military personnel, and he tore it in half and handed the other half to me. I then rode a few metres up from the booth, stopped at the roadside, hastily unravelled the cords from the orange bag and rummaged through the bag to get the pullover and heat packs. Once the stuff was out of the bag, the pullover went under my jacket, and the heat packs were slotted under my feet and inside the hand gloves – at the palm area. However, the heat packs didn't instantly give me the warmth that I needed as it would take some time to get heated up. But waiting for it to heat up wasn't what I wanted to do as I was still shivering pathetically. With that said, I had to go on.

I got back on the bike, and off I went to continue with the steep climb; a sudden gust of chilly air blew on my face, which created a not recommended words in my mind: *FAAAK THHIISS SHHHITTT!*

The temperature dropped lower and lower as I continued to ride up the last 8 kilometres to the summit. Focusing on the gear changes between one and two made the climb slightly easier, but when I inadvertently changed to a higher gear on a steep slope, it made the momentum of the climb dead, and the bike struggled to get the distance.

The engine started to lose power as I got higher in altitude. Full throttling, but the sudden drop of engine power while on a steep climb made the climb even more frightening. A close metaphor would be like a roller coaster cart that slowly goes up in elevation; then a sudden fall comes making a person feel like popping out of the cart. That was how I felt.

I kept going and going, and I came to the final stretch where the road expanded in which I see silver Toyota vans, yellow Toyota pick-up trucks, and other white vans parked on both sides of the road. All these are tourist vans, but I wasn't enthralled to see them. I was more enthralled to see a sign telling me the peak was nearing.

Then another hundred metres ride, the road brought me to a car park. And that was it. That was the summit ride. But the summit wasn't at the car park. There was this sign that directed me to a flight of steps which would lead me to the summit. I got off the bike and left the helmet on the side mirror and quickly hurried to the steps.

I climbed up the steps as fast as I could with much heart palpitation. Then much steps climb; I came to a halt at one point to look up at a large signboard where lots of tourists gathered to take pictures of the sign. And that is where there was a triumphant smile sprouted on my face.

"THE HIGHEST SPOT IN THAILAND."

The cold and teeth chattering ride up to Doi Inthanon mountain was well worth the struggle; the multiple bends and steep climbs were worth the struggle; the many gears changes were worth the struggle; the many profanity words that created in my mind were worth the struggle too – but not recommended, and the long journey from Singapore was well worth the ride.

I sighed as I looked at the sign and remembered telling myself: "I will be up there *one day*." That was when I was sitting at my home desk looking at the pictures on the internet of this place and envisaged myself taking pictures with the signboard. That *one day* came to life, and it was just in front of me. What a journey though.

Many tourists clustered around the area of the signboard, and many were waiting for their turn to take a picture with it. I was all-readied to take pictures, but I didn't mind waiting long for my turn as this was what I had come for.

My turn came eventually, and I passed my phone to a tour guide to help me snap a shot. I sat on the concrete ground before the signboard, and the tour guide asked, "Handsome! ready?!" I smiled triumphantly, and the shot was taken.

***

Not only was a signboard around, but a boardwalk around the summit led to other amenities such as a souvenir shop, sacred statues, an exhibition centre, and even a restroom to have an accomplishment of *letting it go* at the highest spot in Thailand. The one thing that also fascinated me was the signage that displayed the temperature of the summit. Well, it was 5 degrees Celsius.

I returned back to my bike where my bike was the only motorcycle in the car park. But this time, I now have a different view of my bike. I pat the bike seat like patting a cat and stared at it for a moment, and mentally told myself how grateful I was to have a bike like this.

The helmet was on, and the ride went back down. But not far off from the summit, I rode towards the spot where I had earlier caught a partial gleam of a crown-shaped-like pagoda.

As I reached the parking area for the pagoda site, I saw tourists walking up a steep slope, and there were military personnel marshalling the vehicles to the parking area. I parked the bike and took my helmet off, and made my way up the slope after paying the entrance ticket of 40 baht.

Nearing the end of the upslope, everything out in the vicinity looked vibrant. There's a roundabout with flora plantation. Then looking slightly up, there's a slope of flora plants blossoming out its beautiful colours. Looking further up to the left, a blue-sheltered stairway leads up to a purple pagoda. Looking to the right, there's also a blue-sheltered stairway that leads up to another purple pagoda too. Both the pagodas have somewhat similar intricate features all around it but both have a different meaning to each other.

The pagoda on the left is called *Naphamethinidon*, which was built to honour King Bhumibol Adulyadej's 60th birthday in 1987. And the pagoda on the right is called *Naphaphonphumisiri*, which was built to honour Queen Sirikit's 60th birthday in 1992. I have to say, these gifts are well maintained, and I have a better picture of why there is a need to pay for an entrance fee.

I climbed up the stairs that led me to the left pagoda, and as I reached the pagoda's walking platform, I see a viewpoint that has an exceptional view of many mountainous peaks that covered my whole viewpoint, including my peripheral vision. The mountains that were closer to me, were lit up by the sun's rays, and I could see the intricate details of how the mountains were shaped and the vivid colours of the green trees that covers the mountains. Moving my eyes at a farther distance, the mountains appeared dark blue due to the clouds above shading the mountains and as I looked further and further away, the dark-blue mountains transited into white colour mountains that on the whole, my viewpoint filled with a spectrum of colourful mountains. What a magnificent view can this be.

To be able to see what I was looking at, I have to say; I was truly grateful for it. Thanks to the bike again, a marvellous machine that brought me here, and a simple bike that helped to create a story for me. To better describe it, it's just a *tool*. It's how one uses it to make one happy. But first, one has to learn how to use it, then understand it, and then be proficient with it. But at times, it does give problems, right? Then meddle with it till it works. Then back on it and make full use of it again. The cycle will repeat itself many times till it can no longer be used, and one will think back to the good old days of how amazing the *tool* was.

Just about then, I thought about the years left before I part ways with my bike, and it gets scrapped away. Sad to think about it in the future, but for now, the *tool* I have, I have to make full use of it, and be proud of what I have.

***

It was even colder when descending, and the three layers of clothing I wore didn't help much to keep me warm. The heat packs in my gloves and under my feet; barely gave the warmth too. And being under the freezing weather, my mind didn't work like it used to, whereby I would be intrigued to stop here and there to take pictures of whatever that compels me. All my mind wanted was to get my butt down the mountain as fast as possible.

The cold weather changed back to hot and humid just a few kilometres before reaching the intersection of Route 108, where I first made the right turn to Doi Inthanon national park. My jaw stopped chattering, and my body didn't do that sudden spasm. It was an instant relief to get the warm weather back, and never would I want to ride up any summit without having proper warm wear next time.

I stopped at a petrol station close to the intersection to refuel the tank, and I happened to see a pizza restaurant right at one corner of the petrol station, which nudged me to reward myself for riding up the highest peak in Thailand.

An eight-inch pepperoni pizza, a small basket of popcorn chickens, and a large cup of coke were all down in my throat fast. Not a grandeur meal, but it was just enough food for me to tackle the upcoming bends ahead, and not worry about over-bloating and stopping here and there to puke from the dizzy bends.

I continued with the ride to the destined place where I had planned to stop for the day. After kilometres of riding, looking at a suburban town with buildings on both sides of the road, both sides changed to greenery, and the chilly weather returned to life again. But good thing that it wasn't as cold as the ride up to Doi Inthanon mountain.

The roads started to become curvy, with more hairpin bends to negotiate with. My eagerness to dive in and out of the bends like those dexterous MotoGP racers was in a high state. But my cautious mind came to warn me, *"Go on if you want, but later don't say I never remind you."* It was tough not to follow, but I tried my utmost best to be a good boy on the road.

Then again, after covering some kilometres, the drudgery repeated itself. Not one goods truck, but *three* trucks were in front of me, and they were a distance apart from each other. The first two were the same type of truck that I had tackled in the Doi Inthanon ride up, but the last vehicle – in front of me – was a white pick-up with boxes strapped on its bed. Taking over the trucks one by one appeared more viable to me. But not only did I want to take over the trucks, but the white pick-up was also trying to take over the goods trucks too. I watched the pick-up take over one by one dexterously and swerved in and out to the opposing lane then disappeared after it took over the foremost truck.

The same thing went on for me, but I became more circumspect about my surroundings because I had promised myself not to overtake after almost getting sandwiched between a goods truck and a pick-up truck earlier. However, looking at this situation, I have to take over the goods truck somehow; if not, I would probably be reaching Mae Sariang the next day as it had already turned to 6 in the evening. That said, I have to alter my promise and overtake these trucks as safely as possible.

I rode close between the two lanes and peeked out to the opposing lane for incoming vehicles and a straight road ahead. A straight road appeared, and no vehicle approached the opposing lane. I went on to overtake one truck at a time till I got to the front. Well, at times, promises have to be altered.

The ride went on negotiating left and right bends, and I watched the bright orange bulb that lit up the atmosphere, go down slowly and watch it move from one position to another. The orange bulb is in its still position. It was just me doing the bends that made me see the bulb all around my horizon.

The ride kept going on and on, meeting up with goods trucks along the way, and the same procedure went on for me to overtake them one at a time. At one bend, there was a badly crashed goods truck that looked like it had smashed into the hillside and spilt numerous corns onto the road. I had an intrusive thought that wants me to pick up some corns on the roadside where the road sweepers were sweeping the corns out of the road. However, the road sweepers seemed more like they had infiltrated the truck and kept an eye on whoever tried to pick up the corns on the road. Too bad, I had to continue riding and abort my new mission.

The greenery on both sides of the road turned darker and darker, and the orange bulb had gone down the horizon. The greenery on both sides of the road had already turned dark, and the temperature went way down even lower. Looking far ahead, there seemed to be a blue colour road sign and I intuitively knew what it was. A sign that states, "Welcome to Mae Hong Son Province." This is not the actual town of Mae Hong Son, but the start of the southern province of Mae Hong Son.

After another few kilometres of ride, I finally reached the town of Mae Sariang. But coming into this town, the brightest thing I could see were the road lightings. The vendors and the houses around on both sides of the roads appeared dark, and in some areas, it was completely dark as though it's an off-working hours for the town. There are some makeshift food carts on the roadside with bulbs of light dangling on the cart's canopy. There are lit-up advertisement banners, some small automotive repair shops, and many dark areas. I had trouble picturing what was around in the vicinity. It looked like a silent night of Mae Sariang town, or perhaps, it was just that I came to a road that wasn't lit up well. I don't know, but the only infrastructure that looked modern and well-lit-up was the PTT petrol station which I had to stop by to fill up the tank.

Tank fully fuelled then back in the Café Amazon as usual in the PTT station. I scrolled down the booking app on my phone to look for accommodation while I sipped a cup of hot chocolate. There weren't many accommodations here in Mae Sariang apparently. Only a handful of hostels and hotels were available at that moment. Unfortunately, the better-looking ones and the relatively affordable ones were fully booked up. Other accommodations didn't seem to convince me due to the parking area. However, I decided to just pick one, and check out the place.

I rode past different alleys fearing that I might get robbed anytime. The alleys were silent as hell, and some paths appeared creepy where I could even hear the cricket sound evidently. I kept riding to the wrong alley as my phone received weak signals, and in certain areas, GPS lagged so I had to use my innate navigation skills to locate the accommodation.

There was it, stopping right at the front of the hostel. This hostel building looks like a three-story terrace home that had been converted into a hostel. Next to the hostel building, on the left, is a terrace house. But on the ground floor, it had been converted to a snack shop. And in front of the snack shop, there's a sheltered porch with a few men drinking beer and munching sunflower seeds. It seemed like they were there imbibing for a long time as there was a half-foot-tall pyramid of sunflower seed shells on the table. Not only were they munching the seeds, but they were also staring at me with much fear in their eyes. It was perfectly alright for them to stare at me as my tube scarf was still up on my nose bridge, and the way I wore it looked as though I was going to rob them.

Looking at the façade of the hostel entrance, the glass sliding doors have several country flags pasted on them, such as Brazil, Cambodia, China, Germany and Australia. At the entrance of the ground floor, there's a reception desk and high chairs on the right. On the left, there's a sofa, and further in − still on the left, there's a pantry table. Looking all around, no one seemed to be there to invite me in.

I pulled the tube scarf down my neck, got off the bike, and got in the hostel's entrance. "Hello!" I hollered in a low tone and waited for a few seconds. No reply came. "Hello!! I hollered slightly louder, but still, no one came to rescue me. Further in on the ground floor, on the left, there's a wooden shelf with white sheets like bed sheets were shelved up. Next to the shelf on the left, there's a door. But it was closed. I dragged out a highchair closest to the hostel's entrance and made a screeching sound to let the men on the next door know that I had sat down, and to tell them that I came in peace, not to rob the place.

Five minutes passed, and still, no one came. There's a call bell on the desk and I went pressing it, "ding, ding," and waited. Still, no one came. Perhaps the receptionist was busy doing something that takes a longer time to get back to the receptionist's desk? I don't know. I continued to wait and scan around the place.

I looked out to my bike; it was lonely there parked in front of the terrace, and turned to see the men having a fun time laughing about and imbibing their beers. I turned back to look in front of the desk, still waiting with a bold expression on my face. I pressed the call bell again, but still, no one came.

"Ding, ding…Ding, ding." Still, no one came. "DING DING DING DING DING," I pressed the desk bell harder thinking that the receptionist could hear it. But still, no people came. I turned back to see the men laughing vociferously, but once they had an eye on me, they looked at me sceptically, then back to their vociferous chatting again.

"Maybe, I should ask them?" I thought but not move a single bit.

Half an hour passed. I couldn't believe I had waited this long. I could have gone to other hostels, but I had come to a point where I didn't want to get off the highchair as I was too worn out. But I made up my mind to walk out and ask the men.

"No one… inside?" The men looked among themselves and said something in Thai, and one of them stood up and walked me in the hostel. He looks around then walks to the door beside the shelf, opens it, and disappears behind it.

The door opened after a few minutes, and the man came with a woman who hurriedly walked toward me and apologises, saying that she was manning the gym, which is not in the same building. Once she came out of the door, I didn't have anything to say, but I was indeed glad that I was going to get a bed soon and was just too tired for any nonsense. I nodded, pretended that I just arrived, and thought I should have opened my mouth way earlier to ask the angels outside. That could have saved lots of unnecessary waiting and the ding dings sound.

Before the receptionist brought me up to show me my bunk

bed, she walked out with me and showed me a very particular area to park my bike. The parking area was between the two sheltered porches to the next terrace on the right of the hostel, and it was just enough space for the bike. I pushed the bike up to the spot, locking the wheels to a prominent railing and then covered the bike with the picnic mat. That was the end mission for the day, and the receptionist then gave a small tour in the hostel and went up the stairs to show me the dormitory room. Once she opened the door of the dormitory room, she said, "Sir, today no one booking, you can choose any bed." Glad that I had come to this hostel although I waited impatiently.

***

I got back down to the snack shop next to the hostel building to get something to eat as I was told by the receptionist that most of the restaurants were already closed.

My presence at the convenience shop was odd choosing what was on the shelf. When I inadvertently happened to look at the group of men drinking, I was amazed to see their actions. I was offered beer by one of the men and later, all of them asked me to join them for a drink. I smiled and thanked their friendly offer but instead got myself a Tom Yam cup noodle and a small bag of potato chips.

I got back to the hostel and went over to the pantry table, where there was a thermo-pot to fill up water in the cup noodle. I peeled the cup noodle's clear wrapping, pulled the lid in half, tore the seasoning packet and poured it into the cup. Then finger flicked some red ants that were crawling on the dispense button of the thermo-pot, then pressed it to fill the hot water into the cup. Then finally, I closed the lit back and waited for a few minutes before consuming it.

Upon opening the cup noodle lit after much waiting, I saw lots of dead ants floating above the noodle, and some appeared to be glued to the noodles. I opened the thermo-pot lit to see many dead ants floating, and a few ants got onto my hand, which made me go flicking my hand while the thermo-pot lit slams to close. I threw the cup noodle in a trash bin below the pantry desk and went up to my bed to snack on the potato chips disgruntledly with a thought of, "I should have joined those angels to have beers together and munch along the sunflower seeds. Wouldn't it be a great session, right?"

Oh well…

Pai
Mae Hong Son
Thailand
Namtak Mae Surin Waterfall
Tuang Bua Tong Fields
Chiang Mai
Mae Sariang

13

Certificate of Conquest

I trundled down the stairs carrying my stuff and made my way to the foyer to see no one present at the receptionist's desk. I dropped the room key on the desk and walked out of the premises to my bike with a restless look on my face, but it changed once I approached my bike after looking at something that appeared odd to my eyes.

On the next terrace house from the hostel, a man wearing a red apron, swung up and down a chopping knife on a thick meat, but I couldn't perceive to know what meat was that as my view was obscured from his body position. But from the masculinity of his right arm and the vigorous up-and-down swings of the knife through the meat, I knew without a doubt that the animal being butchered wasn't given any chance.

As I got closer to my bike, there was no need for a second look at what the man was chopping. The three pig heads on the aluminium table reveal everything about what he was doing.

It was odd to see a butcher shop in front of a modern terrace house. Or is it a regular thing here in a rural area to have this kind of setup? I wondered, but I wasn't satisfied to see my bike covered with lots of tiny flecks of meat scattered around the picnic mat.

And some bits of flesh had landed on the side fairings of the bike, which disgusted me much.

I dropped all my stuff to the ground, which probably would have made the butcher jolt out from the sound, but I didn't care about it. I calmly opened the top box and took out the wet wipes tissue, and picked up the meat flesh with a disgusted look on my face. While I picked them, I made a swift glance at the butcher to see if he felt remorseful about it. Nope, the butcher wasn't remorseful and continued chopping with that high lifting of the chopping knife and storms it down to the meat. I picked up as much meat flesh with the wet tissue, scurried back to the hostel, tossed it to the trash bin under the pantry table, and then returned to my bike with a poker face as if everything was all right. Giving any contemptuous look or confronting look to the butcher is a no-go thing to do in a rural area like this. If I were to, I would probably be a special ingredient for whatever delicacy he would probably make, I guess.

Once he was done chopping the meat, he sat on a red plastic chair, holding on to an improvised fan that is made up of a long thin twig with an attachment of a translucent plastic bag at one end; he fans above the meat to shoo off the flies from colonising it.

After several runs to toss the filthy wet tissues in the bin, I got back to my bike and removed the picnic mat. Then a voice punctured the air that sounded English.

"You from which country?" I turned my head everywhere around but missed looking at the butcher intentionally. But I had no choice but to look at him as he was the only person around. And so, I looked at him, and yes, he was staring at me.

"From Singapore," I replied.

"Sing…ga…pore?" the butcher gave a confused look and stood up to have a better look at my bike.

"You come here… this bike?" asked the butcher in his surprised tone.

"Yep, long way here."

He nods without saying anything but thoroughly looks at the bike again and asks,

"Yamaha?"

"Yes, Yamaha."

He nodded and gave me a strange look on my bike, and then he gave me a thumbs up to me.

"Very good," he said, and finally, I saw a smile on his face.

"You live here… this house?" I asked and thought if the question was a foolish one.

"Yes. This is my brother's house," he said.

I nod and stare at the sliced meat on the aluminium table on the porch and ask, "Good business?"

"Every day not same. Sometime, people buy, sometime, no one buy. If raining… sleep better," he laughs at the ending phrase and continues, "Few months back, I in Chiang Mai, I work chef. No customer. Business not good."

I nod to his choppy words, but somehow, I understood him easily.

"My boss close shop. I no work. I come here stay with my brother."

I nodded to his words with sympathy while I started to load up the bike.

"At least you do this rather than staying at home do nothing. You are a very hard-working man." I didn't know what to say, but words just spilt out of my mouth.

He then talks about his past jobs, his troubles, and some things that I could only nod to, and in some instances, not a word came out of my mouth. Everyone lives in a different story of their world and some stories are too complex in a way one would hesitate to give a piece of advice. But what can I do in this type of situation? I just gave my ears and listened. I listened to his story. I listened and comprehended how fortunate I was to do this type of ride and thought of the people who have opportunities like me but not do anything about it.

A road trip need not be the same as mine, nor does it have to be a road trip. It can be anything. But the thing is, when people don't use their opportunities, they will never know when will their next opportunity be. How do we know that's the actual opportunity that brings success? I, myself, I don't know. But it makes sense to *try*, as one may never know if that's the actual opportunity to success.

Once I had done loading up my bike, I pushed the bike out to the main road and was all set to start my day-eight ride.

"Good luck bro!" the butcher cheered.

The first time I saw him, I had different views of him. As I was about to leave the place, I had a different perspective of him, and there was a smile on my face. I waved him goodbye, and he waved me off using his improvised hand fan, waving me off like the start of a MotoGP race.

***

The ride went slow watching life pass by me as I rode close to the road edge looking for any shop vendors that compelled me to have breakfast. It was just 9 in the morning; hence, most of the shops were still closed from the look on the shutters down and the upside-down chairs on the tables.

As I looked and looked, I thought through the task for the day. The main task for the day is to ride up all the way north and stop at a town called Pai. But before reaching Pai, a critical sub-task I need to accomplish before reaching the town. I need to obtain a *certificate of conquest* for completing 1864 bends that can be obtained from a Chamber of Commerce in Mae Hong Son town that comes before Pai town. It also means that I would have completed the 1864 bends from Chiang Mai to Mae Hong Son town. But that is only possible if I make it to the town. Also, I have a slight conundrum to it. I wondered what it would be like to get a certificate when the ride isn't organised by any organisation, and there isn't any finish line for me to pass through and be rewarded with a token of accomplishment. Who would even validate that I had ridden from Chiang Mai and not taken any lift from any pick-up trucks? It was peculiar to think of, and thought about whether do I even need to get a certificate. But since the Chamber of Commerce in Mae Hong Son town is before Pai town, it made sense to stop by there to get a certificate anyway.

I checked the GPS of the distance between Mae Sariang to Mae Hong Son, it came up to be only 165 kilometres. Not too far off but as I zoomed in on the GPS map, I saw many hairpin bends ahead of me.

"Wouldn't it be rewarding to have a treaty meal after tackling the bends and then obtaining the certificate in Mae Hong Son town?" It seemed worth it, and there's something to look up for. And so, I skipped breakfast and made my way targeting the town for the certificate.

The usual greenery on both sides of the road appeared, with tall trees seen ubiquitously around. The sun casts brightly as usual, but the ride felt as though I was riding in front of an air-conditioner that blows out cold air from its outlet. The previous day's heat packs in my gloves and under my feet hadn't been replaced yet. I mean, I didn't have additional packs to replace them after they became unworthy to use. But even though the heat packs weren't giving any warmth, I carried on having them and mentally told myself that they would provide an additional layer of warmth. I have to say, I hoped for it though.

The scenic views came as I covered distance, showing off its smooth green grass fields, greenery hills, and the exceptional curves of the mountains ridge lines and the hills with the backdrop of the blue skies. There were some tourist spots where tourist vehicles stopped for a while for the tourists to take pictures of the scenery. I can do that too, as I am too a tourist. But I couldn't possibly be stopping by at every single spot to snap a picture of the many scenic views out there. I let them pass but visually loaded up what I had seen, and it was more than enough. But some, I just have to stop to satiate the beauty of what was around.

The asphalt was smooth and surprisingly better than the regular roads in a main town or a city. There were proper road markings on the tarmac, road speed numbers painted on the tarmac, and even red-painted roads indicating that it was nearing any key area. Then more bends came ahead of me, which I had to tackle, and I dived in and out of the bends enjoying what was around and not being obstructed by the goods trucks.

As I rode on, I thought of the several waterfalls I had missed yesterday. Not having to see one where I'm already in the loop seemed like a wasted opportunity. But the thing is, I'm not a fan of a waterfall nor someone who appreciates viewing a waterfall. But something tells me I should see at least one for this trip.

I got off the road and checked the map for any waterfalls that were ahead. The one that looked decently good to see from the picture on Google was the *Mae Surin* waterfall which is located at Namtok Mae Surin National Park, and it's just before Mae Hong Son town. Without thinking further, I set the GPS to the waterfall site and started off with the ride.

I tackled more bends and covered more distance. Then just less than two hours of ride, I reached a small town in Khun Yuan district and changed to Route 1263 and then changed to Route 4009. It was the route that would lead me to the waterfall.

As I rode on Route 4009, the temperature dipped, and the road gradually became steep in different sections along my ride. It reminded me of my ride to the Doi Inthanon summit as I started to shiver pathetically again. It still baffles me a lot as the whole vicinity was brightly illuminated by the sun, but oddly the temperature felt insanely cold. I think the problem was me, as I couldn't withstand any temperature below 23 degrees Celsius even in Singapore.

I kept riding but realised that the views around me were even better looking than what I had seen earlier in the day. There were lots of green hills evenly shaved, and buffaloes were roaming about in the valleys. Looking at them was remarkably eye catchy. But as I covered more distance, I happened to notice patches of yellow flowers starting to pop up from the bushes on the roadsides.

Then as I continued with the steep climbs and bends, something changed. On both sides of the road, more patches of lush yellow flowers appeared in the roadside bushes. Then after one left bend, the tall usual green trees that I usually see on both sides of the road, didn't appear, but instead, I arrived at a hilltop to see my whole vicinity filled with Thung Bua Tong flowers. (It's a type of wild sunflower that is smaller in size compared to a typical sunflower.)

I rode to the parking area where other tourist vehicles were parked at, and my curiosity went towards a green platform deck where I see tourists lingering around. To fulfil my curiosity, I stopped at one side, and went up the short steps and the deck to witness the view.

My front view displayed many peaks of hills and far away mountains that it created a concoction of wavey peaks with smooths contours all around my viewpoint, for which I intuitively knew that I was back in high altitude again. The viewing deck surroundings were surrounded by carpets of lush yellow Bua Tong flowers all around the hill, making the hill appear as though it's painted with brilliant yellow paint. It was pleasant looking at the scenic view, but didn't want to linger too long as it was cold up here. And so, I had to go on with my ride.

I got back to my bike, and off I rode on passing the yellow field, and a thought came into my mind: "I know where to bring my future girlfriend or my wife to."

Just after a few more kilometres of the ride from the Bua Tong field, I slowed down drastically again to look out for what was there on the right side of the road. There's a wooden platform and a few grass-thatched roof huts on the roadside that seemed like a coffee stopover. But it wasn't an ordinary one. A few people were seated near the edge of a wooden platform, swinging their legs freely in the open air, sipping coffee, and enjoying a view of finely cut grass fields, greenish hills, and watched the sheep roam about on the field, munching on the grass.

I smiled and continued to ride on, thinking, "She should be really lucky to get me in future."

The last few bends and straights of steep climbs brought me up to the entrance of the waterfall sight. I see a woman standing outside the ticket booth wearing a retro jacket on top of her military uniform. I hollered, "Waterfall!" from a distance as I approached the booth. She heard me and pushed the rolling gate barrier open for me to ride through. I came to a stop next to the ticket booth and to see another woman in military uniform inside.

"How much is the entrance fee?" I asked the jacket woman.

"200 baht," said the jacket woman and pointed up at a pricing board, but the pricing were partially faded off to which I was looking at the children's fee, which is priced at 100 baht.

"I, baby, 100 baht," I said, and the two women giggled.

"From where?" The jacket woman asked.

"I from Singapore."

"So far? Alone?" The jacket woman asked.

"Yep. One person. I come alone."

Both looked astonished by what I said. "You, brave man. No small baby, big baby," said the jacket woman, and then both chuckled at me again. I took a single 500-baht note from my wallet and passed it to the jacket woman. The jacket woman then muttered something to the woman inside the booth. The jacket woman returned me the 500-baht note and said, "Big baby, many money," then chuckles at me again.

"No, no… I pick up from the floor," I made a terrible joke but got them chuckling again.

I took out two 100-baht notes and passed them to the jacket woman, and she said something to me that I couldn't comprehend. The jacket woman then hands me an entrance ticket and a 100-baht note to me. I looked at the 100-baht note and the entrance ticket, paused for a while, and thought about how much did I even handed over to her in the first place. Then I look up to see the jacket woman say something in Thai and point at the pricing board, but to the children's fee. I immediately sprouted out laughter and they instantly chuckled along with me.

Well, if I could save some money, why not?

As I rode past the entrance after metres away, there came a voice from my back, "Big baby ride motorbike!" and laughter afterwards.

I smiled as I rode on, thinking that I had made a bold joke of myself but saved one good meal for later.

My bike parked at the open parking area, and I walked towards a middle-aged couple to ask the directions to the waterfall. "Oh, it's over there," the man said in fluent English while pointing to a direction.

I walked towards the direction of where the man pointed, it brought me to a curvy declining step, but as I looked straight ahead, *voila*, there's the Mae Surin waterfall. It's far off from my viewpoint, but I could see it obviously as it is a huge waterfall. It's a single-tier waterfall that falls from a height of 180 metres to the ground. The waterfall looks silky white, and the sound of the water plunging to the large rock at the bottom can be heard clearly. I went down the curvy steps to a small platform where I saw people taking turns snapping a selfie shot with the background view of the waterfall. I took some shots of myself, and again, I continued on to my bike as it was already noon.

Walking back to my bike, the couple I had approached earlier to ask for directions, and the man who gave me the directions came walking alone with both his hands in his trousers pocket.

"Bro where are you from?" He asked.

"From Singapore."

He looked surprised, and then he continued, "With this bike?"

"Yes." I replied with slow nods. He then pulled his hand out from his trouser pocket to shake my hand.

He shook my hand and said, "Oh wow, you are amazing," with a surprised look on him.

"Is that a spare tin?" He asked, referring to the jerrycan.

"Yeah. In case if I miss a petrol station."

"Good that you have it," he said, "I also used to tour around with my bike. But now, I'm married. My wife won't let me ride bike." He laughs at what he said.

"That's my car," he points at a Toyota pick-up and continues, "today is my off day, but my wife wants to come here, so, I have to follow her order." He laughs at what he just said again, and I join along.

The usual questions came like how many days on my ride; where I am heading to later; when I will be returning to Singapore, and so forth. But the last bit of his saying, got me to ponder.

"I used to tour around with my friends to have a good time… you know, what I mean…." I smiled and gave a slow nod to it. "Then one friend married, another friend married, then more friends get married, then I get married. Then everyone become busy with their own life. My group riding slowly fades off after everyone get married. But I still meet my friends to have a meal with them occasionally. Sometimes we talk about doing a road trip, but just talking only. Not easy to do one road trip especially after all my friends are married and have their own responsibilities." I slowly nod and continue to listen.

"I am not saying that you can't do a road trip after you get married. It's just that you may not have the ability to do something easily as before, especially when you have a child." I heed his words but said nothing as I am too unsophisticated in this type of conversation.

"Good that you are doing this. Enjoy what you can enjoy now but ride safely," I nodded to his saying, and he continued, "You should be around your twenties, right?"

"Yeah, twenty-five this year."

"I can see that you are a brave man. Go….," his wife hollers something in Thai at him from a distance, interrupting what he wanted to say.

"Oh, got to go. Have a safe ride," he said and shook my hand once again. He rushed over to his pick-up, and I watched the pick-up ride off the parking lot like a typical movie scene I had seen somewhere before.

***

The ride went back down to where I had come up from and had to see the exceptional view of what was around again, then back to the main route 108 to continue with the ride to Mae Hong Son town.

The last few kilometres to Mae Hong Son town made me apprehensive as I got closer and closer to the GPS pin-drop. Far ahead, something appeared from a distance. As I got closer to it, it reminded me of what I had seen on the internet back home. I had seen bikers jumping up triumphantly to take a jump shot with it as they had finally reached their destination for their ride. It's an entrance pillar to Mae Hong Son town. But it's not just an ordinary entrance pillar. It's an entrance and exit to the many road-trippers who have finally completed the arduous 1864 bends from Chiang Mai.

The GPS brought me into a premises along Khunlumprapas Road, and I see a white- corrugated-hut-like-structure that surrounds a tall green tree in the middle. The structure has an attachment of a sheltered patio on one side with tables and chairs, and all the walls of the structure were mostly made up of glass pane. But much of it was hijacked by past biker's club stickers. But it didn't look like the one I had seen on Google with club stickers all over the façade from a Chamber of Commerce. I Google searched and learned that this is another branch of the Chamber of Commerce. Or I might be wrong as it appeared more like a coffee shop to me.

I parked the bike next to the patio and went into the coffee shop to see a bald male staff on the desk giving me a naïve look as though I was an officer in disguise with a body camera on my chest coming in to interrogate him. I smiled and tried not to look like a hostile person and told him I was on a road trip. But still, he continued to give me a naïve look on me.

There were a few certificate designs stuck on the glass pane next to the counter desk. I chose the design I liked and the staff went on asking me to fill up a form online. Once the online form was done, I told him what I wanted to be written on the certificate and he typed it, and the certificate prints out from the printer. Lastly, he took a small gold sticker that had the year 2019 on it, and pasted it above the pseudo name that I gave to him and then he handed it over to me.

I smiled as I looked at the certificate, but got interrupted by my triumphant moment: "Sir, it will be 60 baht."

It wasn't free.

It was strange getting the certificate, but at the same time, it somehow felt worth getting one after all the laborious ride that had gone by. Anyone can just walk in to purchase a certificate, and there's no one there to validate whether one has ridden from Chiang Mai or took a helicopter here – if there's even one. I mean, who cares, right? Coming to Mae Hong Son town takes a great effort; even if one arrives from a tourist van, one still has to go through the weather change and the bumps from the potholes. Why not reward oneself with a certificate, right? But well, for me, I took it as a souvenir and shall look back in future and tell myself that I once arrived here with an incredible bike.

I rode over to have a treaty meal at a restaurant on the roadside that was recommended by the staff. A cup of rice was finely placed on the centre of the plate with a sunny egg that made it look like a hat, and spicy basil mincemeat was delicately placed on the side of the plate. The plate came with a small bowl of soup, and I ordered a cup of tea to complete a meal. Not an extravagant meal to celebrate the achievement of obtaining the certificate, but a simple meal was more than enough as I still had to ride to the next town, and I didn't want to stop halfway along my ride to dig a hole in the forest to let it go.

Before I got going to the town of Pai, where I needed to stop for a night, I rode over to the other Chamber of Commerce.

As I arrived at the Chamber of Commerce, the façade was fully hijacked by thousands of motorcycle club stickers, and this was what I was looking forward to. I parked the bike at the kerbside and walked towards the office door to see an A4-sized paper taped on the middle of the door with a pen written note that stated: 'Go Bank'. Well, I didn't mind waiting because, by the time the person returned, I don't think I could complete looking at all the stickers though.

Some sticker designs were comprehensively designed, and some stickers have dated back to the year 1999. That's a really long time ago. Just imagine revisiting back here after 20 years to see the sticker one had stuck before; wouldn't it bring back the nostalgic days of the fun, the excitement, and the youthfulness in them? And think about the days when there weren't smartphones to make use of the GPS to navigate to places easily. Nowadays, it's much easier to get around using a cheap phone with a useful GPS application. It can bring a person far away from one destination to another fast compared to those bygone days when people widely relied on paper maps and took longer time to reach a destination. However, I have to say; I'm always fascinated by the many travellers who have travelled around the globe by just using maps back then and still managed to get to places they wanted to get to. It's not an easy thing to do and my salute goes to the people who have done that.

Half an hour passed, and I spent much of the time looking at the stickers; an aged woman came with her scooter and hurriedly got into the office. I walked in, went to the only office desk, and requested another certificate with a different design.

Well, since there are two places where I can get certificates from, why not get one from each place, right?

Once I got the certificate, I made my way to Pai town quickly before I get any intrusive thoughts on purchasing certificates for my whole family.

***

It was another 105 kilometres for me to reach Pai town, and the hairpin bends were still ongoing. The weather was chilly as usual riding between the greenery on both sides of the road, and steep rides came along with many viewpoints along the ride.

"10! ... 9! ... 8! ... 7! ... it's too early! (Background laughter) ... Now! 10! ... 9! ... 8! ..." A group of aficionado tourist eagerly watches the sun goes down slowly behind the mountains far away. The viewpoint I came by is called Doi Kiew Lom. Not only it has an exceptional view of the hills and mountainous views, but there is also a peculiar old adult-swing-like structure, and somehow, it's a famous swing here. And adjacent to the swing, there are five small wind turbines.

"3! ... 2! ... 1! ... almost there ... Again! .... 3! ... 2! ... 1!" The crowd cheers vociferously out to the atmosphere, and some no-children-under-16-admitted kissing scenes happen afterwards.

The ride went on to complete the final kilometres to Pai, and thankfully, I finally arrived at the town looking at the vicinity that was lit up well. Many tourists and locals were flocking about on the streets, and many fluorescent bulbs were hanging around the canopy of the shops. I rode on passing different shop vendors and restaurants along the roadsides, and to see colourful lanterns hanging above on a road that gave me a new eye on this town. I wondered what event was going on, but I have to say, this town looked lively at night.

The usual religious thing went on, stopping at the kerbside to browse for a good place to stay. Fortunately, there were many accommodations in Pai, and from browsing through the number of them, most of the hostels and hotels' pictures looked compelling. But since it had already turned 7 in the evening, why not stay in a hostel instead of a hotel, right?

A receptionist walks me over to a dormitory room to assign my bed. As she opened the dormitory door, I intuitively knew that other people had fully utilised other beds. Cluttered bed sheets; bags on the floor opened up for the spider to crawl in; toiletries scattered on the floor and on their beds. It was just clutter in the room. The only pristine-looking thing in the room was the bed above the upper deck bed. That was my bed for the night.

For the bike, I was told by the receptionist I could park anywhere on the lawn in front of the dormitory. So that became the deal maker for the day.

***

It was cold out here as I strolled and walked in a night market. There were a variety of cart vendors on the street selling food and beverages, which made me go on a food tasting. I got myself a potato twist on a stick sprinkled with artificial cheese powder, a chicken taco, a few varieties of sushi types, a part of fried chicken, and the wholesome dessert that I truly devoured much was the banana pancake with Nutella spread on it. Oh my…

Not only I munched the food to myself, but also a dog came and sat close to my leg, and it gave me a pathetic look when I waited for my sushi to be prepared by the vendor. When I got my sushi, I dropped one sushi slice to the ground, and the dog walloped it and then walked away. I walked to the next cart vendor to get a chicken taco. Again, the dog came back and sat close to my leg, but this time round, it didn't give a sympathetic look at me but decently sat still like a guard dog. The cart owner laughs, looking at the dog and says something in Thai to it. Probably knowing the cheekiness of it. I got my chicken taco and dropped some chicken slices on the ground. It ate it and walked away again.

As I stroll along, munching and looking about, I watch other dogs luring about on the street doing the same thing to other tourists. The witty thing about these dogs was that they don't go all to one tourist. One dog to one tourist at a time. Smart doggo.

Not only carts with food and beverages were around, but there were also bars, tattoo shops, massage shops, varieties of restaurants, handicraft stores, artistic painters who paint on the spot and sells their paint work above ground sheets.

There were many apparel shops too. I came across an apparel shop that sells prints of the "Pai" name on some t-shirts, and some have prints of "762 bends to Pai." My curiosity wanted to know what it meant, so I asked the seller. The seller went on to say that in the anti-clockwise direction ride from Chiang Mai to Pai, there are 762 bends to complete to arrive at Pai. That meant that I had 762 bends left before reaching back to Chiang Mai the next day. Well, since I will be riding back to Chiang Mai the next day, I left my apprehensiveness for the next day and went on enjoying my banana pancake with Nutella spreads with no regrets.

I continued to stroll on and munch on and came to a section where I was surprised to see booth-like vendors run by white foreigners besides the locals. A white man with a fedora hat busked with his guitar and sang along to a jazz song. In the adjacent booth to his booth, which was a yoga booth, a woman made some yoga stretching moves and synchronised with the busker's rhythm. People came to watch them both, but the Yoga woman stole the show obviously, as she wore tight stretchy clothing and made some moves that would make a man be interested to watch. Well, not going to lie; I was there watching too.

As I nod along with the jazz music playing in the background and having a bite of my banana pancake, there came another dog and sat next to me.

Myanmar
Chiang Rai
Pai
Chiang Mai
Thailand

14

Not What I had Expected

Around 1 am, a loud noise pierced my eardrums awakening me with a bewildered look on my face. I slid the bedside curtain and surreptitiously looked down to see what was going on. A few other dorm occupants entered the room with a beer each in their hands and started singing vociferously. I closed the bedside curtain and told myself that it would be a brief moment of their drunken revelry. However, I was wrong. They kept singing and singing with additional music from the feet stomping to the ground, which made the room like an enclosed concert hall.

I concealed my head under the pillow, but it didn't help much to subdue the cacophonous sound. I tried sound effects like "Shhhhh," and "Arhhhhh." And even made a yawning sound. But to no avail, it helped. I guess that I was the only outsider in the dorm and they could do whatever they want. I thought of confronting them, but my peculiar mind feared that I might see a flying Molotov on my bed. With just another two days left to reach Golden Triangle, I didn't want to get into any commotion whatsoever. I cupped my ears under the pillow stoically and just hoped that they would end their nonsense soon.

It did stop. But it was after an hour.

***

The lawn was misty, and the bike's seat and fairings were covered with droplets of water vapour. I was already out of the dorm, fully donned my usual riding wear, and had brought all my stuff out to the porch with a sweaty palm of mine. Anxiety was running high in me even in the early hours of the day.

After the clowns stopped singing and dancing, I had trouble sleeping afterwards. Not only because of the clowns who had disturbed my sleep rhythm, but there was something that made me think that I had an impending load of responsibilities that would come ahead.

It was the 9th day of the ten days to Golden Triangle and the day where I would complete the full loop that ends back in Chiang Mai. This gave me an instant obligation to ride as safely as possible and be very wary about whatever that comes ahead. And apart from that, I need to precisely plan where I would be stopping for the day as it's the deal maker if I could even reach Golden Triangle on time the next day, and not reach after the sun goes down.

Other thoughts roamed in my mind, such as the bike would reach its servicing period when I reached Chiang Mai. Like I have said before, I would religiously do the servicing on time and never like to hold myself back on this as I ride almost every single day. But for this scenario, should I do the servicing before reaching Golden Triangle, or should I do it after? A question that made me ponder much even though it was just a trivial matter.

I feared that if I were to do the servicing before heading to Golden Triangle, I might do something stupid in which the bike may give a problem that would hinder my ride to Golden Triangle. And on the other hand, if I did not do the servicing before heading to Golden Triangle, I feared the bike would give me trouble along the way. Who knows, a problem might suddenly pop up if I don't service the bike on time. High chance it will work just fine. Like again, who knows if something were to go wrong, right? The thing is, I just don't know. And so, with what was running in my head, I think it is alright to feel both sweaty on my palms and my feet.

I left the dorm key on the receptionist's table and made up my mind to target completing the 762 bends to Chiang Mai first as the more I overthink about all the dilemmas in my mind, I tend to daydream and not resolve a problem. With that said, I had to go.

The ride went on under the cloudy greyish sky with doubts if the rain would fall, which made me focus on tackling the bends instead of stopping at the many tourist spots for picture taking. But I did stop by at certain spots and one of the spots was to Pai's very own *canyon*. However, it wasn't a pleasant experience for me though.

After the 100 metres hike up to the canyon landscape – and also after slipping here and there from the slippery terrain that even made me fall on my butt, I reached the canyon landscape to see an atmosphere appearing misty and foggy to which it seemed like I had come at the wrong time and it appeared like it wasn't a picture worthy to me. It was early of the day and I can't complaint about it. Well, not every day is Sunday, right?

There were other spots I had stop by like the serene background of terrace hillsides, and also stopped by at a memorial bridge that was close to Pai. Not that I was fascinated by the history of the bridge, but there was this guy in *Jack Sparrow* costume at the bridge taking pictures for the tourists with his professional camera instead of holding a ram bottle in his hand.

As my game plan was to ride cautiously and target to completing the loop, the last 762 bends slowly went by without causing me any trouble and the cold chilly weather eventually superseded by the hot and humid weather. The usual greenery on both sides of the road slowly vanished off and was taken over by low-rise buildings and shophouses. As I got closer to the centre of Chiang Mai, all the wonderful sceneries I had seen became a memory, and the 600 kilometres of loop riding had all gone off like blowing the dust off my shoulder.

I made my own finishing line by stopping at a PTT petrol station in Chiang Mai. As I got off my bike, I sighed as I looked down at my bike and pat the bike seat like dusting off a precious item. I smiled, and I could finally say this to myself again: Been there, done that.

***

I rode on after fuelling up the tank and came to a stop at a relatively quiet street and sat on the kerbside to think about if I should service the bike or not.

Since I had been consistently servicing the bike on time, and it usually works like a charm afterwards, I resolved to do the servicing. But where would I be doing the servicing at? That was the question to tackle at the moment. I looked around and saw locals walking past in front of me every few minutes although the street looked decently quiet. But some looked at me as though I was going to rob them.

I have to remind myself to pull down the tube scarf whenever I get off my bike.

I thought that it would be odd for me to blatantly do the servicing at a random area or next to a roadside street. Furthermore, with my apprehensive mind, servicing the bike myself may bring me problems that I may not know. With that said, it made sense for me to send the bike to a servicing shop instead of me working on it. But my apprehensive mind admonished me to keep an eye on the mechanic somehow.

I rode over to a Yamaha servicing outlet after searching for it on Google. I arrived at the shop entrance and a man approached me as I arrived. From the look on his polo top attire and his clean hands, he didn't look like a mechanic but looked more like a salesperson to which I explained to him precisely what has to be done on my bike. As I was explaining, there came another man who wore a plain black top and stares at my bike and went on picking on his nose. I assumed that he is an intern.

The salesman then nods and says something in Thai, and draws a vertical rectangle in the air with his index fingers. It has to do with a receipt or a piece of paper. I shook my head not knowing what he was asking and thought for a moment if I did have any heredity of the local Thai people. I told him that I came from Singapore and instantly, his eyes widened and he gave a baffled look at me.

When I shared similar skin colour with people from another country, it seemed like I instantly became part of their people.

He called another man, and the man came and visually checked on my bike. From the look on the man who checks my bike, he seemed to me like a dexterous mechanic. Not from the look of his dirty hands or his attire, but the shoes he wore were bright orange that hadn't had any nick of dirt invaded on it yet. A weird assumption I made to call someone dexterous from the colour of their shoes.

I took out the last bottle of engine oil and the oil filter from the top box, handed over to the dextrous mechanic, and explained what needed to be done on my bike. All he said was "Good, good", with a thumbs up to me. He then said something in Thai to the polo top guy, and then the dextrous mechanic showed me thumbs up again, and he went on pushing my bike to the hoist platform. The intern then followed him behind and I watched him clean his filthy finger on his pants.

I stood at a distance away and watched my bike, not because I love watching my bike get its health cleaned up, but to have an eye on the intern after I stopped him from doing something stupid.

When the bike was hoisted up and when the oil-waste-collector-pan went under the engine, the intern used a wrong-sized socket head – that was attached to a rachet, and aggressively tried to unscrew the drain plug nut while the other mechanic was away. When I watched that right in front of me, I feared that the drain plug nut might get rounded. I immediately went over to stop him and told him the actual size of the nut. Then came the dextrous mechanic who saw what happened, apologised to me, and worked with the intern on my bike until the bike's servicing was done.

Sometimes, it's alright to feel apprehensive. Like what Murphy's law says: "Anything that can go wrong will go wrong."

***

Mae Hong Son loop completed and servicing completed. Two major tasks for the day were accomplished and the last task for the day left was to find a place to accommodate. The time had already turned to 4 in the afternoon. I sip through a straw from a Coke cup and stare out through the glass pane of a Mexican restaurant, glancing at my bike after checking the GPS for the total distance left to reach the Golden Triangle the next day.

The GPS showed me that I had 261 kilometres left, and I had two options in my mind. Either I continue with the ride or just find an accommodation here in Chiang Mai. But if I were to choose the former one, then the next probable place I could stop at – given the available time left before the sun goes down – came up to be Chiang Rai, which is 188 kilometres away from me. And from there, the next day, the final day, it would only be 70 kilometres of ride to Golden Triangle. It seemed like a good deal for me to not ride far for the next day and reach at a comfortable time, which I was targeting to reach by noon.

"Isn't it better to suffer now and let tomorrow be easy?" I thought.

It would take me less than 3 hours to get to Chiang Rai if I were to make my move soon. That includes stopping to refuel the bike and rest my butt. But the part that will inevitably slow me down is when the sun goes down and the vicinity becomes dark. But, looking at the bright side, it seemed like this would be the last ride where I would ride at night in northern Thailand. So, why not just pull it through, right?

It seemed appealing for me to carry on with the ride and I resolved to go for the ride targeting Chiang Rai, but this time round I had already set the GPS endpoint to a randomly picked accommodation in Chiang Rai rather than setting it in the middle of the city.

Getting off the city was fast, as the roads weren't as busy as I had anticipated. Then slowly the same old vicinity appeared all around – greens on both sides of the road. And there was also something unusual that I had come to notice along the road: it appeared sandy.

As I kept riding, I started to see the roadsides appearing under constructions. I could see loose rocks piled up in some areas, and there were excavators excavating rocks on the ground on the roadsides. Then as I kept riding on, roads in front of me became even sandier and my grip on the handlebar intensified further.

Then after a few kilometres of ride, there came the drudgery. The road surface has overtaken by a mixture of muddy, sandy, and uneven ground that got me to bump up and down on the bike's seat. Well, it became a dirt road.

Everything on the bike shakes and vibrates aggressively from just riding at the speed of 40 km/h. I slowed down further and rode between 20 to 30 km/h to reduce the vibrations and the loud rattling sound from the jerrycan that kept knocking on the handlebar's fairing. However, there wasn't much difference even if I rode faster though.

The horrendous ground kept going for kilometre after kilometre shaking along violently with the bike. The suspension for the bike was supposed to do much of the ground shock absorption; however, it had included me to absorb the shock too. This is the punishment I get for not modifying the bike for my comfort. But thank goodness I had the intuition to change to a new seat before this journey. If not, it would be a doomsday for my butt.

The construction path gets narrower in certain area. But in some, the traffic became congested with vehicles close to one another due to some vehicles getting into accidents from rear-end collisions. This was something that I was trying to avoid, and no driver would want to get into this situation, especially on this type of terrain.

The slower I rode behind a vehicle in front of me, the harder it became to control the bike. The bounce from the bumps on the ground was sharper, and my eyes were more focused on the vehicle brake lights that kept lighting up my eyes red so that I could brake on time.

Shouldn't I just not ride close behind the vehicle or just stop at the side and wait for the traffic to ease down? The thing was, the whole traffic was already going slow, and the vehicles were all back-to-back to each other. Stopping at the side of the construction path, erm, there wasn't anyone doing that, and apart from that, I was trying to abstain from riding on this type of terrain when the sun goes down. But how long will this terrain go on? I just couldn't possibly know. With that said, it made sense to keep on going.

The horrendous dirt ground changed to tarmac ground after

many kilometres passed and the ride on the tarmac felt like the smoothest road surface I have ever ridden on.

But not long after, it changed back to dirt ground again.

The dirt ground intermittently changed between the tarmac ground and the dirt ground which then made my body stiffen up from the prolonged ride on the bumps and humps. And for my hands that gripped tightly to the handlebar, became numb and strained. My thoughts went back to the Mexican restaurant where I figuratively told myself: *"...suffer now and let tomorrow be easy."* But never have I thought that I would be suffering literally.

After over 30 kilometres – or longer than that – the tarmac appeared more evidently but the sun had already gone down. Then came the intense night riding where I was already bodily fatigued from the dirt ride, but didn't let my guard down on my focus. The usual pitch-dark roads appeared on certain sections along the way and the chilly weather came along too. But thanks to the auxiliary lighting from other vehicles that lightened up everything on the ground for me to see.

The ride kept on going, and from all the night riding I had ridden on from the past few days, this ride was by far the most intense one I had ever done. Then after a prolong focusing on the road, I finally arrived in the city of Chiang Rai, but it wasn't an extravagant thing to me after entering the many other states before Chiang Rai.

The same usual thing passed me was a series of bright well lightened up automobile outlets, large signboards of advertisements that are surrounded by flood lights, and cart vendors along the streets.

I came to a stop in front of the hostel that I had randomly set earlier before the ride, and just as I was about to look at the façade of the hostel, the receptionist had already made her way out of the hostel waving to me like my arrival was predicted.

The receptionist welcomed me with her bright smile, but my mind only wanted to know if there was a bed to sleep in. Much of my energy had gone to the riding, but still contented that I had finally arrived where I wanted to arrive to. The receptionist then said that only one bed was available for the night, and it was in a dormitory room. My mind instantly brought me back to the clowns who sang and danced last night. However, I was too battered down and too exhausted to look for another place. I accepted it but swore to myself that if anyone were to have a live performance in the room in the middle of the night, I would get the hell out of the hostel and sleep on my bike.

For the bike, I was told by the receptionist to park just right in front of the hostel as there are closed-circuit cameras outside the hostel that could monitor my bike. At first, I was hesitant, but then again, I didn't want to trouble myself to find another place. I parked the bike and did my due diligence to lock up the bike, and all I had to do is to hope that the bike was still in the right spot the next day. Else, I would have to take a cab to the Golden Triangle.

***

Despite being worn out, I still had the eagerness to get myself out to see what was there on the night of Chiang Rai. But too bad that I came on Friday, as the well-known night-walking street is only open on the weekends. However, the receptionist told me to visit the food court that has live performances, and it's just less than 100 metres away from the hostel.

The short walk had brought me to a place that gave me something unique to my eyes. It's a large, squared food court with many yellow tables and chairs that were occupied by the patrons. People imbibed many bottles of beer, having a huge feast on their table, and the atmosphere was lively with live performances on a large stage. There were particularly many groups of families here, but there was something unusual to my eyes.

The majority of the patrons were much fairer in tonality, and some had 'paste' or in other words, *Thanaka*, applied on their cheeks. (It's a paste made of ground bark and it is commonly applied to the face). I intuitively knew that most of these people weren't Thai but were from Myanmar (Burmese). To confirm my assumption, I stopped at one of the food vendors and went asking: "The song playing on the stage, Thai song?" And the reply I got was, "No, no…Myanmar…Here many Myanmar."

I stroll about looking at the concoction of food and beverages displayed at the vendor's storefront. There were Turkish kebab vendors, fruit juice vendors, sushi vendors, seafood vendors, western food vendors, and many others. Most of the vendors had different varieties of either raw or partially cooked food dish plates displayed in front of their stores. All one should do is pick a plate that they like, and the chef will do the job by cooking it or deep frying them. However, there were lots of patrons who were having a 'hot-pot' meal at their table. It's widely called *'chim chum'* in Thailand and they are usually served with a basket full of a variety of green vegetables and a plate of the patron's choice of meats.

If I had eaten less at the Mexican restaurant earlier, I would have had a feast on my own. I ended up having a plate of steak with fries and the usual happiness in me looking at the price tag that displayed only 80 baht. I munched and enjoyed the live performance of a rock band performing on the stage, then it changed to a group of beautiful women who were on their traditional ethnic rope doing delicate dance, and then came another performance of a woman singing or was she screaming on the mike, I didn't know. But the speakers that were close to me were vibrating madly.

The night hadn't end till I got myself a full body massage

and a good foot massage. I walked further out to a street called *Phaholyothin*, where there were massage shops, restaurants, a pharmacy, and other standalone stores on both sides of the road. However, there weren't many tourists or locals flocking about on the street. Probably the food court was the main place to mingle about at night here, I guess.

I went to a massage shop to get a Thai body massage and it came out exceptionally good after the many stretching, twisting, and cracking done to my body. But when the masseuse changed to another masseuse to do the foot massage, it was a hilarious foot massage I have ever had in my life.

I sat on a declined chair and scrolled through the social media application on my phone while I got pressed on my foot. After half an hour into the massage, I felt a tickle sensation on my right foot which made me off-look my phone and heed forward to see the masseuse. She was sweating profusely under the air-conditioned outlet, and I asked her why she was sweating that badly. She just shook her head not saying anything and continued to press on my feet.

After another 15 minutes later, the tickle sensation returned to my foot. I off-look from my phone to see her again. But this time round, she winked at me and gave a seductive look at me. I rested my head on the headrest behind me, looked up at the ceiling above, and muttered to myself, "Oh my… She could be anyone's grandmother."

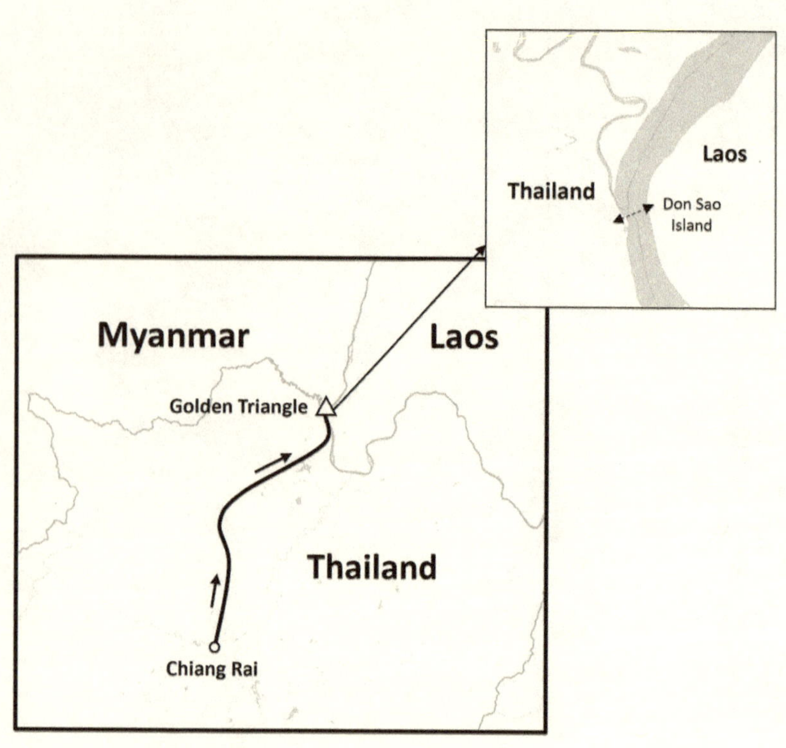

Myanmar
Laos
Golden Triangle
Thailand
Chiang Rai
Thailand
Laos
Don Sao
Island

15

Tiger What?

A mini kitchen was at a mezzanine level landing in the hostel. There were eggs, bread, several types of coffee sachets, and assorted bread spread jars on the pantry table. There was also kitchenware and a stove to make use of, but it was all self-service. I made myself a terrible scramble egg that looked slightly burnt, brew a coffee, and sat at a corner on the mezzanine level to consume my meal.

I ate and watched the early riser kids screaming and running up and down the stairs and around the mezzanine level. Eventually, one kid tripped himself over a chair which infuriated his father, who appeared like he had been holding on to his temperament for a long time. The kid's father then admonished the kid loud enough to wake up other guests in the hostel. And there was I, just metres away from the scene, munching on my burnt scrambled egg like I was invisible to them. But it was strange looking at what was happening though.

Although something was happening in my surrounding, it felt like I was oblivious to what was going on as I munched on my meal. I wasn't feeling apprehensive like in the past days of the ride, when I would have something on my mind that would elevate my anxiety level. I questioned myself and focused my mind to get a better look at the father and son scene. Gradually, I became more conscious of my surroundings and asked myself why I was behaving that way. From a single 'why', it grew into many questions in my mind that soon led me to realise I had to accept something sooner or later: the northern ride was coming to an end.

***

The orange bag got on the seat, securely wrapped tightly down and hooked onto the rack. All the other stuff that had to be in the top box had all gone in. I walked around my bike to do a final check and was satisfied that it was all good to go, but not so satisfied with the chain and the tyres that looked muddy from yesterday's dirt ride. Well, what can I say? It was not what I expected, but good thing that I had somehow gotten through yesterday's ride.

The bike was checked, my riding jacket fully zipped up, my body camera was switched on, and the Google Maps set to Golden Triangle Park that is mere 70 kilometres away. I smiled as I looked at the final destination name and set off to achieve my last mission.

It was sunny and the sky was blue with only a few puffy clouds hovering above the sky to which I assured myself that it would never rain for the day. For the first few kilometres, the roads were busy with commuters; then, as I got to the highway that would lead me to my destination, the highway became silent with only a few vehicles passing by me on my right.

The atmosphere appeared wide open, and the landscape seemed so flat that I could see tiny shapes of far-distant mountains and finely cut green fields around my horizon. It seemed like this highway ride compared to all the previous days' rides; it was by far the noiseless highway I'd ever ridden on. It's like a reward to ride on this highway after passing all the congested roads and packed highways on my past days of rides where I absorbed much of the toxic fumes that comes out from the vehicles.

Well, that can be one reason. But the real reason seemed like I was riding on a newly opened highway as the GPS appeared to have trouble reading the route.

Since the northern journey was about to end soon, I tried like how a movie would flashback the protagonist's past stories and slowly build up the chronological story until the present moment. To be frank, it was hard to chronologically run my thoughts from the start of day-one till the present ride. It was a mess in my mind. But some vivid moments popped up in my mind like the failed border crossing, the tree fall, the *black figure* that I had dodged during the ride to Kelantan, the insanely shivering ride in Mae Hong Son loop, and oddly, much of other thoughts were foodstuff that I ate along my journey, and the one that I had fond of was the spicy stir-fried chicken with rice.

I don't know why, but I really liked that Thai dish.

From all the cluttered thoughts I had in my mind, the one that really made the difference for me to ride all the way to northern Thailand was the tree fall on the day-two ride, and I could evidently remember that scene. Hadn't the tree fall, and hadn't I met the Malaysian man who told me not to give up and to try all the other borders, I wouldn't have reached this far. I have to say; I was really fortunate to have met great people along my ride. And also, thanks to the tree that fell.

As I got closer to my destination, the kilometres passed relatively fast, and I came to the final kilometre to Golden Triangle where I see a blue information signboard above a pole on my left that had Thai and English descriptions on it. The English description was what made me feel jubilant and amazed at how far I had come. I smiled as I looked at the signboard with words written on it: *1km Golden Triangle.*

The highway ride changed to a single carriage road. Then more brick buildings no taller than 6-story high appeared on both sides of the road and there were several tour buses parked on the roadsides. As I got closer and closer to the GPS pin-drop, and before I made the very final left bend to my endpoint, I passed by a huge Golden Buddha statue that sits above the bricked walls and the statue lit up brightly from the sun's ray that kind of made my presence here even more welcoming.

Once the last left bend negotiated and a few metres of ride on a straight, the GPS stopped displaying the route. And that was when, I knew, I had reached my endpoint.

I rode slowly and turned my head to the right; I saw a Golden Triangle arch gate with blocks of white letters of tri-countries names on it and tourists were flocking about at the pillar to take pictures of it. There were also a group of men and women in dark blue top, and some wore sleeveless leather jacket like that Harley Davidson jacket. Some sat on the benches under a tree, some flocked about waiting for their turn to take pictures with the gate, and some looked at me from a distance as though I had done something wrong. Whatever it was, my main focus was all on the arch gate. That was what I was looking forward to since the beginning of my ride from Singapore and I had come to view it right in front of my eyes.

The mission hadn't ended until I took a picture with the arch gate and my bike. That's the final ordeal to call the *10 days to Golden Triangle*. I went pushing the bike up a short ramp and then to the walkway with much anxiousness in me while I looked around to see if there were any security personnel around that would chase me off from the walkway. As I approached the gate, more people looked at me, and I became pretty nervous that I might get chased out. But I kept on pushing the bike with a mindset of "*I got to fucking do this"*, and then there came the voices at me. But it wasn't to chase me away, but a series of questions came to me.

"Dari Singapore (from Singapore)*?"* .... *"Bang, dari mane* (Bro, from where)*?"* .... *"Bagus arh di nie* (Good arh this guy)*"* .... *"Single ke taken* (Single or taken)*?"* And many more questions came flying towards me from the group who were on their blue top and leather jackets. I went on answering their questions and when I said I was single, the women in the group cheered on me and everyone laughed along afterwards.

The questionnaire was quick, and my turn came to take the triumphant pictures with my bike parked right in front of the gate. I quickly double-checked my phone to see if the camera worked fine before handing it over to one of the group members to help me out with the picture-taking. Then the moment came as I took off my helmet and hung it on the side mirror and then positioned myself. When the cameraman echoed the countdowns before snapping the shot, I knew one thing for sure – that I have made it.

The crowd grew, watching me pose for shots and some of the tourists took pictures of me as though I were a celebrity. *"Abang, pegi belakang* (Brother, go to the back) ... *power!"* cheered the group member and I did different poses while the crowd applauded me. I have to say it looked pretty odd, but I liked that moment. More people came snapping pictures of me, and I was smiling throughout the moment. I remembered setting off from my home parking lot where I envisaged a scene at the Golden Triangle gate where I creatively plotted people around the scene and the people were applauding me and taking pictures of me. That peculiar imagination apparently came true but not as obscured as I had thought of. But what was happening around me, was more than enough to put a smile on my face.

But there was one thing that discontented me much. The

letter "L" was missing from the blocks of letters that made up 'THAILAND' word on the arch gate. It would have made my pictures more appreciable to see than having to see 'THAI AND.'

***

The great moment went off, and I pushed the bike back to the parking area and went over to the cameraman to thank him. As I continued conversing with him, I learned that he and his group were on a motorcycle road trip but instead of using their bikes, they had flown over to Chiang Mai via a plane and rented bikes there instead. That is way much better than what I did. But mine is a different story, so I can't compare. He later advised me to take a boat ride to Don Sao Island, which is at the Laos border and told me that it cost 500 baht for the boat ride. My mind instantly went over to my disastrous-looking passport but I kept silent about it. But as he continued on, he said that I need not have a stamp on the passport as the immigration would hold on to my passport until I get back to the Thailand border again, which it lit up a bulb in me.

Before heading over to check out on the boat ride, I roamed about looking at the many monuments and statues around then walked behind the arch gate to witness the tri-country borders. Laos and Thailand border looked lively with infrastructures near its borders and speed boats were around at the docking area, and some were on the go bringing the tourist to the other neighbouring border. However, looking at the Myanmar border, it was utterly dull and monotonous to see. There wasn't any boat docking platform or any interesting thing to look around at the border. All I saw was overgrown cluttered green bushes and grasses on the contours of the border. And from a distance, I see a few red-tiled roof buildings. That was about it.

Well, good thing that my mission wasn't specifically just to view the tri-borders. If it was, I would have been immensely

222

dissatisfied.

After much roaming around the Golden Triangle Park, I walked over close to an immigration office called Chiang Sean. In front of the immigration office, there were four to five booths selling boat ride tickets to the Laos border. Before I even walked over to the booth, I see people at the booths were all beckoning me to their booth to buy their service.

I went to the nearest booth from me, and a man asked me how many people to Laos.

"One person," I replied, and he showed me a clear file with only three papers inside it. The first page had a few sentences describing the boat ride. The second page had pictures of a small speed boat and last page was the same type of boat but a longer one.

"You want to go big boat or small boat? Big boat 1000-baht, small boat 500-baht," he asked. By looking at the pictures, the difference between the big and the small boat was just the longevity of it and had no canopy to shelter the passenger.

"How long is the trip?" I asked.

"Take boat, go Lao, go shopping market, come back, two hours." He replied like a robot, and it rang in my ears when he said 'Lao' without the 's' in it.

"My motorcycle?" I asked.

"No motorcycle. Only you," he said.

My mission had been completed, and the very least thing to worry about was the bike and the stuff on the bike. If someone were to steal my bike or the orange bag on the seat, I would be unconcerned about it. I will just take a taxi or hitch a ride over to Chiang Mai and take a cheap flight back to Singapore. It would save me a great deal of time and energy than riding back to Singapore. But then, I realised that I still had to do food delivery back in Singapore, which I had to take back my words and not let my bike get stolen.

I told him to give me a minute, and I scurried to my bike to lock the bike wheels and covered its existence by using the picnic mat. It didn't help much, but at least I did what I was supposed to do. But I still had some concern. I noticed an ice cream cart vendor who kept looking at me ever since I started to lock up the bike. He looked suspicious to me and I thought that he might be the one who would steal my bike. I ran to him – which terrified him, but when I reached next to him, I took out a 50 baht note and told him to look after my bike. His terrified look changed to smiles on his face, and he said, "no problem."

Sometimes my ingenuity is one of a kind.

I went to the ticket booth again, chose the small speed boat, and handed over my passport and 500 baht with guilt-ridden in me. He then filled up a form and sent it with the passport to the immigration office behind the booths. He returned a few minutes later and passed me a slip for collection of the passport once I got back to the Thailand border.

"What time are we going to Laos? I asked the ticket seller. Another man cut past the man I spoke to and instantly handed me a life jacket. "Sir, we go now."

That was quick.

The speed boat zoomed along the Mekong River at a freaking fast speed. The wind gashed on my face and it felt like a huge hairdryer blowing on me, and my hair winded back like a cartoon character running fast. Every time the boat skipped the water surface and then slapped back down on the water, it felt like the boat would break apart into pieces at any given moment. I held on to my phone tightly to video record my ride while being very cautious not to let it slip out of my hand. Then at one instance along the ride, the boatman slowed down, and the boat stopped in the middle of the Mekong River. The boatman points to the border on my right and says, "that one… Lao border." I nod to it. He then points to the opposite sight of the riverbank and says: "that one… Myanmar border." I nodded again, and that was it. That was the tour speech. And there was no other tour speech afterwards.

The speed boat then headed over to the Lao border and stopped at a docking area of Don Sao Island. With the relatively fleeting time I had in hand, I spent the time strolling about at a market looking at the repetitive things that were sold on the vendor tables. Many vendors seemed to sell the same products, like meditative muscle pain creams that come in variant types of packaging and sizes, a wide variety of cigarettes brand in cartons that were stacked up high on the tables, and the many apparels that have a variety of designs prints of the tri-nation on the t-shirts. What heed my attention were those glass bottles in different shapes and sizes that had a 'thing' or two inside each bottle.

A glass bottle may contain a snake, a scorpion, or a lizard inside. Or any combination of the two inside the glass bottle and it is filled up with liquid. Many other large jars contained snakes and other uncanny things inside them and were filled up with liquid too. Having a better look at them and also asking the seller, I was told that some were wine and some were whiskeys. The eye-catchy ones were those bottles with a snake coiled up perfectly inside the bottle with its head biting onto its tail. If not, the snake bit on the scorpion's tail. It was interesting to look at and I saw some tourists having a shot glass of liquor poured from a large jar.

"Sir, you want to try?" asked the vendor, wanting to hand me a shot glass. I politely declined the offer and told him that I was riding. But I was curious to know what the thing inside a large glass container that looked like a gut, but not like a gut.

"What is this?" I asked curiously.

"This one, *Tiger penis*…very good sir. Make you strong like tiger. Want to try sir?" The way he said it like as though it tastes like chicken soup.

Part 3: An Endeavour to Create a Better Life Story

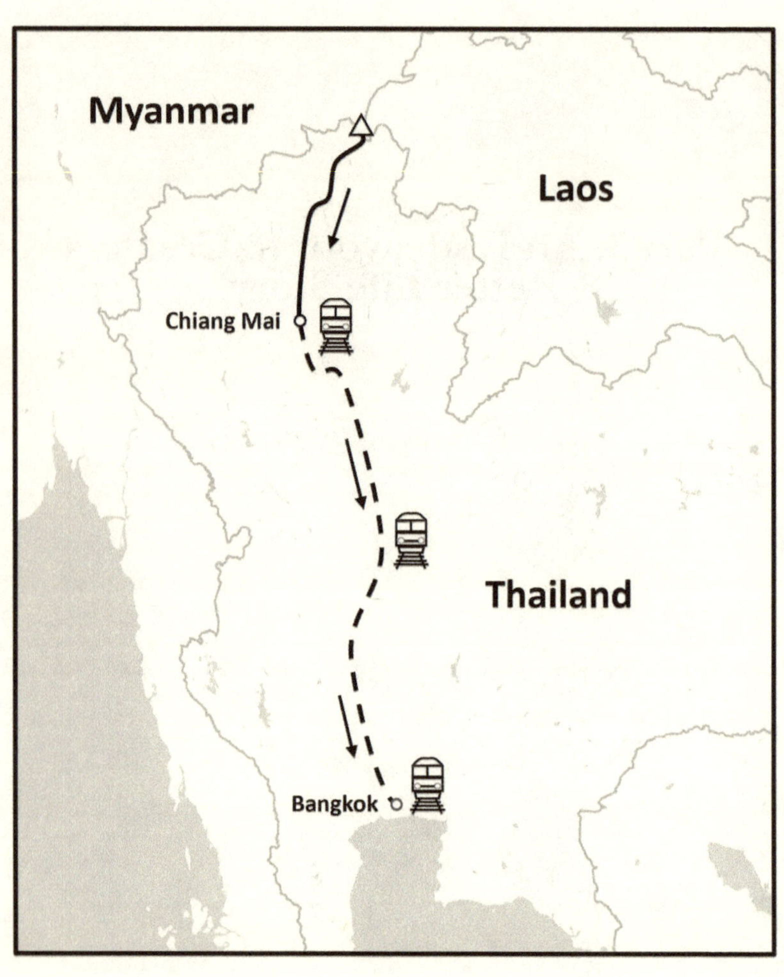

Myanmar
Laos
Chiang Mai
Thailand
Bangkok

16

Not Like Movies

The northern ride ended, and the return trip back to Singapore commenced. I stopped just 200 metres away from the Golden Triangle Park to get the same usual meal of a spicy stir-fried chicken with rice from a food court. I was good with a simple meal and I munch and stared at a brown stray dog outside the food court that was circling around itself trying to bite its tail.

I sighed as I took a spoon bite thinking about the long journey back home. It's about 2,680 kilometres to reach back to Singapore. Just by saying the numbers, it seemed like an astronomical number after glancing at the bike parked metres away from me. Then out of the blue, a bulb lit up in me that brought me to remember talking to a fellow delivery rider just a month ago.

When I was on my way to a vendor to pick up an order, I met another delivery rider who happened to collect an order from the same vendor as me. We conversed about our job while we waited for the order to be prepared, and he happened to take notice of my bike's top box that has route stickers from the Phuket road trip, which intrigued him to ask about my trip. I told him about my road trip and the conversation grew till I got even more intrigued hearing the story of the road trip he made with his friend. He and his friend had ridden to Golden Triangle before and even rode up to China with their lower-capacity motorcycles too. The part that heeded me to the conversation was when he explained about his return trip, taking a train at Chiang Mai Railway Station that ended its journey at Bangkok Station. Their bikes were loaded up onto the cargo carriage, purchased first-class ticket with bedding, and they relaxed throughout their train ride.

"Isn't that a fantastic idea to take a train back? I could sleep, I could see the landscape pass by, and not waste my energy on riding, right?" Why burn myself from the sweltering heat where I can just take the train and munch on potato chips, right?" More questions came back-to-back in my mind, and it seemed illogical to spend much time on the road. The major goal to ride to Golden Triangle had been accomplished, and there was no reason for me to be on the road for long after that.

"Since I have never been on a long train ride before. Why not give this an experience?" I thought.

***

The return trip went on riding back to Chiang Mai. Riding back on the construction path again seemed easier this time round and the over 250 kilometres went by pretty fast. I guess I was too accustomed to whatever surface I had been riding on in which it seemed to me that the construction path wasn't a big deal to handle.

I touched down back to Chiang Mai before the atmosphere became dark and rode back to the same hostel when I first arrived at Chiang Mai. Actually, it was for the sake of easy parking for the bike.

This time round opening the door of a dormitory room, almost all beds were taken up. However, I wasn't concerned about it as I had done what I had to do. But still, deep down in me, I hoped not to see people starting a live band blatantly in the middle of the night like the one I had experienced in Pai town.

I settled down fast, not because I wanted to get to bed, but because I was rather thrilled to visit the well-known Saturday Night Walking Street that's along the road of *Wua-Lai*, which was recommended by the hostel receptionist.

As I arrived at the walking street and approached the market entrance, it was packed with people and the crowd was moving at a snail's pace. All the vendor stands were lit up well, and there were many souvenirs and handicraft products in the vendors' stores for a person to choose from on both sides of the walkway. If one has to introspect much on purchasing a particular item, one may find another similar item or find the same item further up the walking street and need not have to overthink about it.

As souvenirs and handicraft stuff weren't a thing to me on this road trip – not even in any other trip I had been to, I went on to fulfil my purpose here by heading to the food section to get my stomach filled up.

The food tasting commenced, but there were too many to choose from. Trying a bit of what I know from vendors displaying on their tables, such as sushi, lasagne, gyoza dumplings, and marinated chicken meats stacked up on skewer sticks. And again, I got myself a banana pancake with Nutella spreads after reminiscing about having it in Pai town.

There were various types of food and beverages in the food section, but one stall that caught my attention was selling unusual meats on skewers. On the vendor's table, there were scorpions, ostrich meats, deer meats, and even crocodile meats were displayed for people to choose from. I wondered if these were even legit meats to speak of, but well, Thailand always surprises me. And my intrusive mind persuades me to try everything.

To find the exit was more like a wish. I kept walking and

walking and on certain sections of the walking street, the crowd lessened, and I thought the end of the walking street was nearing. However, I was wrong. The walking street kept going and going, and I never failed to see more handicraft vendors on both sides of the street.

The long and slow walk eventually came to an end, but what surprised me was when I checked my location on Google Maps, I discovered that the Saturday Night Walking Street stretched over a kilometre long!

***

The next day, I spent the early hours of the day roaming about the central part of Chiang Mai looking at the moat, the ancient-looking-large-gates, and the magnificent bricked walls that were still intact on certain areas along the moat.

The *Phae Gate* is a populous area for the locals and tourists where they would hang around taking pictures of the gate and the bricked walls. There was other thing that was happening around the *Phae Gate* too. There were people sprinkling rice on the flock of pigeons that gathered around the *Phae Gate*. Not for the sake of feeding the pigeons, but to startle the pigeons by swiftly rolling a wooden pole across the ground while capturing a picture of both the tourist and the pigeons taking flight, creating an Instagram-worthy shot. Interesting.

Walking along the wall's perimeter was tiring enough as each side of the evidently seen square in Chiang Mai is dimension roughly about 1.5 kilometres or longer than that. Taking that as my morning exercise, I went over to get breakfast at a restaurant close to my accommodation. While I waited for my dish to be sent to my table, I started to plan my return ride back to Singapore and thought through whether I should stay longer in Chiang Mai. Despite working extra hours before this journey to cover up my non-working days, the extra hours only covered up to 15 days. With that said, I was left with only 5 days – including this day – to get back to Singapore and start work again.

As much as I would want to stay longer and venture around the city, I didn't have the gusto, the zeal, the true liberation where I could freely travel without thinking about time and money. Perhaps in future, I may have the ability to venture around nonchalantly. But for this journey, I had to make my way home.

Aside from that, I was ambivalent about my decision if I should take the railway train. I was naïve about what the process of loading the bike would be like on the train, how I would get my bike back once I disembarked from the train, and wondered if I would even see my bike arriving at the destination. I was naïve in this train ride thingy and I didn't have any friends who knew a thing about this, nor I had the number of the delivery guy who told me that he took a train from Chiang Mai to Bangkok. Thinking through all these dilemmas, it all came up for me to try it out and see it for myself.

***

I was already in my full gear before the check-out time, and I waved a final goodbye to the receptionist and made my way straight to Chiang Mai Railway Station.

Reaching Chiang Mai Railway Station was a new thing to me. I parked the bike at one side of the station and walked to the station hallway to see an information counter desk. The naïve me, not a good conversational starter, went over to the information desk and started talking about my bike first.

"Hi, that's my bike outside. I want to take the train and load up my bike."

"How many cc, sir?" She asked while she stood up from her seat to look at my bike.

"Erm, like 135cc…but it looks like 130cc…erm…should be 125cc," I said with a poker face trying to make it seem like a lightweight motorcycle. She giggled and went back to her seat and gave a look as though many people had tried saying like how I said it before.

"Erm, 135cc then."

She giggled again and turned over to type on a keyboard to check the train availability then back to me again.

"Going to Bangkok?"

"Er…yes."

"Sir, today, 3:30, sitting with friend, 3rd class only."

Sitting with friend? I came alone…

I was baffled when she said "3rd class only" in a way that it won't be a pleasant one. But until I asked her how long the train ride would be, it got me to hesitate.

"What time will I reach Bangkok?"

"5:25 am, morning," she said and smiled at me.

"Morning?" I asked, double confirming what she just said.

She nodded with a smile on her face, but my ear wasn't pleased with that.

I paused and mentally tabulated the hours in my head and approximated that it would take about 14 hours to reach Bangkok.

"What…14 hours?"

"Yes."

"Er…How much will the ticket cost?"

"271, for you."

"For the bike?" I asked curiously.

She thought through for a moment and replied, "800, up."

I paused for a while to think again and thought about riding back to Bangkok where the distance approximated about 680 kilometres to reach Bangkok. However, looking at the time that had just passed noon and the long rides that I had made on the prior days, it didn't motivate me to do another long ride again. Furthermore, if I were to ride back to Bangkok, it would take me over 12 hours including breaks and re-fuelling. With that said, I would reach after midnight.

"Hello sir?"

"Oh sorry, sorry. My brain. Alright, I will take it."

She went on to explain to me whatever questions I had in mind, and I specifically asked about the transportation of my bike.

"Buy ticket at the counter first. Take motorbike, go outside, go behind, you see cargo," she said pointing at the few ticket counters.

I walked over to the ticket counter to re-confirm the train ride at 3:30 and asked her about the 3rd class train again. The same type of answers came in my ears, and it wasn't pleasant to hear it again.

"Only 3rd class train left for today. No lie down. The seat cannot recline," the counter staff said.

The way the ticket staff said it like as if they didn't encourage tourists to board the 3rd class train. I was ambivalent and unable to make up a decision and told the ticket staff that I needed some time to think about it.

I walked about thinking if I should just ride my bike to Bangkok.

If I don't take this train, I still need to find an accommodation to sleep, right? Then, the next day I still need to either ride back or take the train, right? Why not just take the train today? Since I've never taken the 3rd class train before, why not just go for it and experience something new?

Deep down inside me, I was hesitant. But well, I gave it a try.

"How much is the ticket again?"

***

The cargo department was just a walking distance from the ticket office, but to bring my bike over, I had to ride out of the station and enter from another entrance gate at the back of the ticket office.

Boxes of cargo were around the cargo department, and there was a small office with one wide open window, and a man watched me walking towards him.

"Hello, I want my bike to be transported to Bangkok." He peeked out of the open window to see my bike.

"How many cc?" He asked sternly.

"Erm…130…125…135cc," I said in a way to try my luck with the numbers to see if he would give a discount for my bike as I happened to notice a poster next to the window with different pricing for different capacity bikes. But I didn't really look at it closely before talking to the staff.

"Ticket, passport, log card," he replied like an automated machine then pointed at my bike, "bag take off, box take off, rack take off."

I nodded looking at my bike but thought that it would be a hassle to dismantle the rack off as it's mounted internally which I have to unscrew the side fairings to take off the rack which is just a hassling job.

"I take out everything, but can I leave the rack?"

"No. Take out. Only motorbike." He said without giving him any chances.

I was still reluctant about it and went over to my bike and pretended to work hard on dismantling the rack.

"The rack cannot take out," I lied. He became sceptical about it and asked one of the stevedores around to check on my bike. The stevedore came, and I instantly had second thoughts of taking back what I just said. The stevedore bends down to look at the rack and then says something in Thai to the man inside the cargo department. The man nodded and didn't say a word afterwards. I guess the stevedore was on my side for this, as he did seem like lazy to be bothered about me. That meant that I could just leave it as it was.

Sometimes, lying to save trouble does help a lot. But not always.

I passed him everything he asked for and he looked at them thoroughly then quoted me the cost for the cargo which I instantly knew that there wasn't any discount given to me. The transportation cost me 1030 baht. But I thought about the expenses like the fuel, food, accommodation, and energy that I would have to use if I were to ride back to Hat Yai. It still somehow seemed logical to take the train anyway. And so, I paid for the cargo ticket.

I dismounted the top box off the rack; brought the orange bag after unravelling the cords; took off the helmet from the side mirror; took the jerrycan off the basket, and the other stuff that was in the front basket was all put into the orange bag. That was all I had to do, and I left my bike to the stevedores to bring it up to the train.

With less than three hours to spend before boarding the train, waiting at the train station wasn't something I wanted to do. I took all the stuff and placed them onto a trolley, changed into my comfortable clothing to prepare myself for the long train ride, and then placed my stuff in a cloakroom for a deposit so that I could head out of the station to roam about and get a good meal before boarding.

I came back to the station just in time to see a stevedore push my bike to the cargo carriage and watch them load up my bike without the need to use a hoist. Two stevedores were stationed on the ground, and they lifted my bike and handed it to another stevedore on the cargo carriage platform, and then he pushed the bike to one side of the cabin. He then ties ropes around my bike and ties it to whatever prominent mounted objects on the cabin side walls to prevent the bike from falling.

"Bro, this bike, tie good, good," I said. He further ties tightly, then looks at me and shows a thumbs up.

The train boarding time came. I got my stuff back from the cloakroom, and I was the first few people to board the train. As I scurried through the narrow aisle carrying my top box, I realised that I wasn't the first person to board the carriage. Three young Thai men had already come before me and had occupied the 2-seater seats that faced each other, leaving a seat unoccupied.

40, 41, 42… I looked at the red numbers on the cabin walls that denoted the seat numbers and came to a stop at the number 46 – which is my seat number, and it is where the group of three Thai people were and the one empty seat next to the aisle, it came out to be mine. Not sure if this was an unfortunate meeting, but they gave me their sub-conscious smile, and I gave my sub-conscious smile back to them and placed the top box on the railing above the window.

I scurried in and out of the aisle carrying my stuff in, and once all the stuff was placed up on the railing above, I had no option but to sit on my seat and give them my subconscious smile again.

All three wore funnel tops with an inner t-shirt and the person who sat next to me had his sunglasses on. I wasn't the type of extrovert to start an ice-breaking talk to people. But since it would be a long journey, I tried to start a conversation. I smiled and nodded to the person sitting next to me and he instantly initiated to speak to me, but it was in Thai. I shook my head not knowing what he meant.

"I'm from Singapore. I ride my motorcycle here. Going back to Singapore." I said while demonstrating some hand gestures of me riding a bike to get him to understand. He didn't comprehend what I said, and he looked at his friends in front of him, and then all looked at me with baffled looks.

Well, it was already the 11th day of my road trip, and I was already well intellectual enough to handle this type of situation. When there's Google Translate, what is there to worry about, right?

I translated what I wanted to say and showed my phone screen to the guy next to me, and he nodded with amusement.

"Singapore…Singapore!? …. aww…." The person next to me said it enthusiastically, and he spoke something in Thai to his friends. All gave a fertile smile, and that was when the phone conversation began.

We exchanged conversation enthusiastically, and all used their phones to communicate through Google Translate to ask me questions and I answered back using my phone. They were so interested to know what I had done on my ride for which, I showed them the pictures and videos I had taken along the ride which awed them much. Then phone conversation continued for over half an hour till we even laughed, and one even invited me to make fun of his other friend. I became a part of their group and thought that I was indeed fortunate to meet these people. Or is it the Thais who are easy to get along with where I didn't feel the hostility from their presence? I very well think so.

The time went really slow and every minute waiting for the train to depart felt like an hour. I became restless really quickly and the humidity inside the cabin was at an obnoxious level. The conversation with the newly made friends became on and off after 45 minutes of phone conversation. I ran out of stuff to say and ask as the interesting topics were already done saying. I stopped using my phone to conserve battery power so that I could use it during the middle of the train journey.

The railing above the windowpane filled up fast, and I watched with guilt conscience as I had taken much of the space leaving some of the passengers to place their stuff under their seats. As the passengers slowly filled up the cabin, I watched many peculiar eyes on me when they walked past the aisle. There weren't any foreigners that I took notice of, and it came out to be me the lone foreigner in the cabin.

The cabin was fully filled by 3:25 pm and the long dreadful wait for the train to depart started to depart exactly at 3:30 pm. I sighed as I watched the train move off, and many of us sprouted smiles on our faces, but the screeching sound that came along from the train wheels made the moment maddening.

As the train slowly moved off, a strange-looking man walked through the aisle and sat on a seat adjacent to me on the opposite aisle. He wore kaftan-like clothing that was in red, and it had many flower prints all around his clothing. His eyes were pretty red, and he just sat still and stared at his front, hugging onto his grey sling bag. The passenger next to him tried to talk to him to try to break the ice, but he didn't answer a single word and continued to stare at his front. Somehow, he appeared like the one who steals someone's seat and just does not talk to anyone.

An hour passed after the train move-of-time, and I finally got off my seat to experience something that I always wanted to try: What is it like to hold onto a railing and stick my head out of a train door? But never have I thought that it would be so terrifying to do in reality.

The train jerks a lot as it moves and by just walking close to a train door – that is between two carriages, it terrified me much that I might get thrown out of the door. As I got closer to the door, I could hear the gushing sound of the wind and I forgot about what I had seen in those Bollywood movies where the protagonist grips the handlebar with their bare hands, and nonchalantly swings their body out of the door and sways along with the headwind. But in reality, I put my whole arm around the handlebar that's next to the door, hugging it close to my chest before sticking my head out of the opened door. The wind gushed on my face, and it pushed my spectacles tightly onto my nose bridge. As I looked up, down, left, and right, I knew all the dangers out there.

One wrong miss-step, I could send myself falling onto the track and down the many stories high train track. Stretching out my hand wasn't the right thing to do as the prominent poles that passed me every few seconds were so close to the train. Singing and opening my mouth wasn't in my mind too. There were lots of bird shad can be seen on the track when the train slowed at different areas and birds were flying close to the train. Just imagine a bird poop and it directly lands on someone's mouth while the person tries to imitate singing like a Bollywood actor; it would perhaps be a taste of a lifetime.

I meant it in a gross way though.

After all, I got the feel of how it feels like to stand close to the train door while it moves fast and slightly stuck my body out of the train's door. That was more than enough, and I am done with my Bollywood triumph.

To extrapolate my experience, one should not do what I did if one fears much. Don't even think about getting near an open train door while the train moves.

Two hours into the train ride, the cabin was relatively silent, but the atmosphere outside the window was in its brilliant appearance. The atmosphere was in orangey-red in hue, turning passing building into elegant silhouettes. Many passengers gazed out the window to see the mesmerising orange sky and appreciate what passed by. I was too immensely pleased by it, and watching the sky on a train, was a unique experience for me.

It was turning dark outside, and it was also getting cold and humid in the cabin. The Thai guys tried to latch up the windowpane as the cool wind started to gush in from the window. But it kept sliding down every time they tried to bring it up in which they gave up trying.

The conversation with the three Thais wasn't fertile anymore as my phone could not get any signals. I was taciturn and expressed annoyance with my phone as I was frustrated that I couldn't make use of it during the night. However, here and there, the three Thais tried to speak a little English to me. I tried configuring in my brain what they were trying to say and tried to say it in a way they could comprehend, but still, the time passed slowly.

The red kaftan-clad man alighted after a man – who looked like a ticket inspector, came next to him and said something to him in a demeaning manner in which he scurried out of the aisle fast like a scared bunny. Still wasn't sure if the seat was his, but from the look on the passenger that was next to him, he was immensely contented to get the two seats to himself.

Some of the commuters were either talking amount each other or using their phone. I envied those who could get the signal on their phone but not on my phone. I looked about everything there to see in the cabin, scrolled through the videos and pictures I had taken, and even saw a tiny caterpillar crawling on someone's shirt. But still, the time passed slowly. My default setting of how I sat was to fold my arms, lean back on the seat backrest, lean my head against the vibrating handle pole behind my head, and stare out the window watching the continuous motion of the pitch-black screen. What a view.

The only entertaining moments were when the train stopped at each station and the *walking vendors* came walking through the aisle holding onto a tray or baskets or a pail with either food or beverages filled on it. Some who had their eyes closed were automatically woken up by the yelling of the walking vendors and then rummaged through their pockets to get cash to buy something they liked. Some of which that I could conceive of were the sticky rice that was wrapped in plastic, fragrant yellow rice with fried chicken, mango sticky rice wrapped in plastic, fried chicken wings, hot dogs, fish balls, assorted cut fruits, ready-made assorted Thai iced flavoured drinks in plastic cups, and there was even a walking-vendor carrying a pail filled with ice, and it has many assorted can drinks from carbonated to non-carbonated ones inside it. The ones that I couldn't conceive of were Google Translated by the Thai guy next to me. Not all were walking vendors were walking back and forth the aisle, but some of the vendors were walking outside the station selling it through the window opening. Usually, the ones outside the train were selling hot bowls of soup noodles. It made sense that they should walk outside instead of walking on the cabin aisle.

There was a variety of food to choose from each walking-vendor and it was difficult for me to choose what I liked. But not all walking-vendor came at once. For every few stations past, a new set of walking vendors boarded the cabin. After a few subsequent stations, a new set of walking vendors would walk into the cabin. This made me look forward to them and wonder what new stuff were to go past the aisle on future stops.

The best advice for someone taking a similar train class is to have enough change in hand and avoid giving large denomination notes to the walking vendors. It may hold them up from finding change and hinder their ability to sell more to the other passengers.

At around 10 pm, most of the commuters had already closed their eyes. Some were all prepared till covering themselves with a blanket, and it astonished me much of how well prepared they were. In the opposite seat next to me, the man who was contented to see the red kaftan guy left the seat, his girlfriend sat next to him and they literally covered themselves with a white bedsheet. A bedsheet? Yes. They brought along a bedsheet.

I watched each and every one of how they slept and envied them a lot. The Thai guy who sat next to me covered his face with his hat and had his feet stretched out, resting on a small space between the two Thai guys in front and his body slouched on the backrest like a boneless person. The Thai guy in front of him brought along a blanket too, and covered himself up. And the Thai guy in front of me leans his head on his friend's shoulder and snores sporadically. Wow, the ability to snore on this type of discomforting train ride really mystified me.

Sometimes the screeching sound of the wheels was so loud that it awakened some. But only a few. The rest were in their deep sleep, somehow not hindered by the sound. "What kind of people are these," I thought. Unlike me, a light sleeper, I couldn't get my eyes closed for long, and the loud screeching sound was too loud to even have my eyes closed.

At one point, the Thai guy in front of me wakes up from the screeching sound and sees me still with my eyes open. He tapped the small seat space next to him and hinted me to rest my feet there if I wanted. But I shook my head not and showed him a thumbs up. But to him, he didn't comprehend what I meant, for which he bent forward to grab my ankles and wanted to lift them to the seat. I stopped him hastily and thanked him for his overly gracious act and told him it was alright.

The long awaiting for what food to choose from the walking vendor had come till midnight, but there weren't many varieties of foods after midnight. The snacks that I had bought before boarding the train had been sandwiched between the orange bag with the other commuter bags on the railing above which I didn't bother reaching for it. I regretted that I didn't purchase any of one of the foods earlier from the walking vendor as there weren't any more good stuff going past the aisle after midnight. I made my decision to purchase an instant curry cup noodle. In real-time, the vendor tore open the cup noodle's lid, tore open the seasoning sachet, and poured it into the cup. He then poured hot water from the thermal flask that hung on his forearm, into the cup noodle. That was the supper for the train ride.

I had short interval sleeps, but each was mere 10 to 15 minutes in length. I get awakened by all sorts of things, such as the train screeching sound; the train halts to stop at nowhere; the yelling of walking vendors who, even past 12 midnight, were still ongoing with their sales. But most of the commuters were already in their so-called comfortable position where they weren't bothered to be awakened by it. It was cold too and my face oiled up by the humidity every half an hour; I would wipe my face on my shoulder and stare out the window with a tired eye of mine.

After a long, tiring, frowning, and past many screeching noises from the train's wheels, the time had reached 5 am. I somehow survived that long, gruelling ride and had seen many peculiar sleeping patterns from all the people around me and did many face swipes on my shoulder. Then I see a few commuters start to disembark the train a few stations before the train stops at my destination. Then more people disembarked at a station before Bangkok and the group of three Thai friends I made all disembarked at once and waved me goodbye.

The train moved slower when it neared Bangkok and my disembarking time was delayed. I sat sluggishly next to the window with a black-ring mark around my eyes, with bodily aches from the prolonged sitting, and the restlessness in me was at the superiority level. However, I was slightly relieved when I neared my station, looking out the window to see the streetlights and the infrastructure lights illuminating the vicinity.

Just past 6 am, the long train ride came to my destination, and finally, I disembarked from the train.

To think back on the total time, I was on the train, it came up to be more than 16 hours.

What a ride...

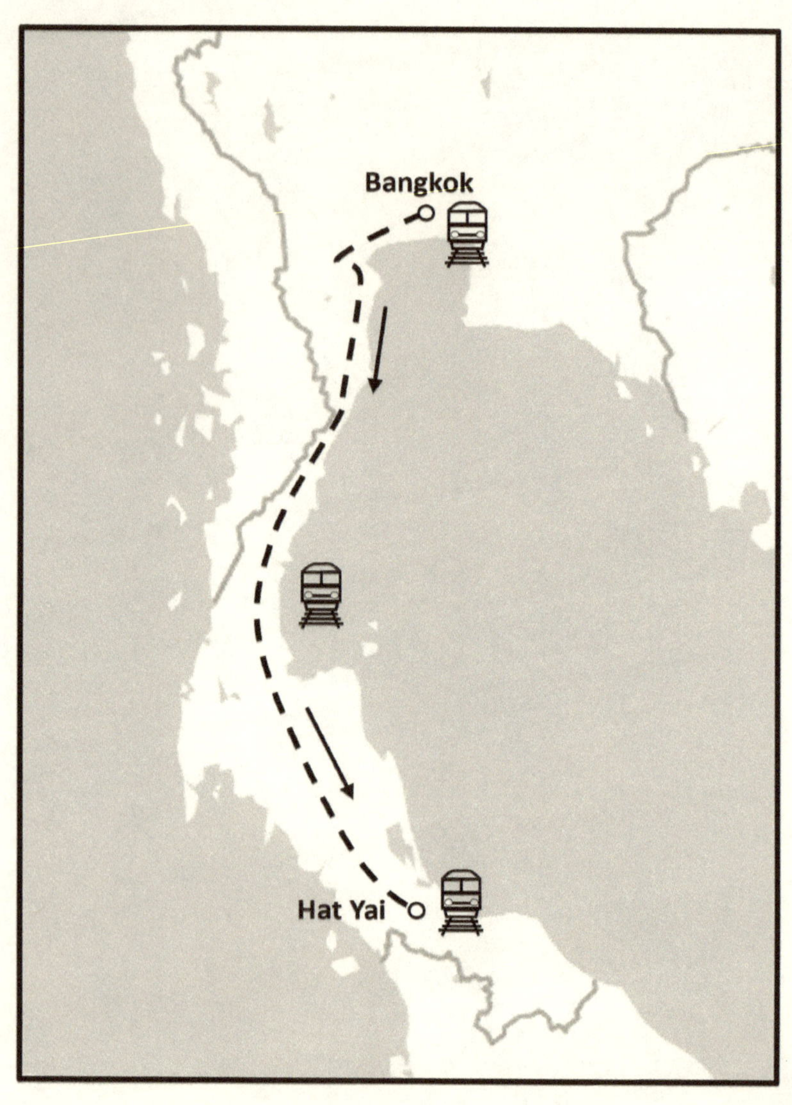

Bangkok
Hat Yai

17

False Meditation

I restlessly brought my stuff out from the train to the station platform. Once my stuff was brought down, I walked over to the cargo carriage and watched my bike being brought down by a few stevedores with contentment in me, looking at my bike still in one piece without any parts dangling.

I took out the receipt and hand it to one of the stevedores. He checked the receipt and said 'OK', but straight after the OK, he unexpectedly said something that I didn't have any impulse nor zest to say anything back to him.

He continuously chipped out like a parrot saying, "tip tip tip…" with the beckoning of hand asking for money.

What a start of the day.

The top box was fixed back to the bike's rack and all the stuff was loaded back on the bike. I pushed the bike out to where I saw several other bikes parked at one corner of the station. Then put the bike on the main stand, sat on the bike, and scrolled through the accommodation application for a place to stay.

This time round, I had an aim. I aimed to find a hotel instead of a hostel as I long to get a good sleep without having to be disturbed by any sound or whatsoever. But there was a dilemma.

It was too early to check in to any accommodation. However, it is still possible to check in early, but that is provided if there is a bed available for me, and also, it shouldn't be an expensive hotel.

I could call and check with the hotel receptionist on the room availabilities, but after much scrolling on the application looking at the many hotel listings and checking on their room rates, I stopped searching for one. The thing is, who would even want to entertain me at 6:30 am?

Some hotels would be keen to take me in and entertain me if I'm willing to pay for the previous day's night which would require me to check out before noon or earlier on the same day. And then I would need to pay for a new night stay after the check-out time, which meant that I would be paying for two nights for a night stay. Well, I could pay for two nights, but then, I wasn't the type of person who would want to spend my money meaninglessly. It may seem like a miser, but the real reason was that I preferred to splurge my money on food instead of spending much on a hotel room.

Well, it's just me.

As the morning was still early, I switched off my phone and leaned back against the orange bag covering myself with my riding jacket to take a nap. However, the light sleeper me, I couldn't sleep for long as the station became busier with people walking behind me, forklift drivers driving back and forth taking cargo and unloading the cargo, and sporadically I heard station speakers announcing anything that's related to train services. From all the noises, it was better off to leave the station.

As I sat up on my bike, I sprouted out an idea after looking at the atmosphere outside the station brightening up by the sun's light. It wasn't an idea apparently. It was actually the promise I made on the day-five ride that I would venture around Bangkok with my bike and get to the centre of Bangkok, which I didn't get the chance due to the terrible traffic at that point of time. That said, it seemed like a good opportunity to fulfil that promise I made before.

Jacket on, helmet on, gloves on, off from the main stand, the engine started up like a charm, and off I went to fulfil my new mission. But it was only after a cup of coffee.

****

Bangkok's atmosphere was already bright and sunny in the early hours of the day. Everything around was brightened well enough to see and it was already hot under my jacket and in my helmet. The roads were fairly busy, but when I stopped at a right turn pocket at four junctions, it was hilarious to see more than ten motorcycles in the right turn pocket. The turn pocket extends as much as it wants whenever a motorcycle fills up from the sides of the imaginary pocket. Saying ten motorcycles on a right turn pocket seemed like exaggerating. But in reality, looking around over my shoulders, even twenty motorcycles didn't fit my computation.

And I have to say; when the light turned green for the bikes to move off, I felt so safe turning along with the other motorcyclists as though they were securing me all around like a wall.

The road surface was perilously smooth like a polished-up tarmac. I could even see some distorted reflections of buildings that shine on the road surface. That didn't mean that it was a good thing. It can be worrying if the rain were to fall.

As I approached the Bangkok centre, the roads became increasingly busier. When the traffic light shows red, the junction front of the stop line or what can be said as fading off stop line would be packed with lots of motorcycles. Some would look left and right and if it's all good to go, they will ride off even if the traffic light shows red. But the majority of the motorcyclists would wait patiently for the traffic light to count down to zero before riding off. (Most of the traffic lights in Thailand are the countdown timer type).

However, there's this particular incident I had experienced on the road that made me realise something fascinating about the local Thai people when someone beat the red light and cut across other motorcyclists in front of them.

It was when the traffic light turned green for my direction traffic to ride off. But there was this motorcyclist who beat the red light from the perpendicular junction and then crossed past my front and other motorcyclists around me. I did get angered by it, but when I looked at the other motorcyclists on my right, I was amused to see the other motorcyclists showed no reaction to the rider nor reacted disparagingly. They ride as normal after the red-light-beater rides past them, and life goes on as normal. If this were to happen in Singapore, and from my everyday experience as a delivery rider on the road, I would see all kinds of reactions from the road users and all types of profanity spewing out from the drivers' mouths. I have to admit; I have an itchy mouth too.

Maybe it was just one incident that I was lucky enough to see the good motorcyclists on my right, right? Nope. As I rode to the many junctions in Bangkok, I had seen the same occurrence of someone beating the red light and I would see the same reactionless from the other Thai motorcyclists. But definitely, there would be someone being angered by it, right? That's possible. But the many I had seen, many were reactionless.

It made me realise that it was indeed the right thing not to react to some things that aren't worth keeping in mind. I could think back to those times when I became infuriated when someone abruptly braked hard in front of me, or those times when someone cut into my lane dangerously which would provoke me to flick my universal middle finger or say something profane. But to think back, it was all unnecessary. Why should I waste my time, my energy, and my brain synapses on someone I don't know? Wouldn't the rider be offended if I were to say something profane and show my universal middle finger? Wouldn't the rider come after me if the rider is a mentally unsound person? Wouldn't I have to deal with something meaningless and have the rider renting space in my brain so I can criticise him whenever I want? All these can be avoided by just not reacting to anything nor even looking at someone, like how the Thai motorcyclist showed no resentfulness to the rider who beat the red light.

I thought about it and realised how easy it was to not react to something, and I thought of adapting to like how the Thai motorcyclist reacted. It may not be easy for the first few tries, but it is doable if I persistently try. With that said, I promised myself to practice displaying a reactionless face whenever shit happens.

I rode past Ratchadamri Road and Phetchaburi Road. My unbelievable eyes of mine were amazed to see the large malls that were around me. Central World Mall, Big C, Platinum Fashion Mall, and Palladium Mall were the few malls that I had passed by that looked huge and grander with many advertisements' brands embellished to the façades of the malls, and there were also huge LCD screens displayed ads on the mall's facade.

Mesmerised by what was around, it reminded me of walking on the walkways next to the malls on my first solo trip to Bangkok a few years ago. I remembered wandering about on the walkway drinking that pomegranate juice in plastic bottles sold on the street vendor carts and taking pictures of whatever compelled me. At that point of time, I had no motorcycle licence, nor had I even thought of getting one. But just within a few years later, things changed so much. I was once a person who hated motorcycles, but ironically riding a motorcycle on the road of Bangkok now. How hilarious can that be, and how things have changed in just a few years? It somehow made me think that just making a small change could make me achieve a new milestone, even if it weren't a grand achievement like owning a Rolls Royce. Well, I'll leave that for the future perhaps.

With more available time left before looking for a hotel, I rode over to find for tyre shop as the rear wheel tyre tread depth had gone down dangerously low and also, it was the perfect time to have it replaced.

Fortunately, the tyre shops were open early, and the rear tyre was changed within less than half an hour. After which, I got back on the road again to venture around Bangkok to see the many monuments that were around, such as *Victory Monument, Democracy Monument, King Tak-Sin the Great State Monument, King Rama Vi Monument,* and also rode over to Bangkok's very own Chinatown at Yaowarat Road.

At all the places I have been to, I took many pictures with my bike and myself as something told me that it would be my last time here with my current bike and there would never be a next time again. It seems true to think of, as I have only a few years left before my bike's ridable statutory period ends, and I can no longer ride this bike. I have to accept that in future. But in the meantime, spending the best times with my bike is the right thing to do before heading over to find a place to stay for the night.

*****

The hotel room had turned dark, and I was dazed as I woke up looking at the darkness in the room. A sudden panic ignited in me, thinking it was already morning and I wondered how many meals I had missed. But after checking the date and the time on my phone, I realised that it was still the day I had check in on, and the time had turned 7 in the evening.

My stomach growled and I had an apprehensive mind that told

me that I had missed much of what was out there in Bangkok by just taking a long siesta in the afternoon. It should be the continuous ride from the past day's afternoon ride that made me think that I was missing much. Nevertheless, I made a new mission to do night riding in Bangkok but not wear heavy wear this time round. Simple wear of a dry-fit top, shorts, and shoes was more than enough to see Bangkok. But not a recommended wear, of course.

The road wasn't as busy as I thought, and the weather was just right to ride on. Street vendors can be seen along the many soi out there, and many locals were having their meals on the roadside stalls. There's no way one would go hungry saying there aren't many foods vendor in Bangkok. There were many food vendors everywhere on almost all the soi I had passed on.

The malls looked even more exclusive at night than during the daytime, with their façades decorated with Christmas themes embellishments and the streets bustling with locals and tourists. There were several night markets I had passed by, and the common ones were the *Silom Night Market, Palladium Market* and also the well-known market called *Patpong Night Market,* where the market is just next to go-go bars and strip clubs, which made the market appear lively. I had already walked on all of these markets on my first trip to Bangkok, and all these markets sell comparable items that can be seen from other markets too. At one of the markets, something had excited me to take a picture of myself with my bike at the entrance of the market. It was the entrance of the *Patpong Night Market*. I don't know why, but I had to do it.

I stopped at the front of the *Patpong Night Market* entrance to see a lit-up pin-drop signboard. And around the area of the sign, people were standing around holding onto a laminated card in their hands and smiling at me. I asked one of them to take a picture of me with my bike and with the pin-drop signboard. He took many shots then handed my phone back to me and asked, "Wow, you come very far, my friend?"

"Yes bro. Very far."

"Since you come far away, you must see Ping Pong show," he said, showing me the laminated card of the many types of *shows*. Some of the few shows on the card were "shooting balloon", "chopstick", "blowing candle", and "open bottle". Normal shows, right? But I have yet to complete the sentences. I've intentionally missed out the first word of each show as the word resonates with a body part that starts with 'V', and it's not v for vertebrae.

Oh my…

I shook my head laughing while passing the laminated card back to him and thanked the person as I mentally knew what all these were. Well, it was just easy to comprehend what the words meant on the laminated card.

***

The following morning, the fourth day of the return trip, I woke up dreadfully tired and yearned for a helicopter to take me back home. Probably it all started from the long train ride from Chiang Mai to Bangkok that made me yearn for that. It made me ponder whether I should take another train down to the south of Thailand or ride back on my own.

However, I didn't have a tough time rationalising which mode of transport I should use to head south. Taking the railway train still came up to be the best option after looking at the Google Maps that showed me a freaking 940 kilometres from Bangkok till ending at Hat Yai city. I chose Hat Yai as the city to disembark – about 80 kilometres north of the Sadao border, Thailand – to merely get the route stickers from a well-known sticker shop in Hat Yai, along the street of Sripoovanart Road. It's where many overlanders from both Malaysia and Singapore would stop by to get route stickers or do a custom design sticker.

But which border will I cross back after purchasing the stickers? Having entered Thailand from the Betong border on the day-two ride, and considering both Thai and Malaysia immigration allowed me entry despite the state of my passport, shouldn't I exit from the same borders I had entered from? It made sense to me I should indeed exit via the Betong border. That also meant that I must ride from Hat Yai to the Betong border after purchasing the route stickers.

I checked the distance from Hat Yai to the Betong border. It came up to about 260 kilometres. Well, what is 260 kilometres when I had ridden over 700 kilometres on day-one?

I tried my best not to be complacent.

The first thing for the day was to ride to Bangkok Railway Station with the goal in mind to get a first-class ticket. I arrived at the station and parked my bike in the same area where I parked when I first arrived at this station.

The station was busy with people walking about carrying lots of luggage in their hands, loudspeaker announcements informing the train boarding time, and there were also lots of backpackers walking about the station. I walked straight to the ticket counter to queue up and saw some backpackers queuing up in front of me. At one moment, I heard disgruntled voices at the front, which made me peep to the front and see a dissatisfied look on the face of a backpacker at the ticket counter. An instant thought came to me that I have a 50 per cent chance of getting a first-class train ticket with bedding in it. But I couldn't complain much about it. It was already half past eleven when I arrived at the train station and it was considerably late to get a ticket if I want to board a train that is few hours later.

The long queue I was on had come to my turn and I was exhilarated to know that there were two available timings for first-class trains with bedding in them. But the conversation with the ticket staff cut off when I said that I would want to transport my bike to Hat Yai.

"You check your motorcycle?"

"What do you mean by that?" I replied with a perplexed look on my face.

"Go there and check your bike," he points in a direction that points to the wall next to him.

"You mean on my left?" I asked after taking a wide look around on my left, but to see only people walking in and out of the main station foyer. He then stood up from his chair and came close to the counter glass front with a disdainful look on him.

"You turn left, turn right, you go check your motorcycle," he replied scornfully and sat back down and looked at the computer screen. I was still perplexed by what he meant, but I didn't ask any more questions after his scornful reply. I said OK and walked to where he pointed and like what he had said, "turn left, turn right," but it brought me just out of the main station foyer. I became even more perplexed about it and recalled my memory at the Chiang Mai Railway Station, where I first purchased the ticket before even riding to the cargo department. I thought maybe I should get my bike checked first before getting the ticket so that the cargo department can check if there was enough space for my bike to fit in the cargo carriage. I walked looking around for signs and tried to figure out what the ticket staff meant, but nothing visually heeded my attention and I wondered whom I should look for to get my bike checked. But there was one wooden-hut-like booth near where I parked my bike, and it had an English sign above that stated: Scales. I went over to ask a man inside the booth where I could get my bike checked. However, in return, the man gave a perplexed look instead and then replied, "You have ticket?"

"No ticket," I replied.

"You buy ticket, you come here."

I nodded and walked back to the ticket counter to look for the staff, but he wasn't there in his seat, and the seat was empty. I got back to a new long queue again and waited for my turn. When my turn came to ask the staff for the first-class train, guess what, there wasn't any first-class ticket left!

"Sir, we have 2nd class train," the ticket staff replied, and my ears eased off slightly as I was thankful that it wasn't a 3rd class train.

"Good. So, can I load my motorcycle in?"

He stopped for a moment to think and then said, "Cannot. The train no cargo." The small happiness had faded off fast.

"How many cc your motorbike?"

"135. I asked them already. They say can. They say my bike no problem," I lied. I lied to avoid getting the same answer: "You check your bike?"

He nodded while he checked on something and told me that my bike could be put on another train, and said that I had to check it with the cargo man.

"Sir, do you want to get 2nd class, sitting with friend at 3:10."

That "sitting with friend" resonated back to the woman I spoke to at the information counter in Chiang Mai Railway Station. That meant I was going to sit for long again. But it's 2nd class this time. Better than 3rd class train, right?

"Is there other train?" I asked.

"Yes we have, at 1 pm. 3rd class, sitting…."

"Er…I will get the 2nd class train then."

I had about three hours to board the train. I rode back to get all my stuff in the hotel, checked out, and returned to the station. Back in the station, I parked the bike at the usual spot again, then purchased the ticket from the Scales hut I had earlier been to. Then again, I brought down all the stuff from the bike, and then I waited for stevedores to take my bike away to the cargo carriage. But no one came. I waited and waited, but still, no one came. There was this man, standing metres away from my bike wearing an orange vest like other stevedores which initiated me to ask him about my bike. I asked who would bring my bike over to the cargo carriage, and an instant answer came saying, "Sir, let me help you. You relax."

I thought to myself that I met a good Samaritan who was trying to help me out. He checks my ticket and writes down the train number, and then calls another stevedore to pick my bike up, but before the stevedore even pushes my bike over to the cargo carriage, both the men which I had perceived to think as good Samaritans, had instantly changed my preconceived thought after they said something.

They both stand side-by-side and then start to parrot off: "tip tip tip…."

Not all are good Samaritans though.

***

The boarding time came. I carried my stuff to the cabin walking through the aisle looking at the seats split into two-seater seats and all facing one direction. This time round, the seats could be reclined to a certain degree and I got the window seat. Besides that, everything appeared the same, from the luggage storage railings above the windows, the dusty ceiling fan, and the same window type that would require me to pull up the windowpane to shut the window. This is what a 2nd class train is like and I wondered who would be my 'sitting with friend'.

The majority of the seats were already occupied 10 minutes before the train departure time at 3:10 pm. However, the seat next to me wasn't occupied, and I hoped no one would do so as I was already planning how to use both seats to sleep at night later.

While I waited for the train to depart, three kaki uniform personnel came up to the front of the aisle and randomly picked some passengers to check on their passports. Rather than looking at the passport stringently, they looked cheerful to the passengers and there were even passengers taking a selfie picture with the uniform personnel. Then, one of the three officers, who seemed like the most senior officer of the three, picked a random passenger and posed for a picture with the passenger as though the officer was doing his checks stringently. Once the pictures were taken by the other officers, the officer and the passenger would laugh and have a quick chat before moving over to the next randomly picked passenger.

One of the officers came next to my seat with a smile on his face, and I instantly handed him my passport. All he does is leaf through the passport pages to a random page, look for a second, then close the passport, and then look at the passport cover that has the Singapore name and a heraldic symbol on it.

"Singapore?" He asked.

"Yes, from Singapore."

"Welcome to Thailand," he said cheerfully, then returned the passport to me. Not sure if it was the power of the Singapore passport or is it just that the Thai people are generally amicable. Well, the latter one seemed more true to me.

The train engine started, and I could feel the train's vibration evidently. But still, no one came to occupy the seat next to me. As I thought of the several sleeping patterns I could do on both the seats for the night, an older man came walking on the aisle and stopped right next to the empty seat. He wore a Panama hat, a brown short-sleeve shirt that that resembled a traditional Indonesian batik shirt, paired with long black pants. And in his right hand, he held onto a black briefcase.

Outside the window, a family stopped right next to the window. A woman and a man were holding onto a child on his arm, and they waved at the older man. The time I had spent planning how to sleep with the two seats had all gone to waste. But once the older man smiled at me while taking off his hat and then wearing it back on, I forget what I thought about as the 'hats off' thing he did somehow resembled an olden movie where one does it to be polite. I smiled back and thought about whom I was going to handle for the train ride as I was too naïve to speak to a professional gentleman.

He lifted his briefcase to place it on the luggage railing above, but his arms struggled to put it up and shook violently. I got out of my seat to help him, and then the older man said thank you and did the hats off to me again. I gave my naïve smile again and got back to my seat.

The train moved off exactly on time and I watched the family outside the window waving off to the older man and he waved back at them. It felt as though I was in those old movies where this type of train scene commonly be seen in a movie.

After the waves parted, the older man spoke to me in Thai, but I didn't comprehend what he said for which I shook my head not knowing what he meant.

"I'm not Thai, sir. I'm from Singapore." He became amused and tried to speak with his little-known English words, but from those words, I was still unable to comprehend what he was trying to say, but I just nodded to him. I tried to articulate the English words slowly, but still, he couldn't comprehend what I was trying to say and we were shaking our heads much of the time. I tried using Google Translate, but still, it didn't help. So, there wasn't any fruitful conversation to speak of, and I was stuck looking outside the window watching the landscape pass by.

Hours passed, and the good old walking vendors walked past the aisle selling their goods, but there weren't as many walking vendors compared to yesterday's train ride. Knowing that these walking vendors would come by even past midnight, I kept myself prepared to have supper since I would be spending more time awake than sleeping anyway.

At one moment along the train ride, the older man took off his sandals and sat cross-legged on his seat, resting both his hands on his knees. The seat itself wasn't wide enough for someone to sit cross-legged, and his left knee was already hitting on my right thigh. I moved closer to the left of my seat to let him have some space as he looked like he was about to do a prayer or meditate on his seat as his eyes were already closed.

Ten minutes passed, and my presumption became all wrong. The older man slept and snored loudly with his mouth open up wide. My kindness in giving some of my territorial seat space to him was a foolish thing to me. But what can I do? I continued looking outside the window and watched the atmosphere turned dark slowly.

Another hour passed, and the older man's snores were consistently going on for a long time. I cramped myself to the left of my seat and leaned my cheek on the window frame watching the dark atmosphere go by. His cross-legged then became more relaxed and loosened out till it took more of my seat space on my right.

What can I do? He looked like a tired old man that wanted to have a good sleep for a long time but chose to have it on the train instead. And the unfortunate me have no choice but to sit still beside him. I let it be and let him enjoy his snore.

But then, it was going on for a long time.

He only woke up when the screeching train sound was too unbearable for him and the other times when the walking vendor walked pass shouting out their goods name. When all were gone, within minutes, he got back to his loud snores incessantly. I wondered how my neighbouring passengers who were around felt having to hear the loud snores for a long time, though.

It was getting cold after 9 pm. I had pulled up the windowpane next to me and ledged. But the couple that was seated in front of me struggled to pull up the windowpane to close the window that kept sliding down. Although the window next to me was shut, the window that was next to the couple blew in the chilly air and aerodynamically flew to the back and hit on my face. To take refuge, I leaned my forehead on the back of the seat in front of me while my left ear heard the gushing sound of the chilly wind, and on my right, unfortunately, the snores from the older man persisted.

"What a wonderful ride," I thought.

It was truly a dreary and boring ride. After many attempts by the couple to ledge up the windowpane, they finally managed to ledged it up, and I went back leaning against the edge of the window frame and continued to absorb the train's vibration.

I was amused by the longevity of the older man's snores that kept going on and on for a long time. But I had an idea. It was an idea not to let him snore as my brain suffered from the prolonged sound of his snores. I tried some sound effects, like making coughing sounds which did help to wake him up and cut off his snores. He became conscious when I did, and he then looked around for a while then went back to his deep sleep. Unfortunately, the snores came back to life again.

Sometimes, giving up does make sense.

The cabin was humid as usual and the many face wipes on my shirt still went on without fail. The passenger in the cabin reduced after 11 pm, and this time round, I slept 30 minutes to an hour interval. But on each interval, I would be woken up by the sudden loud snore that penetrated through my right ear or the loud screeching sound from the train wheels.

The long awaiting to have something to eat after midnight became a nightmare. No walking vendor came up after midnight, even when the train stopped at other stations. I was really hungry and angry, and I dreaded thinking that I had made a wrong assumption thinking that the walking vendor would still come after midnight.

I still kept myself motivated and hoped for the walking vendor to come on the train at 1 am. But still, no one came. After one, after two, after three, no food passed the aisle. The sad and hungry me just tried to close my eyes and cover up much time and waited for breakfast in the morning.

At around 4 am, I awaken up to see the older man getting off his seat and heading to the toilet. But when he returned to his seat, he passed his seat. I pretended to stretch my arm and turned back to look at him, he sat several seats behind me, and he was back to his cross-legged sitting again. I guess my attempts to stop him from snoring only came to his consciousness only after his toilet break.

My endeavour had been proven triumph perhaps.

Even though I felt contented after the older man sat far away from me, I came to a point where I couldn't get my eyes closed but just stared out of the window till the dark atmosphere slowly discoloured.

The long hours on the train had gone by, and I somehow managed to survive the great ordeal. The walking vendor came back to life after 6 am. The breakfast that intrigued me to get was the hot coffee and two palm-sized fritter doughs. Not sure if I was overly overwhelmed by the breakfast from the night fasting, but I have to say, the best fritter dough I've ever had was actually on this train ride.

It was already past 8 am, but the train still hadn't come to my destination. The train halted at many points along the way, and the exceptionally tired me, couldn't wait to disembark from the train. As the train got closer to my destination, the remaining passengers in the cabin started to get off their seats and started bringing down their stuff from the luggage railing above.

I did like what the rest did to bring down their stuff, and the older man came back to take his briefcase down. But he struggled to get his briefcase down to which I got off my seat to help him. But this time round, there weren't any hats off to thank me, instead, I saw a grumpy-looking face.

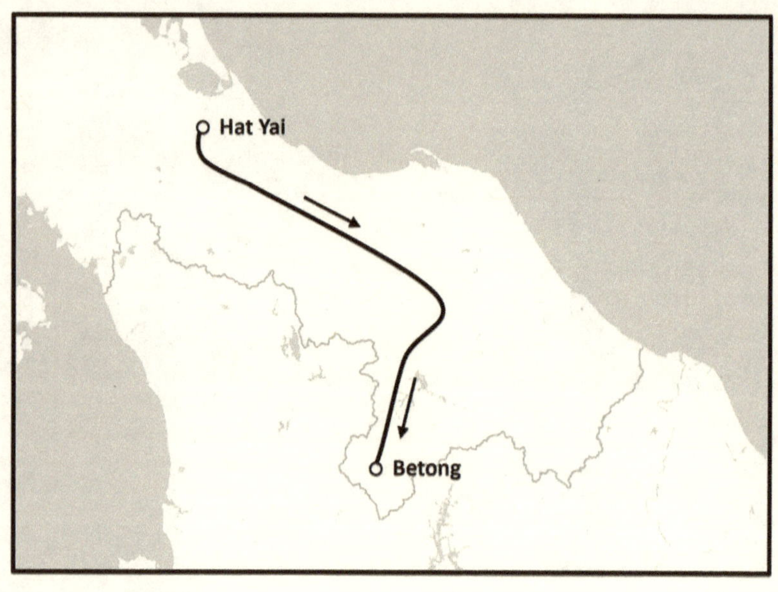

Hat Yai
Betong

18

Double the Trouble

The train came to a halt at Haad Yai Station after half past 8. The long and gruelling 17 hours of the ride had come to an end, and I had finally disembarked from the train sluggishly with deep carvings of dark circles around my eyes. My stuff was brought down to the station platform, and I waited for the train that had my bike in it. But then, I had no clue when will the train arrive at this station after looking at the incomprehensible writings on the cargo ticket.

Too battered to even think about doing anything, I just waited and watched other trains pass by me sporadically. I walked back and forth to the station platform; I stood and stared at the train track; I sat on the station platform leaning against the wall behind me, and continued to stare at the open blank space in front of me. Then finally, I settled down to lie, resting my head on my riding jacket. I was just dead tired.

Only when I heard the sound of a walkie-talkie, I woke up to see a security guard standing next to me saying something in Thai, and like as usual, the words were incomprehensible to me. But the only word I comprehended was the word 'motorbike' that came out from the guard's mouth. I sat up and saw a stevedore pushing a black bike at one end of the station platform which I intuitively knew that was mine. However, I was just too battered to even put a smile on my face.

My stuff was loaded back on the bike as usual, and I set off to make my way to the sticker shop to honour this bike its success before riding to Betong town. Reaching the sticker shop, which is along Sripoovanart Road, I parked the bike at the kerbside and happened to see several other Singapore-registered vehicles parked along the kerbside too. I walked into the sticker shop like I knew whom I should approach and waved to the workers in the shop like I knew all of them. But none of them knew me – except for an older worker who remembered me arriving at this shop on my return trip from Phuket. But the rest of the workers played along waving at me as though they knew me too.

After a while of explaining to the staff what sticker designs I wanted to get, the staff told me it would take a while to get my stickers printed out as they had back-end orders yet to be done. I agreed to wait, and when I was flipping a folder to look at the sticker designs, I noticed that the other Singaporeans who were in the shop were curiously looking at me – probably because of my Singaporean accent when I spoke to the staff. Some went out of the shop to check on my bike and came back to me and questioned me where I had ridden to, whom I rode with, how long my trip was, and many more usual questions that I have heard along my journey came to my ears again. I answered them and received many compliments, and I was indeed flattered by them. However, I have to say; it was the first time I wasn't motivated or in the mood to have a conversation with anyone. Although I hadn't done something physically demanding, I was psychosomatically drained out from the train ride. The exhaustion was different from any other day of my ride, and I thought about my day-one terrible ride in the rain. But still, it wasn't a match for the train ride.

Who should I blame? I had to blame myself as I was the decision-maker for everything that happened on my road trip.

I gave my fake smile to them, tried to stay focused on listening to them, and tried to give my best presentation. But my mouth spewed out short answers which made the conversation short, peculiar, and monotonous to the listeners. I don't know why, but it was also my very first time trying to flee from getting praised for my accomplishments and soon enough, the short conversation with the Singaporeans ended fast. I thanked them before returning to my bike to look for a carwash shop since the stickers would take some time to get readied.

I managed to find a carwash shop which wasn't far off from the sticker shop but to see only one worker in the shop pressure spraying a vehicle. I stopped by and asked the worker if he could wash my bike; I was told that it would take a while to get it done. I agreed to wait, left my bike at the shop, and looked for a food stall to get breakfast. I happened to find one and spent almost an hour there having breakfast and spent much of my time scrolling on social media applications, hoping that when I got back to the carwash shop, the bike would be done washing.

Unfortunately, when I reached the carwash shop, the lone worker was still working on the same vehicle. He then told me it would soon be my turn and apologised for the long wait. Can't fault him as he was the lone person in the shop.

I walked over to the sticker shop, the earlier people in the shop had gone off, and unknown faces were around. Asking the staff if the stickers were done, the reply came from the staff nodding left and right in slow-motion and a sympathising look came. It meant that I had to wait even longer.

It was only after three hours of waiting, the route stickers were done printing, and my bike washed up and dry-cleaned. Within the hours, I had walked back and forth to the sticker shop and the car wash shop, made many scrolls on the social media application, done lots of blank staring in the open space, and even listened to the carwash worker's problems while he worked on my bike.

I wonder why he chose me to tell his problems though. But with all due respect, it was truly the wrong time to talk to me as my exhaustion had elevated, and I was staring at the open blank space nodding and nodding the whole time.

***

Back on the road, my journey to Betong town commenced. The roads were wet as I rode on, and the clouds above were greying as I covered distance. I stopped to wear the rain gear but did not zip up the rain jacket as the weather was interchanging between hot and cold. However, I had to switch off the body camera to better prepare myself so when the rain pours, all I had to do is to stop at the side of the road and zip up the rain jacket.

The roads brought me to the same old curvy asphalt and back to see the dense-looking forest on both sides of the road. Apart from the environment, my eyelids started to close and open involuntarily, and the blinking rate increased exponentially.

As I rode and rode, I felt my eyelids roll much more rapidly than before and they became heavier, to which I had to force myself to stop somewhere to take a break.

I came by to a small town and stopped next to a 7-Eleven store. I got myself a well-known Thai Red Bull energy drink in a 100ml glass bottle, and a ready-to-eat black pepper beef burger to give me at least a certain amount of energy to keep me going. I don't know what rationale I had, but I just wanted something to fill my stomach.

I left the store and sat on the steps in front of the store to consume my meal. Not only did I sit on the steps, but there was also a man in a white top sitting on the other end of the store and avidly uses his phone. And as usual, I would look around my vicinity and inadvertently make eye contact with someone – which was to the white top man now, and the usual me gave a benign smile and a nod. However, he returned a contemptuous look at me instead and returned to use his phone.

As I munched on my burger, a dark grey vehicle with tinted windows all around the vehicle stopped opposite the roadside directly in front of me. A woman in a full black burqa, slightly plump in size, came out from the vehicle and walked towards my direction crossing the road. Only her eyes area could be seen, and from the look at the woman from a distance, her right arm was missing. I was like, "Man... bless her" and felt sorry and turned away from looking at her. But I just didn't know why; I gave another glance at her again. But this time round, as she approached closer to my direction and from the sunlight casting on her, I saw her right hand under her left shoulder that's under her hijab (scarf). I was like, "I take back my words. She was just scratching her shoulder."

But it appeared odd. She was looking at the man in the white top and then walked toward him. That man then saw the woman approach closer to him; he stood up from the steps, said something in Thai to her in a delighted way and took out a blue plastic bag from his sling bag.

Just as I bit on my burger, on my right, I heard a quick footsteps sound in my right ear. I quickly turned to my right to see two young men speed pass in front of me – almost having kneed by one of the men to my face – and they both jumped over to the white top man. And at the same time, two other young men came jumping onto the man from the other end of the 7-Eleven store and pinned him down to the ground. Then, there came a loud cry from the white top man, which spooked the atmosphere around and made whatever sounds around the vicinity silent.

My heart palpitated fast, and I was stunned to see what had just happened. More men came scrambling toward the white top man to grab hold of him. Crowds started to form fast, and many were clad in their *sarongs* (a long fabric wrapped around the waist and tucked at the waist). The odd thing about the scene was that I was the only one close to this scene and munching on a burger.

One of the men took the blue plastic bag from the apprehended man's hand and searched inside. However, I wasn't able to see what was in the bag as the people around the apprehended man blocked my viewpoint. All I saw was a man checking the bag and nodding to the other men around him and said something in Thai. Then more cries came from the apprehended man, and I soon realised I was in the middle of a drug bust. It felt like I was in some kind of mission-impossible scene, and this guy was being extra in their mission. Well, that was me.

The crowd gathered more, and even the staff in the 7-Eleven store came out to see what the commotion was about. The dark grey vehicle that was parked opposite the road earlier came to the kerbside close to me, and a man brought the woman in a black burqa back in the vehicle and they left the scene.

I took out my phone wanting to take a picture of the scene, but one of the men, saw me holding my phone up and he started yelling at me something in Thai. And then all stared at me. Two men shouted "PHONE! PHONE!" at me then the two men scurried fast towards me.

And at that very moment, I knew I f*cked up.

They both came to me and kept yelling at me in Thai, for which I immediately showed them my phone telling them that I didn't take any pictures. Despite showing my phone to them, they kept yelling something in Thai to me and the next thing I did was to say, "I, riding motorcycle, fun, enjoy… I love Thailand." I spoke in a broken manner so they could at least get something out of the sentence and even pointed at my bike parked at the kerbside.

I had another bite on my burger to keep myself cool and mentally told myself that I'm innocent. One of them still wasn't pleased with me and pointed at my body camera which I wore on my upper chest and yelled at me, "CAMERA! CAMERA!". I told them that my body camera was switched off, and I even demonstrated to them that the intermittent flashes of red LED light only show when it's 'on', and when there is no red light, it meant 'off.' It took me a while to make them comprehend, but I was mentally contented that I had switched off earlier before even reaching here. If not, I would probably not see my body camera again.

They looked at my body camera and nodded to themselves like they have understood what I was trying to explain to them. But it didn't end there. One of them shouted, "ID! ID!" at me even though I was just right next to him. I told them that I rode from Singapore and only had a passport with me, and then another guy shouted, "PASSPORT! PASSPORT!" Incensed by their unconscionable screaming, I kept my cool and told them that it was inside the top box and pointed at my bike at the kerbside. Then one of the men grabbed my left arm, and the other man grabbed my right arm, lifted me to stand, and walked me over to my bike while I still held on to my burger. I took out the passport from the top box and passed it to one of the men, and he checked on it while the other man checked on my phone.

I leaned on the top box, took another bite of the burger, and watched what they did. The man who checked my passport leafed through the pages, and he seemed unsure of what he was doing;

neither the other man knew what he was looking for in my phone's photo gallery. The man who checked on my passport did the same thing as the officer on the train who leafed through my passport to a random page, then flipped back to the front cover page of the passport, and then gave a wicket smile to me. He said something in Thai to the other man and handed over my passport to him and walked away. The other man then returned my phone, and he did the same thing by leafing to a random page and then returning back to me. Before he walked away, he gave me a wicket smile on me too and said, "Welcome to Thailand." I stood there baffled by what had happened and wondered for a moment if they were even a police officer or were they were all friends pranking among themselves. I just didn't know.

I sat back to where I had sat on the steps and watched the whole scene like a movie but substituted the popcorn with a burger. Another vehicle came and brought the apprehended man into the vehicle and they left the scene. After which, the rest of the men had a popsicle party and I watched them with a baffled look on my face.

The crowd subsided and eventually, everyone went off. Another vehicle came, and the rest went in the vehicle and one of the men who interrogated me, gave a wicked smile at me again and unwinds the door window to close before the vehicle drove off.

I have to say, the man replicated like a movie scene which made me tempted to show my middle finger at him. But then, I stayed sane as I remembered not to show any expression like how the Thai motorcyclists were on the road junctions, which saved me from another trouble.

***

The roads were curvy and wet as I got going with my ride. My eyelids were getting even heavier than before, and my blinks increased exponentially. But my mind still badgered me to keep on going and telling myself, "Paradise is soon to come," but the ride felt like a never-ending one. I thought that my meal earlier would keep me awake, but then, it was working inversely.

I throttle more to cover more distance and negotiate the bends dangerously fast. Then I came to meet up with an old and dilapidated van that puffs out thick black smoke from the exhaust pipe and rides slowly in front of me. The van carried school children, and some of the children playfully pretended to shoot at me through the rear window with imaginary handguns. I dodged the fake bullets and played along to shoot back with sound effects like *pew *pew. It made laughter and smiles on the little faces, and I overtook the van and sped even faster wanting to get to Betong town badly.

Kilometres after kilometres, the weight of my eyelids became even heavier, and I had trouble keeping them open. I closed my eyes for a second longer and then forcefully opened them again. Then an illogical idea sprouted in my mind to intermittently close my eyes for a second and somehow convince myself that it would help me stay longer on the road. I did that many times to which my mind pressured me to keep it close for longer than a second.

At one moment, I closed my eyes for longer than a second, but as I opened my eyes back, it was already too late.

I came fast to a sharp right bend but the handlebar was still level with my shoulder to which I had passed the supposed point to steer the handlebar to the right to negotiate the bend. In fear, I pulled the hand brake lever hard and depressed the foot brake hard that made the rear brake lock the wheel, making the bike slip – like a person falling after stepping onto a banana skin.

I got apart from my bike, and the bike slammed on one side to the ground and skidded off the road and bashed into the bushes. Me, my back slammed against the ground – with my left shoulder being the first contact – and I heard a "squishing" sound from my left shoulder. Then I skidded for a few metres due to the wet ground and finally came to a complete halt.

As I lie on the ground looking up the grey clouds, I realised that I had watched the whole thing with my eyes open.

"I deserve it," my mind sounded.

When I was a kid, I watched WWE a lot and watched the wrestler Undertaker do his sit-up move and make the crowd go wild every time he did that. I would mimic the actions of Undertaker when I was a kid, but at that point of time, never have I thought I would be doing it in real circumstances in future.

I brought myself up to sit upright with excruciating pain in my left shoulder and stared at my unglamorous bike hanging by the bushes. No one witnessed my fall, nor was anyone around. It was me, myself, and I. Reality was there live, and I witnessed everything by myself.

I was in shock and had profound fear that I might have broken my left shoulder. I was in a blank state of mind, not knowing what to do as this was my very first accident. How ironic can it be to have my very first fall in someone's country but not in my home country? I painfully got up and walked to my bike with a fully woken-up mind, and my eyes were no longer blinking fast or heavily closes.

The first thing I looked for was my phone, which wasn't on the handlebar nor was there even a phone holder mount on the side mirror. The side mirror wasn't even there to speak of. As I looked into the bushes to search for my phone, I heard a motorcycle sound come from my back. I turned to see a few people on kapcai bikes, clad in their *baju kurung,* which is traditional wear in Malaysia.

The people hurried off from their bikes to me and asked me if I was OK. I nodded in pain and went to get my bike off from the bushes, but it slipped from my hands as my left shoulder hurt badly. The people around came to help me bring out the bike from the bushes to the road and I saw liquid dripping out from the engine. Still keeping myself positive after looking at the drips, I went on to look for my phone and in serenity, I found it metres away from the bike which was on the grass patch. The phone, phone holder, and the side mirror were all in one piece together when I found them. But unfortunately, the side mirror was broken. As I looked at the broken mirror, there came the old and dilapidated grey van from my back.

The happy children I had seen earlier weren't smiling after looking at me. "Eh, uncle nie!" I heard a kid shout to his fellow friends in the van, and the van driver asked if I was alright. I told him I was good and told them not to worry, but I was internally embarrassed by my position.

The phone still worked fine and there weren't any cracks on it. But the bike wasn't exactly like what I used to see. But the good thing was, the liquid that poured out from the engine wasn't from the engine apparently. Fortunately, the liquid drips were actually from the coolant tank after tracking the drips.

After having a thorough look at my bike, I realised the damages on the bike wasn't that bad after all. Some of the damages were like the brake pedal on the right side of the engine that had bend inwards which I couldn't depress with my foot; the mirror mount for the handlebar mirror had broken off to which it became redundant to screw back the side mirror; the front fairing where the signal indicator lights were at, the side edge of the fairing had broken and was filled with dry mud.

Apart from those damages, there was one thing I had to do that would tell me if I would carry on with my ride or get the bike towed away. I pressed the ignition button several times, but the engine didn't start up. But after kickstarting the engine several times, the engine roared back to life and the feeling of reviving the bike was one of the most glorifying things I have ever done on this road trip.

The people around were concerned about me and kept asking me if I was alright. I tried lifting my left arm parallel to the ground, but it couldn't be raised any higher, and it was excruciating pain to even lift up. The instinct that came to my mind was to get to the nearest hospital as I had no clue what was going on with my shoulder.

I asked the people around if they knew any hospital nearby. The looks on their faces were blurred as though they need not have one near their homes. But one told me that there would be one in Betong town as I told them that I was heading to the town. Since Betong town is another 79 kilometres and it was where I was heading to, I resolved to continue with my ride there.

One of the group of people came to me and patted my non-injured shoulder and looked me straight in the eyes, and asked me if I was sure to continue with my ride. At that very moment, I was clueless about what I wanted to do. All these were new to me, and it was only 'I' who had to decide what I want to do. I thought about my insurance, thought about the trouble processing it, and thought about the trouble getting the claims and etcetera. This wasn't an accident with any vehicle; it was an accident with me. With the thoughts I had in my mind, an instinct told me to get back on the road and use whatever I had learned from my prior days' ride and not be a fool on the road.

I thanked the people around me for the help, and I got back on the road to Betong town. But this time round, it was all on full awareness.

No phone holder to make use of, so the phone was placed on top of the jerrycan, and the netting on the jerrycan held it down.

But that wasn't an issue. The issue was the handlebar that had bent on one side and misaligned with the front fork, which induced me to veer the bike to one side. However, somehow, I recollected the time when I did this similar ride back when I first got this bike from the previous owner. I remembered riding around the car park getting used to the bike and not having a clue back then issue with the steering cone that caused the bike to veer to one side. As I had the experience of how I handled the bike and still did delivery with it, it made me quickly click on that riding style and I rode the bike like it hasn't been on any accident.

It was odd that I would be using a futile skill, but it indeed came in handy someday.

The atmosphere was turning dark and the feeling of getting to Betong town was like the feeling of reaching to Golden Triangle. As I drew closer to the Betong town, I pondered about whether I should find a hotel first to unload all my stuff or head straight to a hospital. The better option that came to mind was to get to the same hotel I had accommodated on day-two before heading to the hospital as I knew where the parking area for the bike was.

I reached Betong town and rode back to the same hotel and back to the same parking place. As I walked to the receptionist's desk to check in, the receptionist knew something wasn't right from the look on my face. Asking me if I was alright, I told her what had happened and said I wanted to see a doctor. The receptionist empathised with me and instructed a bellboy to carry my stuff up to my room, and I even had two staff to help me take off the rain jacket and the riding jacket from me. The bellboy offered to take me to the hospital using his kapcai bike, which I gladly hopped on to the backseat and off he went.

As I entered the foyer of the hospital, the floor was pretty busy with people standing around and walking about at the foyer. I went over to register at a counter with the help from the bellboy for the translation to the nurse of my situation. The nurse then gave me a ticket, and I was told to sit on a bench and wait for my name to be called out.

One hour passed, and I was still on the bench and watched many patients walk past in front of me and watched the bellboy play *Mobile Legends* game on his phone. I asked the bellboy to head back to the hotel first as I felt like I was holding him back from his work. But he seemed to be contented to play the game to which I forgot about asking him to go back.

Another hour passed, and my turn finally came to see the doctor in the emergency room. The bellboy went in with me, but the nurse asked the bellboy to leave the room. From there on, the bellboy left and then went back to the hotel.

I sat and waited at the doctor's desk and watched a lone doctor and a few nurses walk in and out of the emergency room. The room was practically spacious and only one bed was being used up by an elderly patient, but the patient had lots of tubes around him. I prevented myself from looking at the elderly patient as the curtain around the bed wasn't closed, and the room was filling up with cries from the loved ones around the elderly patient and the loves ones were reciting the verses from the Quran book. There was a Chinese kid too. He was at one side of the room with a worried mother in front of him to block the kid from looking at the elderly patient.

After a while of waiting and hearing the cries, the doctor came back to the emergency room after closing up the curtains around the elderly patient's bed and came back to his desk. I told my dilemma to the doctor and was fortunate to hear that the doctor could speak English. I was instantly told to have an X-ray, and a nurse brought me to another building in the hospital. Once the

X-ray was done, I returned to the bench outside the emergency room and anxiously waited for the nurse to call me back.

Another half an hour passed, and the doctor returned to his desk and told me to go for another X-ray. But this time round, the nurse asked me to walk over to the X-ray department and instantly walked away from me. Probably due to a shortage of nurses, I went walking by myself to the X-ray department, having to lose my way, looking at the creepy-looking building that appeared dark and abandoned to my eyes, walking to a lift lobby that looked like one of those horror movies I had seen before which made me walk back to where I started from.

I returned to the foyer and tried to recollect my way to the X-ray department on the first visit. Then I walked and walked and took a creepy-looking elevator and managed to find my way to the X-ray department. Another X-ray was taken, and I made my way back, waiting outside the emergency room waiting for my name to be called again.

Another half an hour passed, and the nurse called me back to the doctor's desk.

"Hmmm, you don't have any fractures in your left shoulder," the doctor said while turning the computer monitor to me to show the X-ray result, and continued, "but looking at your shoulder, it appears inflamed."

I was content that there wasn't any fracture but didn't understand why my shoulder hurt so bad.

"When will you be arriving back to Singapore?"

I had no idea when I would reach Singapore, but I told the doctor I would reach soon in a few days' time.

"OK, you will get some medications, but when you reach back to Singapore, you should see a doctor to check on your shoulder again." I took his advice, took the prescription paper to the pharmacy to collect the medications, and walked straight out of the hospital with much relief. But never would I want to look back at the hospital again and I hoped the elderly patient lived.

***

I finally got back to my hotel room after a long walk from the hospital and after grabbing something to eat from a cart vendor on the roadside. Everything was tough to do once I had got into my room. From taking off my shirt, taking things out from my bag, and spending a hell lot of time trying to open the cap off the bottled water. Never had I been so weak before, and my left shoulder pain had somehow weakened my right arm too.

It was already 12:15 am by the time I lay on the bed and truly reflected on this dreadful day. From the reflection, one thing I truly promise myself was that I would not rush to do anything nor tire myself for the upcoming days' rides till I reach back to Singapore. That was one goal I made for myself, like a goal to reach the Golden Triangle.

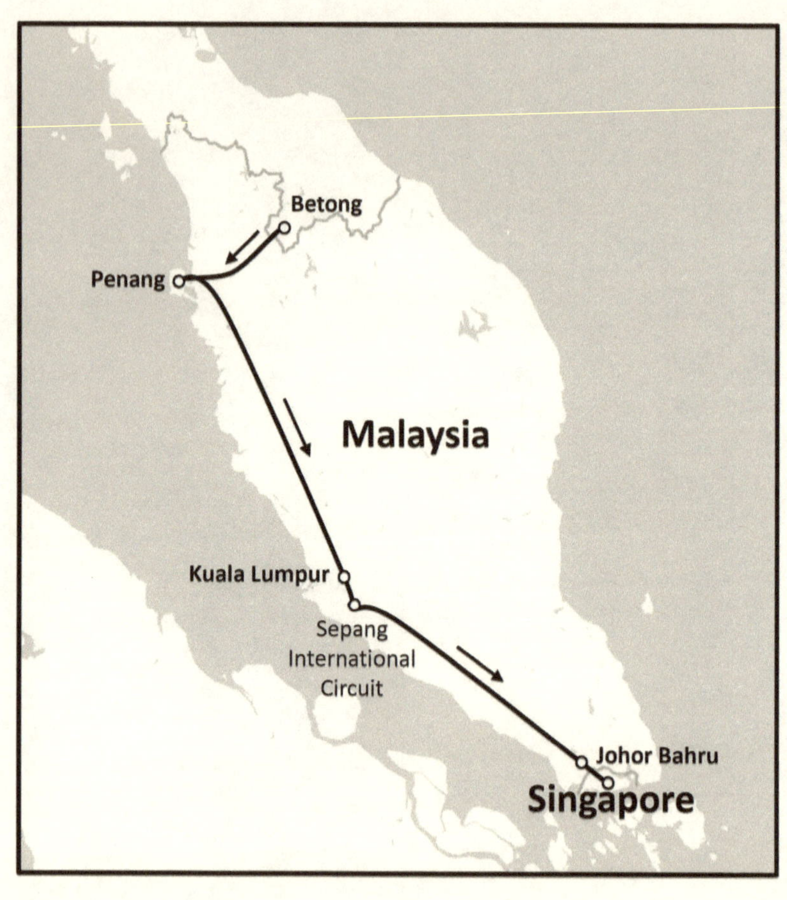

Betong
Penang
Malaysia
Kuala Lumpur
Sepang
International
Circuit
Johor Bahru
Singapore

19

The Final Ride

I woke up looking up at the ceiling realising that I had slept in the same position throughout the night. The pain in my shoulder had slightly eased off but the muscles around my shoulder had hardened up like a rock. It felt like my skin would tear apart if I further squeezed my shoulder. However, I could lift my shoulder slightly higher compared to the prior day but it was just for mere few degrees high only. Still, a great improvement than nothing and from that slight shoulder improvement, I thought about if I should rest longer to further recover my shoulder or perhaps have a few days of break to recover from all the weariness I had gone through.

I thought about it as I slowly got out of bed and somehow resolved to take a few days of break. But having to get the bike's damages fixed and getting the bent parts back to their original position before taking a break seemed more like fulfilment to me as I could rest with ease of mind afterwards and not think about the bike.

I took my time to get changed and got out of the hotel to look around for bike servicing shops, but I learned that there weren't many shops around in the town after searching it on my phone. The shops I had ridden to were either closed from the shutters down or didn't do what I asked for. And one even asked me to get my bike fixed in Malaysia since I would be heading down south anyway.

As clueless as I could be, I gave up finding for a shop, and stopped by at a 7-Eleven store to grab something to eat. But this time round, I was being very vigilant around my surrounding so that I don't get myself into another drug bust where I see myself being lifted by any policemen or perhaps by a thug.

To better caution myself, I ate my ready-to-eat sandwich in the store rather than outside.

As I munched and roamed about in the store looking at the snacks on the shelves, I heard a group of Chinese tourists talk about 'Penang', which popped up an idea to check on the distance to Penang. I got onto my phone and checked the distance between my current location and Penang, and it came up to about 115 kilometres apart. Not a long ride to think of, and I thought that it would be a great idea to get my bike fixed there as it's a haven for motorcycles where lots of motorcycle servicing shops can be found.

More positive thoughts came to my mind of Penang, and I thought of why not have my break there instead. As from the prior Phuket road trip, Penang was only a day stopover, and I hadn't spent much time exploring the island. It seemed like a great opportunity to head there, but in the position of having pain in my shoulder, would I even have the zest to explore the island? Well, it was still an opportunity as I couldn't imagine in future I would specifically ride to Penang from Singapore for any given reason. With that said, Penang was the chosen one. However, it has to be a slow and steady ride.

I rode back to the hotel to get all my stuff and check out before I paid for overstaying. My stuff was brought out to my bike and loaded up as usual, and then I started to paste the route stickers on the top box to reward its remarkable triumph. Just as when I was pasting the stickers, the same man who tried to pester me to get a woman on my day-two stay here in this hotel came walking towards me.

Nothing changed in him. His overwhelming smile remained intact, and his enthusiasm sprouted on his face as he approached me. He then asked me if I was about to leave soon. I told him I was, and he saw my bike's damage and asked me what happened. I told him about the fall and he empathised me and encouraged me to stay longer in Betong town.

But his encouragement wasn't an encouragement though. He then recommended me to get *three* ladies instead one and told me that one lady to massage my shoulders, another lady to massage my legs, and the last one, well, let me referred it as a joystick.

I shook my head, laughing at the way he said that, but I also had an intrusive thought that told me it wasn't a bad idea after all. And just then, two Chinese tourists walked past us, and he then diverted the conversation to them and walked away promoting them with ladies. That saved me. I quickly pasted the stickers and rode off to my new destination before I got offered more ladies.

***

Betong customs was less than 10 kilometres ride, and getting through the border of Thailand was surprisingly easy without anyone stopping me to ask about my passport. My passport had already dried up but the stamps had overlapped to other pages which can be easily spotted as an anomaly and can be very questionable to someone looking at them. Guess that I was lucky enough to get through, but as I stopped next to the passport stamping booth at the Malaysia border, I had to go through a small hiccup.

Two officers were inside the booth, and one was a higher-ranking officer with a nicer embroidery decoration on his shoulders.

Once I handed my passport to the lower-ranking officer, and an instant look of dismay appeared on his face. He then thoroughly checked the other pages and then passes my passport to the higher-ranking officer, who later wore a dismayed expression after seeing my passport.

"*Nak pergi mana ni?* (Where are you going now?)," the higher-ranking officer asked.

"*Nak pergi balik Singapore* (Want to go back to Singapore)," I replied.

"*Passport ini tak boleh pakai* (This passport can't be used)."

I explained to them the whole story, and both the officers nodded as I spoke. The higher-ranking officer looks at my passport once again, then looks up at me and says, "There's no point for me to hold you back. But when you reach Singapore, you must change your passport, Ok?"

I nodded to his saying and didn't want to say anything else. I got the stamp on a page, but he wrote something below the stamp print. As I got back the passport to see what he wrote, it stated, *'Change PPT'* with a signature next to the words.

The ride to Penang was relatively slow, and I strictly adhered to the promise I made the night before to not rush myself. Oddly, I somehow got accustomed to the odd riding style. I intuitively knew when to slow down when coming close to a vehicle in front of me and mastered using only a single brake – the front brake, without the need to use the rear brake as the brake pedal had bent inwards. However, it's dangerous to ride using a single brake. But well, that was what I only had – still not a good reason though.

The 115 kilometres to Penang went by really fast despite riding relatively slow. The roads were busy when I entered Penang, and there were lots of kapcai bikes on the roads. Especially those 125cc Honda Wave model bikes that were ubiquitously seen on the roads.

Just looking at those small-capacity bikes, it had given me much confidence that my bike would definitely be fixed in Penang.

The first thing for me to do was to get to the Yamaha servicing outlet. As I entered the premises, a young-looking man – who looked like an intern and appeared not like a mechanic – walked towards me and enquired about the bike's issues. I explained everything precisely what needed to be done to my bike, but his looks appeared doubtful. He first said something like 'Gu', then cut off what he wanted to say, then called a mechanic to look at my bike. The mechanic came, and I explained if the handlebar and the foot brake pedal be bent back to their right position. Instead of hearing something positive, I see the mechanic scratch his head and give a baffled look at my bike. Then the mechanic explained to me that he could not get both of them bent as it required gas welding to heat the metal parts, and it was against his work. Can't fault him, as it's completely a valid reason, and I resulted in asking the intern to replace parts instead and other parts such as the side mirrors, the bracket for the side mirrors, a few blown-out bulbs, and the front fairing that had its side chipped off.

The intern went over to check the parts stock and came back to me, telling me that there were only side mirrors and the bracket mount for the side mirrors in their inventory. I was discontented to hear that, but I couldn't fault the outlet anyway as my bike is an old model and it is the very first version of the many versions that have succeeded it. But since I have ridden over 100 kilometres to Penang, I resulted to just ask the intern to get the two parts changed instead and told myself to be glad that I had at least done something to the bike.

I sat in the waiting room and stared through the glass window with my palm resting on my left cheek, and watched other bikes that came before mine being worked on. As I waited and searched for other shops to get the other parts changed, the intern came and asked me how the accident happened. I explained to him the whole story and not long after, the conversation extended till we eventually talked about the food in Penang, the weather, and even talked about life in Singapore.

It brought me a reminiscence of my tertiary school days where I had my internship. During my time at the internship, I would spend most of my time going around talking to the workers asking about their work life, their life outside, and everything that I wanted to ask, I would ask them. It has nothing to do with my work, but it was more like burning my internship time fast. Back here at this outlet, this lucky intern – I just assume he was an intern – came to the right person and I was glad to be part of burning his time there.

As we conversed more, it then came to an important part where I learned what he had previously hesitated to say to me. The intern then recommended me to head to a bike servicing shop called "Gu Motors", which is close to this outlet. Saying that I could get my bike fixed fast and most of the parts could be obtained from the shop. I thanked him for the recommendation and eagerly anticipated getting back my bike. Once the small fixes were done, I quickly got back to my bike and rode off to look for the shop.

Like what the intern had said, the shop wasn't far off, but it wasn't "Gu motors" I had perceived to think of. But see a sign on the façade of the shop that states "Ragu Motors."

Upon my arrival outside the shop, I see two Indians working on a kapcai bike. One was an older man, and another man looked like he was in his twenties. The older man then asked me what I want to fix on the bike. I told him if he could find a way to bend back the brake pedal. An instant answer came from him: OK. Then I carried on and asked if he could bend back my handlebar. And again, he instantly said OK and showed me thumbs up. Then I carried on telling him what other parts I wanted to replace. He said, "Oh, no problem," and again showed me thumbs up. I was satisfied to hear his answers but sceptical if he could get the bike fixed by today as there were only mere hours left before the sun went down.

I asked him how long it would take, and he replied, "Very fast, don't worry," and showed me a thumbs up again and instantly started to work on my bike.

He worked on my bike like a simple toy to him. He intuitively knew what screws to take off and where exactly the screws were, and after a while, the other younger man came to work on my bike after working on the other kapcai bikes. The parts that do not require heating to bend the metals were replaced in the shop. And the ones that required heating, the older man brought the bike to another shop nearby to use the gas welding to bend the handlebar and foot pedal back to its near original position.

While they were working on my bike, I chatted with them and from there, I learned that the older man was indeed the shop's owner and his name is Ragu. The younger man is his son who was helping his father out in the business. After a while of chatting with them, Ragu recommended me to watch the Malaysian Cub Prix held in the Sepang circuit in the state of Selangor. It's a national level under bone or moped racing series for motorcycles with displacements between 100 to 150cc. I was thrilled to hear it and was told that entry to the circuit was free to everyone, and it was held on the weekend.

They were heading to Sepang, not as a spectator, but to help in one of the motorcycle brand models. I've never seen this type of cub bike racing before and thought that it would be a good opportunity to have a look. It was Wednesday. I could catch the race on the weekend before heading back to Singapore.

In less than two hours, all the stuff I asked to fix was fixed. The coolant was fully topped up, the handlebar and foot brake pedal back in their right position, bulbs changed, the front fairing cover changed, and the health bar for my bike restored to max like a Pokémon health bar.

I thanked Ragu and his son for the significant help and paid the price for the services but was surprised to know that it didn't cost much for all the repairs and the replacements. Probably due to my bike being ubiquitous in Penang or perhaps all over Malaysia, for which the cost of producing the parts had gone down low. Nevertheless, I thanked them for their work. And from there on, I went on to start my three days break in Penang.

Had I not gone to the Yamaha servicing outlet earlier and not spoken to the intern, I would never have gone to this shop nor would I even know what Malaysian Cub Prix was. I guess I was just lucky after the fall but never want another fall again.

***

Three days in Penang were more of resting, eating, sleeping, roaming about, and repeating the cycle. And on all three days, it was hot and humid in Penang. I avoided doing any strenuous activities and mostly kept myself under the shade. My shoulder movement improved a lot, but still, I had difficulties putting on my shirt.

I stayed in a hostel that had large-shelf-like furniture that had many large compartment pockets for people to sleep inside the pockets. An interesting experience sleeping inside the shelf, and the hospitality from the owner was superb in which I even had private parking right in front of the hostel premises.

I did less riding and walked much of my time in Penang to see what was around. Had a haircut in a famous barber shop in Penang called "Son & Dad," went around looking at the many wall arts on the street walls, had at least a massage a day, devoured the many varieties of food in Penang, and had one of the popular dishes in Penang called "Nasi Kandar." It is a meal where one can choose a variety of meats, such as prawns, fried chicken, beef, squid, fried fish, and other variants of meats and all the meats were cooked with different types of gravies. It was a splendid meal, but to get myself served and get onto the queue at the wrong time of the day – which was at noon, it took almost an hour for my turn to be served. Well, good food comes with long queues apparently.

The three days in Penang went eye blinkingly fast. Getting back to my bike felt disheartening, and to know that I had to ride back to Singapore, was immensely upsetting to think of. Even with my injured left shoulder, I still had the aspiration to venture around and had the spirit to keep on going. However, I deeply knew that the journey had to come to an end and I somehow had to accept it.

***

The return ride commenced. I made my way out from Penang, passed the windy Penang Bridge, and then back to the North-South highway to head south. The total distance came about over 700 kilometres back to Singapore, but I didn't want to ride all the kilometres in a single day. Like I had promised myself back in Betong – not to rush, I broke the distance into two halves. The first halfway mark is to stop at Kuala Lumpur (KL) and plan to stay there for two nights before returning to Singapore for the second half.

My first halfway ride to KL was smooth and easy with many lanes on the highway, unlike my time riding on the eastern side of the Peninsula Malaysia on day-one, where much of my ride was constrained to a single carriage road.

My two days in KL were relaxing, and again I had many satisfying meals. There were a few night-walking streets in KL, and one of the well-known ones was in Bukit Bintang called *Jalan*

Alor Food Street, and it's where lots of seafood vendors, hawkers, and cart vendors can be seen along the street.

Walking around Bukit Bintang was captivating to my eyes. I saw many souvenir shops, food shops, massage shops, and bars on one street, and surprisingly, there were many Turkish kebab stores around which craved me to get myself a kebab.

The streets were intriguing to look at, with artists' paintings, buskers, and other entrepreneurs along the streets. The busiest busking area was the one just right outside of a MacDonald – or the Malaysian way of saying MacDonald would be "Mekdi" – which is at one corner of a four junctions' road. A huge crowd would circle around to see the captivating performance from different buskers, and some would be in large groups where it would be like a live band performance. The crowd would sing along with the buskers, and from the crowd synchronism singing, the sound could even be heard from a distance away.

***

My two days passed incredibly fast, and it was time for me to make the final ride back to Singapore. But before riding back, I headed straight to the Sepang International circuit to catch the Malaysian Cub Prix, which was only 63 kilometres away from KL.

It was captivating to watch different categories of kapcai bikes ranging up to 150cc racing on the track. I have to say, the sound of the exhaust pipes from all the kapcai bikes that zoom past the track was exceptionally loud and to be very honest, I hoped for someone to walk by the grandstand to sell me earplugs.

Having to watch the races on the grandstand for the first time was a unique experience to me. I joined along with the enthusiastic fans who came to support their beloved riders if not the bike's brand model to cheer whichever riders zoom past the track. At times, I would vociferously shout out the bike's brand model out loud for no valid reason. Well, who knows, a brand comes and sponsors me.

Actually, I didn't know what to cheer, so I shouted out the bike's brand model. (As I write this paragraph, it was hilarious to think about what I did on the grandstand.)

What really surprised me were the riders. They were all below 16 years of age, and all wore full safety suits like those professional MotoGP racers. I was really impressed to see them in full proper gear, and everything on the track was professional. When a rider fell, the famous silver Mercedes-Benz safety vehicle drove around the track, ensuring the safety of both the riders and the integrity of the track – just as I had seen on TV before.

Watching the race was truly impressive, and experiencing it in first-person view provided a unique opportunity that I'll remember for a long time. And again, thanks to the amazing people I have met along my journey.

***

The ride from Sepang to Singapore is roughly 318 kilometres. Every kilometre I had passed by was upsetting to think of. Having to think of the end nearing closer felt even more upsetting. Reminiscent of my ride to Golden Triangle was running in my mind like a motion picture. Although I couldn't chronologically recollect whatever when by, I could still remember all the good moments, the places I had been to, the food I ate, and all the obstacles I had been through, be seen vibrantly in my mind. It felt like it wasn't long ago since I left home to embark on the journey.

After hours of riding, I arrived back in Johor Bahru soundly before the atmosphere darkened. I returned to the usual bike washing shop at Lorong Bapok to get the bike washed. As I sat on the waiting bench, I recollected my memory of meeting two fellow Chinese Singaporeans who arrived back from their road trip from Phuket and stopped by this shop. I smiled to myself thinking about it and was also mystified to think that it was just a few months back since I met them. That made me think that one could achieve so many things in just mere months down the future if one is willing to try.

The bike was washed, and the final last ride came for me to cross back to Singapore via Johor Bahru border crossing and then to Woodlands Checkpoint in Singapore. Passport scanned, and back on Singapore roads and off to the last and foremost ride back to my home.

No more weaving in and out of the lanes, and no more riding above the road speed limit. I rode religiously following the road speed looking at the well-lit-up roads in Singapore, and smiled at the days I rode in the dark.

I rode the last bends to my home estate and then back to the parking lot where I rode off from the day-one ride. No one was there to welcome me back, nor was anyone there to celebrate my journey to Golden Triangle. It was all me and a quiet housing block around me. However, I didn't feel discontented about it. I was proud of my achievement and gained so much knowledge and experience from the road trip. That was all I needed and that was more than I could ask for. But one sad thing I couldn't let go of and had to accept somehow was that the ride had come to an end.

The probatory stickers on the front fairing and rear mudguard were removed. I am no longer a probationary rider in Singapore nor a novice rider in Singapore. But still, I regard myself as a novice rider around the world.

"Around the world?" I thought.

My senses tingled.

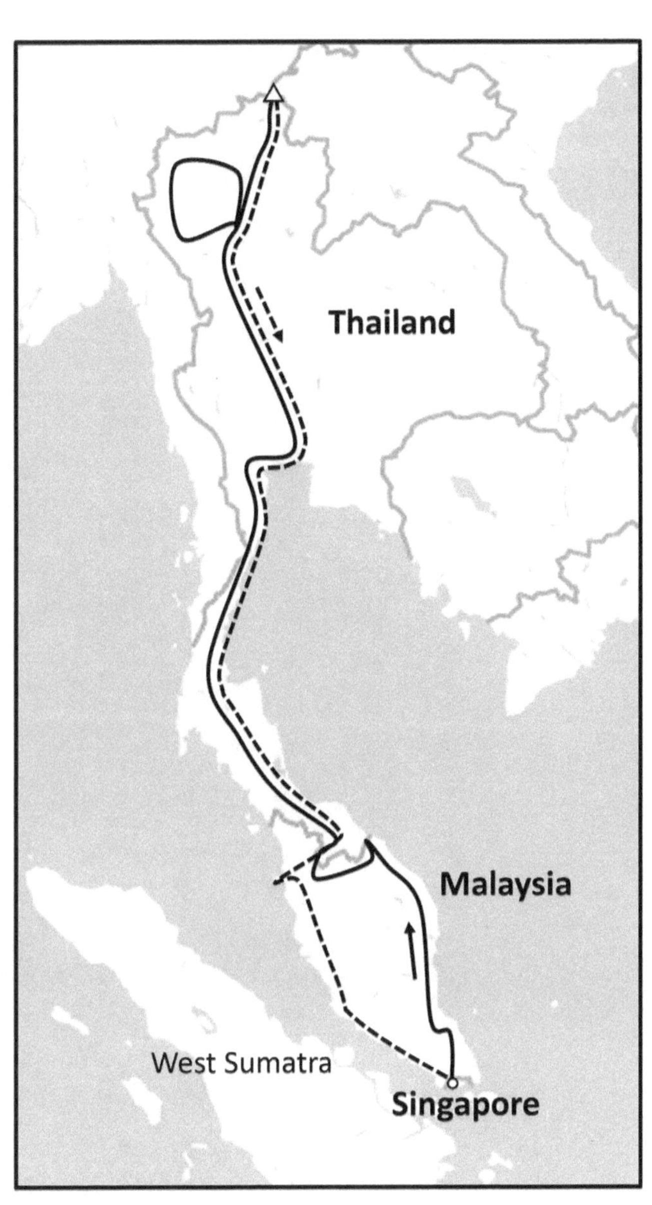

Thailand
Malaysia
West Sumatra
Singapore

Part 4: The Aftermath

20

All You Have to Do Is Try

A few months after the incredible road trip of mine, my left shoulder pain had already vanished off and I had obtained my class 2A licence where I could ride any motorcycle up to 400cc. Within the week of obtaining the licence, I rented a Suzuki DRZ-400 motorcycle and did a day joy ride to Malacca which is about 238 kilometres from the Singapore border. Of course, it was only after I had replaced to a new passport.

But little did I know, that was my last ride before a contagious disease struck the many countries out there causing flights to cancel, land borders to close, ferries to stop ferrying, and the many modes of transportation, came to a halt. Thanks to COVID-19 for the calamity.

Even you would probably know what COVID-19 is or was. So, I have nothing much to say about it.

But I have to say; I was fortunate to have done the whole journey to the Golden Triangle and back to Singapore before the borders were shut. What if I had postponed the ride a few months from the original date of departure or perhaps for a year? My perception and perspective would have differed and all the things I had learned along the road trip wouldn't even exist in my mind now.

During the border closure, it came to my mind that there are, indeed, lots of intriguing scenes of my journey, and I thought, "Why not write a book about my road trip?"

It took me a while to think through if I wanted to pursue writing a book, as I was a super novice in almost anything that related to writing. Drafting a script itself is a daunting task which I had already perceived in my mind, and I even read an anonymous article that stated only mere people out of the many had made it through completing their scripts and publishing them. There was also another alarming thing for me: If someone were to ask me what Grammar or Vocabulary is, I would probably reply, "What language is that?"

I was that incompetent.

But something came bogging down in my mind that brought me back to a kid in the classroom. I remember envisaging myself as an author of a book when I was in my classroom, having just received my badly written comprehensive writing paper from my teacher I dreaded so much. My writing was so terrible that my teacher read my paper aloud to the class, enlightening them, but much laughter was directed at me.

Even though being laughed at abysmally, it made me envisage that one day I would somehow become an author of my own book. For that reason, it gave me a purpose to pursue my childhood envisagement – not a dream – and it appeared to me that this road trip must be it. And so, I asked myself this before even giving my time in: "If not now, then when?"

But most importantly, from what I had learned from the road trip: why not *try*?

I worked on writing the manuscript and the extremely novice writer me, read lots of motorcycle road trip books, watched lots of

YouTube videos, bought textbooks to improve on my English, and read lots of self-help books to help me out with my manuscript. It took me a while to write up this book as I was still working as a delivery rider to earn income. Apart from that, at one point while working on the manuscript, I began learning how to code as I thought of transiting out from the delivery job to do something meaningful in the future.

With the many overwhelming stuff ruminating in my mind and the physically demanding work, I had many setbacks that made me quit working on the manuscript. But after much get backs and making use of the principle of *try*, I slowly, word by word, sentence by sentence, paragraph by paragraph, and yes you got it, page by page, and from there, I persevered to see the manuscript slowly form up to a book size. And that was when, I knew, it was worth the *try* after all.

By the time the manuscript was completed, majority of the borders had opened up for travel, and I had achieved a new feat by travelling to many ASEAN countries and ridden a motorcycle in each of them. Besides that, I was no longer a delivery rider but rather pursuing a degree in one of the local universities in Singapore. Thank goodness I learned how to code.

While I smiled at the arduous times I had been through, I had to face something that was inevitable.

On 5 June 2023, my amazing bike, the Yamaha Spark T135, came to its end time, and it could no longer be ridden on the road of Singapore after the expiry of the COE. If you remember, it's the Certificate of Entitlement that gives the right to own a vehicle and be ridden on the road of Singapore. When the COE expiry date arrives, and when the COE date can no longer be extended, the vehicle has to be scrapped. With that said, I had to say goodbye to my bike.

Saying goodbye to my bike was truly saddening, and never have I teared for a machine before in my life. It gave me fond memories and made me achieve something I could never imagine of. The boring life I once perceived no longer lingered in my mind, and there will never be a time where I would say I have a boring life again. Never.

With that said, I have undoubtedly created an incredible life story with a truly amazing machine. But it was only possible, when I gave it a *try*.

About the Author

Mohamad Khair finds joy in exploring diverse landscapes of neighbouring countries, immersing himself in various modes of transportation unique to each destination. Beyond his love for motorcycling, he has a penchant for seeking adventure in every corner of the region. Currently pursuing a local degree, Mohamad Khair is passionate about sharing his travel experiences and adventures through his writing.

Email: 10daystogoldentriangle@gmail.com
Instagram: @khais_yolo

Appendix

Route

While one has the freedom to create routes in any way they want, the route I took was this:

- Singapore – Kelantan (Kota Bharu)

  (AH18 – Route 14 – E8 – AH18)

- Kelantan (Kota Bharu) – Betong

  (Route 4 – Route 76 – Route 77)

- Betong – Phatthalung

  (Route 410 – Route 409 – Route 43 – Route 4 – Route 41)

- Phatthalung – Chumphon

  (Route 41)

- Chumphon – Hua Hin – Bangkok – Pathum Thani

  (Route 41 – Route 4 – Route 35 – Sirat Expressway)

- Pathum Thani – Chiang Mai

  (Route 1 – Route 32 – Route 1 – Route 11)

- Mae Hong Son loop (Anti-Clockwise direction)

  (Route 108 – Route 1009 – Route 108)

- Chiang Mai – Doi Inthanon National Park – Mae Sariang

  (Route 108 – Route 1263 – Route 4009 – Route 108 – Route 1095)

- Mae Sariang – Bua Tong field & Namtok Mae Surin water-fall – Pai

  (Route 1095 – Route 107 – Route 118 – Route 1)

- Pai – Chiang Mai – Chiang Rai

  (Route 1095 – Route 107 – Route 118 – Route 1)

- Chiang Rai – Golden Triangle Park

  (Route 1)

Motorcycle Essentials

While one can bring anything for a motorcycle road trip, it's up to personel choice. Here are the essentials that I brought along, and some may be useful for your future trip:

- Spare motorcycle keys

- Spark plug

- Chain and locks (disc lock and padlock)

- WD-40

- Chain lubrication

- Tool kit (like spanners, drivers, etc.)

- Funnel

- Jerrycan

- Insulation tapes

- Cable ties

- Portable charger

- Engine oil and engine oil filter (not recommended as there are an abundance of servicing shops in Peninsula Malaysia and in Thailand – unless one is willing to service themselves)

- Mini air-compressor

- Tyre repair kit
- Spare bulbs
- Screws and nuts

Additional Note

I was never a great photographer or videographer before this road trip – even while writing this line. However, I have realised the importance of capturing good shots or videos, as they can be useful for future purposes. For example, creating a memoir video or using the pictures for a blog, book, or anything that one could use to look back at what one had done before.

Most of the pictures I took featured the landscape or various sights with me in the frame. However, they didn't fit well into this book, as it seemed eccentric to see myself in most of the pictures. So, it makes sense to have different perspective shots like some examples below:

- Pictures with various backdrops featuring oneself
- Landscape shots without including oneself
- Panoramic shots
- Video capturing the landscape or other interesting scenes